SOUTH AFRICA

SOUTH AFRICA

The Struggle for a New Order

Marina Ottaway

THE BROOKINGS INSTITUTION
Washington, D.C.

Copyright © 1993

THE BROOKINGS INSTITUTION

1775 Massachusetts Avenue, N.W.
Washington, D.C. 20036

Library of Congress Cataloging-in-Publication data:
Ottaway, Marina.
    South Africa: the struggle for a new order / Marina Ottaway.
        p.   cm.
    Includes bibliographical references and index.
    ISBN 0-8157-6716-1 (alk. paper)—ISBN 0-8157-6715-3 (pbk.: alk. paper)
        1. South Africa—Politics and government—1989– 2. South Africa—Politics
        and government—1948– 3. Apartheid—South Africa.
    I. Title.
    DT1970.088   1993   92-46371
    968.06—dc20   CIP

9 8 7 6 5 4 3 2 1

The paper used in this publication meets the minimum requirements of the American
National Standard for Information Sciences—Permanence of paper for Printed
Library Materials, ANSI Z39.48-1984

Foreword

The lifting of the ban on the African National Congress (ANC) in February 1990 gave hope that the new government of F. W. de Klerk would abandon the policy of apartheid and that South Africa would move quickly toward a peaceful transition to a more democratic system. Three years later it is clear that the transition will be neither swift nor peaceful. Many black South Africans are beginning to doubt that de Klerk ever intended to end apartheid and to suspect that the leaders involved in the negotiations have been more interested in government positions for themselves than in the rights of the majority. Nelson Mandela, in 1990 the revered symbol of the anti-apartheid struggle, has become a controversial and lone figure.

Marina Ottaway analyzes the transition process that began in 1990. She discusses how the conflict has changed from a fairly simple bilateral confrontation between blacks and whites to an increasingly complex and violent multilateral struggle pitting black organizations against one another as well as against the white government. She argues that the complexity of the conflict has not been the only obstacle to a solution. The inflexibility and the negotiating style of the major parties has played an important part in the failure of the process. The convoluted constitution introduced by the National Party in the hope of retaining a large share of the power has made an agreement very difficult. The lack of attention to detail on the part of the ANC leaders has also caused the process to suffer many setbacks.

The author shows how international events have influenced the transition process. The collapse of communism in the former Soviet Union and elsewhere forced the ANC leadership to moderate its long-standing economic demands for resdistribution; and the explosion of ethnic nationalism in Eastern Europe gave new arguments and a new legitimacy to those leaders of the ethnic homelands who did not want to see their territories reincorporated into South Africa. As a result, an alliance began to emerge between black ethnic leaders and conservative Afrikaners, further complicating the transition.

Marina Ottaway is an adjunct professor at American University and Johns Hopkins School of Advanced International Studies. She wishes to thank all those who influenced her thinking about South Africa and thus the contents of this book. The people involved are too many, and their influence often too difficult to trace, to allow her to mention individual names. South Africans who helped deserve special thanks and an apology of sorts from the author, who came and asked questions and went home with a book, while they remained to live through all the conflicts and crises she has had the benefit of discussing with detachment.

Donna Verdier edited the manuscript; Khalid Medani checked it for factual accuracy; and Kirsten Soule provided secretarial support. Max Franke prepared the index.

Brookings gratefully acknowledges the financial support provided for this book by the Rockefeller Foundation and the Rockefeller Brothers Fund.

The views expressed in this study are those of the author and should not be ascribed to any of the persons or organizations mentioned above, or to the trustees, officers, or staff members of the Brookings Institution.

BRUCE K. MAC LAURY
President

February 1993
Washington, D.C.

Contents

Chapter 1

The Changing Conflict

The year 1990 marked a turning point in South Africa. On February 2, State President Frederik W. de Klerk unbanned the African National Congress (ANC) and other antiapartheid organizations. Shortly afterward, he released Nelson Mandela, the ANC leader who during twenty-seven years of imprisonment had become the symbol of black South Africans' struggle for political rights. From the front pages of newspapers, Mandela and de Klerk stood side by side like old friends, smiling broadly, ready to lead their countrymen out of the dark years of apartheid and into the new South Africa.

On December 20, 1991, the Convention for a Democratic South Africa (CODESA) opened in Johannesburg. Delegations of nineteen political organizations, supported by teams of advisers, prepared to negotiate the future of the country. At the end of the first day, they listened in stunned silence as Nelson Mandela delivered a scathing attack on President de Klerk, accusing him of behavior despicable even by the standards of the illegitimate and discredited apartheid regime. The new South Africa, it was clear, would not emerge from a friendly agreement between the two leaders and the political movements they represented, but from protracted, difficult, and acrimonious negotiations among many political organizations. Six months later, the second meeting of CODESA ended in deadlock, dispelling any lingering illusion that an agreement would be reached soon.

On June 23, 1992, after a particularly nasty outbreak of violence that left more than forty people dead in Boipatong, a township south of Johannesburg, the ANC announced that it was suspending constitutional talks. The enthusiasm of early 1990 was a distant memory. The veil created by a combination of hope, misunderstanding, and deliberate obfuscation that initially surrounded the negotiations had been lifted. The events of the year and a half that followed revealed

1

in all its starkness the gulf that separated the two sides. The ANC still sought a transfer of power to the majority, hence to blacks, but above all to itself. The government remained determined to engineer a complicated political system in which the power of the majority in the end would not be any greater than that of the minorities—particularly that of the current white leaders. The first phase of the transition process was over; it ended with no progress toward narrowing the gap between the two positions.

THE FIRST TWO YEARS

A thumbnail sketch of the major events of 1990 and 1991 helps explain the change from elation to gloom. The unbanning of February 2 and the release of Nelson Mandela were long-demanded steps that nevertheless surprised nearly everyone. Blacks were jubilant; whites expressed concern, but mixed with it was some relief that the inevitable step had finally been taken; all sides had many questions that needed answers. The country had embarked on an open-ended process that could lead anywhere. Except for the Conservative Party and extraparliamentary right-wing organizations, South Africans seemed to judge developments positively. The press, even its more conservative members, welcomed the decision to unban the ANC and gave de Klerk high marks for courage. Once-dreaded subversive organizations and banned leaders were freely mentioned and discussed. Editorials hailed the change. The state-controlled South African Broadcasting Corporation showed full-screen pictures of the ANC flag, whose display had hitherto been forbidden, and interviewed Nelson Mandela.

For the ANC, the first few months after Mandela's release were marked by a series of triumphal rallies all around the country. After twenty-seven years in jail, Mandela was not an eloquent orator, but crowds listened in reverent silence to his slow delivery of lengthy speeches in English, a language many in the audience did not understand well. At home and abroad, the unbanned ANC and Nelson Mandela were acclaimed as symbols of the antiapartheid struggle.

In the general atmosphere of goodwill prevailing then, no one looked too closely at the demands of either side or questioned how their divergent goals might be reconciled amicably. The first round of talks-about-talks between the government and the ANC went off very smoothly in April 1990, prolonging the illusion that a solution would be found soon. Groote Schuur, Cecil Rhodes's estate in Cape Town, was the incongruous backdrop to this unprecedented friendly meeting among former champions of apartheid, leaders of the liberation struggle, and Communist Party members. The Groote Schuur Minute they all signed established working groups that would discuss how to remove the obstacles still standing in the way of constitutional negotiations and prepare a timetable for the completion of this preparatory phase. Following the meeting, both President F. W. de Klerk and ANC Deputy President Nelson Mandela embarked on foreign tours, reaping praise on all sides. As far as the world was concerned, apartheid had ended and it was time to celebrate its demise.

The conclusion was premature. The Groote Schuur meeting and the leaders' foreign tours that followed it marked merely the end of a phase in the change from apartheid, a phase that had been long on symbolism and short on substance. What came next was the discovery of the enormity of the problems to be tackled. The process of conflict resolution, it became clear, was also one of conflict generation. The approaching end of the primary conflict over apartheid spurred competition for power, and thus a series of secondary conflicts within and among organizations and groups.

All political organizations faced the challenge of adapting to the new situation. The ANC was an exiled organization with a military wing and a loosely structured internal mass movement under the umbrella of the United Democratic Front (UDF). From these disparate pieces, it had to craft a political party capable of undertaking serious negotiations with the government, and eventually of competing in elections and playing a major role in the future government. To become such a political party, it had to sort out the relations between exiled and internal leadership, as well as between two generations with widely differing political cultures (one had come of age politically in the 1950s and 1960s and the other in the 1970s and 1980s). It also had to clarify the relationship between the political organization and the military wing, Umkhonto we Sizwe—the Spear of the Nation (MK).

The de Klerk government was preparing for negotiations while continuing to run the country, but its legitimacy was shaky. Always representative of only the white minority, it had won the 1989 elections with less than 50 percent of the vote. Furthermore, the platform of the National Party (NP) had not explicitly called for negotiations with the ANC, and in March 1992 de Klerk was forced to call for a white-only referendum to establish the fact that he had a mandate to continue the process.

Nevertheless, the party had incredibly ambitious goals. The NP intended to continue governing the country until a new constitution was enacted and elections for a new government held, without surrendering power to an interim government. It wanted to maintain the support of the white population and simultaneously to convince the black organizations that it was serious about change. What's more, it apparently had set for itself the seemingly impossible task of introducing the universal franchise and restructuring the political system in a way the rest of the world would accept as democratic, but without allowing blacks, who constituted about 85 percent of the population, to control the government. With supreme self-confidence, indeed hubris, de Klerk and the small inner circle of NP leaders remained convinced they could pull off the stunt of abrogating apartheid without abrogating their own power.

Other political movements and parties also had to redefine their roles and their goals. The United Democratic Front, originally a stand-in for the banned ANC, had to decide whether it still had a reason to exist or whether it should disband. The UDF affiliates, for their part, also had to find a new niche. The Africanist movements upholding a black-power ideology—the Pan Africanist Congress of Azania (PAC) and the Azanian People's Organization (AZAPO)—faced a difficult choice: they could join the negotiations, where they would be at best the ANC's junior partners, or they could seek to maintain a more radical image and remain outside the process, where they might become marginal.

The dilemma for the leaders of the four independent and six self-governing homelands concerned their territories' position in the new South Africa. Created by the white regime, the homelands had no legitimacy in the eyes of most black South Africans. Nevertheless, over the years many people had developed a vested interest in their survival: the top leaders who enjoyed the perquisites of office; the civil servants who could count on a secure though modest salary; the laborers who had jobs only because the government subsidized plants that were set up in the homelands.

The chief minister of KwaZulu, Chief Mangosuthu Gatsha Buthelezi, and his movement, the Inkatha Freedom Party (IFP), were especially pressed. The best known and most controversial of the homeland leaders, Buthelezi had used KwaZulu to further his career but also to oppose apartheid. In the process, he had earned a mixed reputation, being variously regarded as the leader of seven million Zulus, a stooge of apartheid, or a moderate politician who could be an important counterweight to the radical ANC leadership. Buthelezi's problem after February was to avoid the dismantling of KwaZulu—his guaranteed power base—while maintaining his credibility as an opponent of apartheid and establishing himself as a national rather than simply regional leader. The problem was complicated by his ambition, which compelled him to demand recognition not only as a national figure but as one whose stature equaled Nelson Mandela's. In 1990, that was no mean demand.

The dilemmas faced by the several groups could not be resolved without a great deal of strife, both internal to each organization and among the various movements. Goals and interests of different participants were too divergent, and the stakes too high, for compromises to be fashioned quickly, if at all. Signs of open strife arose even before the initial mood of optimism faded. The first few weeks following the unbanning of antiapartheid organizations saw extensive violence in the townships as organizations jostled for position. Violence between Inkatha and ANC supporters, a constant problem in Natal in the late 1980s, flared up with particular virulence in March. Fighting erupted between ANC and AZAPO supporters in the Eastern Cape. Violence exploded elsewhere as well, although the causes were often unclear. Right-wing white extremist organizations began to issue militant statements and occasionally indulged in acts of sabotage. National Party offices were blown up on the Witwatersrand around Johannesburg; vigilantes patrolled the streets of Welkom in the Orange Free State to keep blacks out of white neighborhoods at night; armories were robbed to supply the arsenals of right-wing groups.

The violence subsided for a while, but in August and September it flared up in the townships of the Witwatersrand. Close to one thousand people were killed in those two months, and scores more in early December. The violence assumed ethnic overtones—fighting between Inkatha and ANC supporters came to be perceived as fighting between Zulus and Xhosas not only by conservative whites but often also by the township residents.

Parallel to the emergence of these violent conflicts were manifestations of new tensions between the government and the ANC. For many months their relations had been good. To be sure, they were rival political organizations with different goals, and they were locked in a struggle for power. Nevertheless, in the early part of 1990 the two appeared to agree on how to proceed to arrive at a negotiated solution of the apartheid conflict. A second round of talks-about-talks held in Pretoria in August saw a breakdown in cooperation, however. Both parties signed a second agreement, the Pretoria Minute, in which the ANC pledged to suspend the armed struggle and the government to release political prisoners and grant exiles indemnity from prosecution. But the document was vaguely worded, and this led to disagreement over its interpretation. The government claimed the ANC had conceded a lot more—and agreed to accept less in return—than the ANC thought. The government became overconfident of its ability to manipulate its rival. The Congress felt cheated. The divergence of understanding was an unpromising basis for further talks.

The international response to change in South Africa also helped deepen the cleavage between the government and the ANC. Mandela had his moment of triumph in June 1990. The hero's welcome the ANC leader received in the United States prompted President de Klerk to postpone his own visit—he knew that he could not possibly garner similar acclaim. But by September the situation had already changed. International approval for de Klerk was mounting, while the ANC was losing some of its luster. Increasingly it was seen not as the symbol of the antiapartheid struggle but as a movement still upholding outdated radical ideas. Economic sanctions were crumbling, giving a psychological boost to the government and spelling defeat for the ANC, which insisted that the time to reestablish normal economic and cultural relations with South Africa had not yet arrived.

In the fall of 1990, there began a period of stagnation in the negotiations. No front registered much progress. Political prisoners were not being released at the expected rate—the two sides disagreed on the definition of political offenses and produced conflicting estimates of the number of people remaining in jail. The situation was even worse for the exiles, hardly any of whom had returned except members of the ANC leadership involved in the negotiations. Adding to the malaise; a still-disorganized ANC postponed its congress, holding instead a consultative conference in December that revealed a considerable amount of dissension in the ranks.

Violence continued unabated in the townships; tensions mounted among political movements. The ANC held the government, Inkatha, and a "third force," supposedly orchestrated by elements of the government's security apparatus, responsible for the continuing strife. Inkatha and the government accused the ANC "comrades" of causing the problem by trying to establish control over the townships. To crown it all, in April 1991 the ANC leadership, convinced that the government was deliberately fomenting violence and frustrated by what it perceived as the failure to implement the Pretoria Minute, issued an ultimatum. It called for, among other measures, the firing of the minister of defense and the minister of law and order and for the formation of an independent commission to investigate the violence. Until the conditions were met, it declared, it would suspend negotiations. Inevitably, the government refused to comply.

What came to be known as the Inkathagate scandal broke the impasse. The government, the media reported, had funded some Inkatha activities. The specific evidence leaked to the press was limited to relatively minor incidents, the contribution of funds to two Inkatha rallies in order to bolster the organization's image. However, the revelations heightened suspicions that government support for Inkatha was much more substantial, lending credibility to the ANC's accusations. In an attempt to restore his tarnished image, de Klerk demoted the two ministers the ANC wanted dismissed, thus partially surrendering to the ANC ultimatum.

In the wake of Inkathagate, the ANC was more confident, the government chastised, and the balance upset by the government's interpretation of the Pretoria Minute reestablished. In July, the ANC held its long-awaited congress, overcoming some of its own internal tensions. Talks resumed; a peace conference was held in September to tackle the problem of violence. Finally, in December CODESA met, signaling the end of talks-about-talks and the beginning of formal negotiations on a new political system.

Like the Groote Schuur meeting, the first CODESA plenary session was followed by a period of misunderstanding and eventually by a deep crisis. The negotiations within the working groups, committees, and subcommittees that constituted the permanent CODESA machinery were marked by lack of clarity and openness. This appeared to be the result of deliberate efforts at obfuscation on the part of the government and of sloppiness about detail on the part of the ANC.

Superficially, the two agreed on the need to form an interim government, which would be regulated by an interim constitution while a constituent assembly carried out its task. In reality, they envisaged totally different processes and outcomes. For the National Party, the so-called interim government should stay in power for years and the interim constitution should be a full-fledged charter, which the NP hoped would turn into the permanent one. This enhanced the importance of CODESA and the small parties represented in it. For the ANC, the interim government and constitution should have a very short life, simply providing a bridge between the rule of the National Party and majority rule. In this vision, the elected constituent assembly, not CODESA, would be the major negotiating forum, enhancing the power of the ANC and reducing that of other parties. When the ANC finally understood the government's intentions on the eve of CODESA II, negotiations broke down.

The ANC announced that it would once again summon its supporters to participate in mass action to pressure the government, and indeed it called for a one-day general strike on June 16, with mixed success. On the night of June 17, a raid on a Vaal triangle township, Boipatong, by residents of a nearby migrant workers' hostel left more than forty people dead. The ANC blamed Inkatha and the government, which in turn chose to view the outbreak as a consequence of the ANC's call for mass action. With tension mounting, de Klerk decided to visit the township in an attempt to appease the residents and show the government's goodwill. The plan backfired. Greeted by an irate crowd, de Klerk left in haste; in the wake of his departure, the police opened fire on the crowd, as it had done innumerable times in the dark days of apartheid.

The incident dealt the final blow to the negotiating process. On June 23, the ANC withdrew from the negotiations, presenting the government with a new list of conditions to be met before talks could resume. The first phase of the transition had ended in failure.

To be sure, much had changed in South Africa since the unbanning of the ANC, but much remained the same. Major apartheid laws had been repealed, but outside the large cities life went on unchanged, except for the mounting violence. Most blacks did not have the money to take advantage of the new opportunities theoretically open to them. Most whites tried to ignore the inevitability of change. "Whites only" signs had largely disappeared, but different population groups continued to live in separate and very different worlds. In the townships, streets remained unpaved, water taps scarce, sewer systems nonexistent. In the white suburbs, council workers armed with watering cans sprinkled herbicide on the crack between sidewalk and curbstone, lest weeds should grow. It was hardly surprising that the ANC should seek majority rule and the government would try to hang on to power.

Some things had become much worse during the first phase of the transition. The year 1990 had opened on a note of optimism and goodwill, but both had dissipated. Mandela no longer called de Klerk a man of integrity—he accused him of duplicity. The government disparaged the ANC, claiming it embraced obsolete ideologies and wanted to impose a communist dictatorship on the country. Other parties, Inkatha foremost among them, had made it clear that they were not ready to automatically accept what the government and ANC agreed to. A strange alliance was developing between Afrikaner nationalists in the Conservative Party and some homeland leaders fearful of losing their power base. Clearly, even if the suspended negotiations resumed and a compromise was struck, there was no guarantee that peace would prevail. The new South Africa remained elusive.

CONFLICT RESOLUTION AND CONFLICT GENERATION

Underlying the events of this period was a conflict situation that was becoming more complicated as the hope of a settlement waxed and waned. The talks between the ANC and the government threatened other political organizations, which feared exclusion from the negotiations and perhaps eventual political impotence. As other parties tried to force their way into the process and gain recognition as autonomous players—something other than simply allies of one or the other side—new lines of cleavage emerged.

Historically, the conflict over apartheid pitted five million whites, who controlled 87 percent of the land and most other economic assets, against the black majority, which consisted of twenty-nine million Africans, three million Coloureds, and one million Indians, largely disenfranchised and very poor. In this conflict, political power and economic resources were in the hands of whites, and population size as well as historical trends on the side of blacks. It was this stark, black-on-white conflict that spawned an antiapartheid movement in most industrialized countries strong enough to cause the imposition of economic, sports, and cultural sanctions, making South Africa a pariah state.

The National Party was acutely aware that the apartheid system bucked the historical trend toward universal political rights and that whites, always a small and now a shrinking percentage of the population because of their lower birthrate, would find it difficult to maintain their dominant position indefinitely. The tactic of the white regime, then, was to try to transform South Africa from a country in which a minority held the majority at bay into what it defined as a country of minorities. "Nonwhites"—the government carefully avoided using a collective term with which blacks might want to identify— were not seen as a homogeneous category. Rather, they were divided into Coloureds, Asians, and ten different African ethnic groups, each of which was eventually given a homeland. It was a divide-and-rule strategy carried to great extremes, and it led to a system that was extraordinarily convoluted, inequitable, and inefficient.

Divide-and-rule found no acceptance in South Africa or abroad. Most Coloureds and Indians rejected the 1983 attempt to give them a place in the system via a tricameral Parliament, and they boycotted the elections. Only four of the homelands eventually accepted independence; those that did never gained international recognition.

What the government's machinations to keep power in white hands did do was unite blacks in their opposition to apartheid. Real divisions did exist among blacks, but by trying to accentuate cleavages and impose ethnic consciousness, the government unintentionally made the conflict a black-versus-white one. Particularly in the 1970s, the prevailing ideology was an all-encompassing black consciousness.

By changing the end of apartheid from a distant goal to an event that would take place in the near future, the unbanning of the ANC and other groups destroyed the veneer of simplicity the problem had assumed, revealing it in all its complexity. The conflict over apartheid dissolved into a set of crisscrossing and overlapping cleavages, leading to open strife. The National Party remained an enemy for many organizations, but it became a potential ally for a few. The followers of different political movements fought for control of the townships, and the clashes occasionally assumed ethnic overtones. Rifts arose within organizations, too. In the ANC, relations were tense within the leadership as well as between officials and rank-and-file members; the Pan Africanist Congress was so wracked by internal dissension that it eventually became paralyzed, unable to decide any question. Violence in the townships was escalating, with the lines of conflict increasingly blurred—rivalries among political organizations, ethnic clashes, and gang warfare overlapped and intersected so much that at times the only certainty was that people were dying.

Whites were no more unified than blacks. The National Party was losing support to the Conservative Party. Extraparliamentary right-wing groups whose goals were similar nevertheless went their separate ways. Attempts to form common fronts faltered.

Increased strife was not surprising. The euphoria of February 1990 had given rise to hopes that were bound to be dashed, leaving people disillusioned and embittered. As the next two years showed, the new South Africa existed only in the rhetoric of politicians. For most people, the changes of 1990 and 1991 had been for the worse—more violence in the townships, more inflation, more unemployment, more poverty, more school failures, more crime everywhere.

Increased competition among organizations was another natural consequence. For many, it was a matter of survival. Only the ANC and the National Party were assured of a major role at the negotiating table. Only the ANC would certainly be part of a future government. Whether other groups would be able to remain viable political organizations in the new system depended on the outcome of the negotiations and the constitution that would eventually be adopted. Most movements had to act immediately or risk becoming irrelevant. At the local level, too, the civic associations that had organized resistance to the apartheid state in the 1980s had to fight to maintain their identity once the ANC began to reestablish itself inside the country.

The government and the ANC, both of which seemed to relegate other groups to a subordinate position, did not help matters. They apparently believed that the solution to South Africa's problems lay solely in their hands. Other organizations did not figure prominently in their calculations. They would have to be informed about what was happening and even formally involved in the negotiating process, but they were expected to line up behind the major players, not assert themselves as autonomous forces.

That expectation was not warranted. By the time CODESA opened, the right of the ANC and the National Party to determine between them the future of the country was being challenged from the Right and the Left, as well as by those who embraced the cause of ethnic nationalism. The government and the ANC were still the most important players by far, but they were not the only ones. The conflict had become more complex and the negotiations more open-ended than either the ANC or the government had expected. The outcome would not necessarily be simply a compromise between the original demands of the principal parties. It would be open to broader influences.

NEGOTIATING IN THE ABSENCE OF CRISIS

The increasing complexity of the conflict was only one of the factors that made negotiations difficult. Another was the main players' conviction that they were negotiating from a position of strength. The talks had started not because one side knew it was defeated but because a few individuals decided the time had come to take a decisive step to break the stalemate. Both the government and the ANC, however, saw negotiations as a means of attaining their original goals, rather than as the first step toward a compromise solution. As a result, there was little sense of urgency to the negotiations, particularly on the part of the government, which would have to surrender at least some power in the future.

What characterized the apartheid conflict in 1990 was stagnation, not crisis. Crises had arisen before. In 1976, the Soweto student uprising had led to a surge of political activism on the part of blacks unmatched since the banning of the ANC and PAC in 1960. The uprising was repressed, but a second wave of militancy was triggered in the early 1980s by the adoption of a new constitution that still excluded Africans from the political process while giving limited rights to Coloureds and Indians. In 1986, the government imposed a nationwide state of emergency, and the turmoil abated.

The underlying problem, however, was not solved—it simply turned from critical to chronic. Repression no longer ensured a peaceful or prosperous life for white South Africans. The townships were in turmoil, the economy in recession, and the country isolated internationally. In the 1960s and 1970s, white South Africa had thrived despite its political problems. In the 1980s, this was no longer the case.

The government's decision to seek negotiations was not an act of desperation but a daring gamble that an agreement with the ANC could be reached that would restore peace, allow whites to retain a large measure of political control and their economic assets, and restore normal relations between South Africa and the rest of the world. De Klerk did not appear to consider himself defeated, and certainly there was no danger that the ANC would seize power.

The government had known for many years that the political system had to be reformed, but it had not found the determination to move. De Klerk finally did. Like Soviet leader Mikhail Gorbachev, he apparently decided that by taking the initiative he could maintain control over the transformation. He could change the system sufficiently to restore social peace and normalize South Africa's relations with the rest of the world, but avoid a complete transfer of power to blacks, moving instead to a system dubbed "power-sharing without domination."

The ANC did not face a crisis, either. In fact, in the 1980s it enjoyed a period of strength. The ranks of the external organization were swollen by hundreds of young blacks choosing the road of exile to escape arrest or join the struggle. The formation of the United Democratic Front provided an indirect but important presence inside the country. A campaign to demand the release of Mandela gave the ANC a high profile abroad, eventually leading to the imposition or the tightening of sanctions against South Africa. On the negative side, the Congress, and particularly MK, faced the prospect of dwindling Soviet and Eastern bloc support as the internal crisis of the communist world hastened disengagement from southern Africa. And the armed struggle was not achieving any results—but then it never had.

So, like the government, the ANC had its problems, but it had not entered the negotiating process out of desperation. Rather, it had done so out of conviction that it could achieve what it wanted through negotiations. As the liberation movement that had spearheaded the antiapartheid struggle, it was confident it would take over after the demise of the white regime. Its concept of the new political system was quite different from that of the National Party, being based on majority rule rather than power-sharing, and both sides knew that negotiations would be hard.

In the absence of a crisis, the negotiations proceeded at a leisurely pace. There was little sense of urgency. Moreover, the government openly favored a slow process of transition, since it was not eager to begin sharing power with other organizations. The ANC, which aimed to negotiate itself into power, did want to see results, but it too moved slowly, especially at the outset of the talks, because it needed time to reorganize and resolve some of its internal problems.

Negotiations thus did not start auspiciously. Lacking a strong incentive to reach an agreement rapidly, the participants settled for scoring points against one another, even if no lasting gain could come from it. The result was that, two and a half years and innumerable documents, statements, and proposals later, the positions of the two major parties had changed very little, if at all. Neither side had made any real concession by the time negotiations were suspended in June 1992. Behind the barrage of confusing verbiage that gave the illusion of progress, the parties remained rooted in their initial positions, convinced that in the end they could obtain what they wanted and avoid a compromise. The result was the breakdown of CODESA in June 1992, followed by the resumption of a halting dialogue between the government and the ANC in the fall.

MODELS OF TRANSITION

The differing goals of the ANC and the government were influenced by historical trends apparent around the world. Three particular currents had special relevance to South Africa: (1) the decolonization process, already ancient history in most third world countries trying to come to grips with economic decay and authoritarianism but a poignant issue in South Africa, where blacks still had no political rights; (2) the transition from authoritarianism to democracy that had swept Latin America and was on the political agenda of most African countries; and (3) the revival of nationalism, which had dismembered the Soviet Union and Yugoslavia, threatened the rest of Eastern

Europe, and was already changing the political configuration of the Horn of Africa. In the rest of the world, the three trends belonged to distinct historical periods; in South Africa, they were telescoped into one.

For the black liberation movements, the formation of a postapartheid government was akin to the attainment of independence in other African countries. The demise of apartheid would mark the end of the era of colonial domination in Africa. To be sure, South Africa was not a colony, and it had not been one since the early part of the century; two of its provinces, the Transvaal and the Orange Free State, had never really been colonies. Nevertheless, South Africa as it is today had come into existence as a result of the European powers' conquest of Africa. Other regimes originating from that subjugation had long since disappeared. South Africa remained the exception.

Leftist intellectuals even defined apartheid as "colonialism of a special type."[1] Without much theoretical elaboration, the Organization of African Unity considered the ANC and PAC to be two of the many liberation movements engaged in the anti-imperialist struggle throughout the continent. The frontline states bordering South Africa saw themselves as the embattled buffer between independent and still-dominated Africa. ANC leaders, particularly those of the older generation, thought of themselves as part of the broad movement that had led to the independence of Africa and the third world. Some of Mandela's actions that whites found most puzzling and upsetting— his warm relations with the Palestine Liberation Organization and Libya, for example—were simply part of this identification with a third world standing up to the Western powers. When crowds demonstrated in favor of Iraq during the Gulf War in 1991, or roared their approval at the mention of Saddam Hussein's name, they expressed a similar solidarity with a perceived victim of imperialist aggression. The perception was distorted, but it was nevertheless very real.

White South Africans rejected with indignation any suggestion that their country's situation paralleled colonialism. Their protestations were sometimes pushed to an absurd point, such as the claim that an analogy with the Meiji restoration in Japan in the middle of the nineteenth century was more helpful in understanding the transition in South Africa than an analogy with decolonization.[2] Their reluctance even to entertain the idea that the end of apartheid might resemble decolonization was understandable. Decolonization had led whites to flee the continent, particularly in the settlers' colonies, where the struggle had been most protracted and the change most traumatic. Independent African countries were not models of democracy and economic growth. Nor was South Africa, for that matter, but life remained good for many whites despite a prolonged recession. Furthermore, decolonization had often entailed an attempt by the new government to repossess the country's wealth. Outright nationalizations, the promotion of Africans to replace whites, and the seizure of white and often Indian businesses by indigenous inhabitants had all been enacted elsewhere. South African whites, then, refused to concede similarities between South Africa and other African countries; for many blacks, however, the similarity was real.

Whites, especially liberals, who searched for a more reassuring scenario found one in the transitions from authoritarianism to democracy that had occurred particularly in Latin American countries.[3] The transition from apartheid, they argued, was but another face of the same phenomenon. This vision was more positive than decolonization. To whites, democracy was less frightening than a single-party African regime: it would be good for everyone and, most important, it would not threaten white interests. Furthermore, democracy worked best if underpinned by a flourishing free-market economy. Whites could hold hope for the future if the transition were from authoritarianism to democracy.

A third possible outcome of the transition was espoused by only a few right-wingers in 1990, but the idea was gaining new adherents two years later. The proposition was that the existing multiethnic South Africa break up along ethnic lines. What mattered was not the emergence of a democratic regime but the exercise of the right to self-determination for all nations, and above all for the Afrikaner *volk*. As in the Soviet Union, nationalism would become the dominant force. For South Africa, this did not necessarily mean the formation of independent states, although at least one of the homelands, Bophuthatswana, envisaged just that. It could mean, however, that the recognition of distinct nations and their autonomy from the central government would matter more than the degree of democracy achieved by each entity. The transition from apartheid authoritarianism would thus lead to a plurality of political units rather than to a pluralistic political system.

To some extent, the idea was a remake of the National Party's old apartheid scenario, but with some important differences. For one, the homeland leaders who most strongly advocated the recognition of their nations' right to self-determination wanted their fragmented territories consolidated within enlarged borders. For another, most Afrikaners realized that they could not hope to have as their homeland the 87 percent of the territory that had been designated in the past as the white area.

Paradoxically, the upsurge of ethnic nationalism coincided with the National Party's decision that the plan to grant independence to the homelands, transforming South Africa into a constellation of independent states, was unworkable. In fact, in 1990 it was generally assumed that even the four independent homelands would be reintegrated into South Africa; there seemed to be no other choice for pseudostates without international recognition or financial autonomy.

But two years later, the leaders of Bophuthatswana and KwaZulu were arguing that their homelands were not apartheid creations but the traditional territories of nations with a long and proud history, which therefore could not be eliminated. An unexpected new alliance was developing between homeland leaders and conservative Afrikaners anxious to have their own state. Ethnicity, around which the dying apartheid system revolved, was thus reinjected into the transition to a new South Africa by ambitious black politicians, not by the National Party.

THE STUDY

The growing complexity of the conflict, the absence of a sense of urgency in the negotiations, and the competing models inspiring different participants in the conflict suggested that South Africa would face a difficult, protracted transition. The timing of the transition, coming as it did when decolonization was history elsewhere, also suggested that South Africa's experience would be unlike that of any other country.

Two years after de Klerk's dramatic unbanning of the antiapartheid movements, constitutional negotiations were just beginning. Even the enactment of a new constitution would be only a first step. Apartheid was such a pervasive system, deeply affecting all spheres of life, that its formal abrogation was bound to touch off a long chain of consequences.

The change would certainly be more far-reaching than a purely political transition from authoritarianism to democracy. It could even be more significant than decolonization had been in many African countries, where governments launched ambitious new policies on paper but had little capacity to implement them. The transition could conceivably be as broad in scope as that from socialism in the Soviet Union and Eastern Europe. Like socialism, apartheid was an ambitious experiment in social engineering, and its abolition would have widespread ramifications.

This book deals with the initial phase of a process that will take a long time to complete. Its aim is not to predict the outcome but to clarify the issues involved in the transition, the groups trying to influence it, the arenas in which they fought with one another, the alliances they formed, and the tactics they used to further their goals. The outcome of this process of belated decolonization with all its accompanying demands and expectations—which is taking place in a world that by and large rejects redistribution in favor of growth and considers narrow ethnic nationalism more inevitable than undesirable—is impossible to predict.

A few comments are necessary about the terminology used in the study. The first point concerns race classification. It is impossible to write about South Africa today, and certainly for the foreseeable future, without reference to the major statutory race groups introduced by the apartheid regime. The government recognized four main groups: Whites, Asians, Coloureds, and Blacks, the latter three being referred to collectively as nonwhites. Following the example of the South African Institute of Race Relations, this study uses the word *Africans* instead of *blacks* to refer to the indigenous population, reserving *blacks* as a collective designation of the people the government called nonwhites. Also, Indians is used in preference to Asians as a more accurate description. For simplicity's sake, the term *Coloured* is maintained, in preference to the clumsy "so-called Coloured" used by members of the group to refer to themselves.

The second point concerns other expressions that are part of the political vocabulary of the country and that will be used in the study without recourse to quotation marks or other qualifications, even though many are highly inaccurate. For instance, independent homelands are not independent, and self-governing homelands are hardly self-governing. In fact, they are not even homelands to many of their inhabitants, whose presence there is the result of forced relocation rather than birth or free choice. Nevertheless, eschewing that lexicon in this book would very likely prove confusing to those who have followed the South African drama.

PART 1
The Actors

For a country with a long history of de facto single-party rule, repression, and censorship, South Africa in the early 1990s was home to a staggering number of organizations with a political agenda. Representatives from nineteen political parties participated in the Convention for a Democratic South Africa, which opened the formal negotiation process on December 20 and 21, 1991. A few weeks earlier about ninety groups had met to launch the Patriotic United Front of antiapartheid organizations. The National Peace Accord of September 1991 was signed by twenty-four organizations, with several more attending the convention. A conference of religious leaders, meeting in November 1990 to discuss the churches' position in the process of change, brought together representatives from eighty-five churches (a few foreign) and forty-five other organizations.

In every quarter, South Africa was a highly organized society. From political parties and movements to churches, from business groups to student organizations in township schools, mobilized constituencies tried to influence events. The importance of these groups varied greatly, and certainly not all equally affected the process of transition, but those that had a significant impact were numerous. The prolonged bilateral conflict between the supporters of apartheid and those seeking to destroy the system had spawned a great variety of organizations, which turned the process of conflict resolution into a multilateral one.

The chapters in this section examine those organizations that could be expected to play a part in the transition at the national level. Some were bound to have a major impact in any circumstance, the ANC and the government being the most obvious ones. Others would become important only if they made certain choices—for example, to turn to violence. None, however, could be dismissed in the initial phase of the process.

Chapter 2

The Government Establishment

In 1948 the National Party (NP) unexpectedly won the parliamentary elections. Although it received less than 50 percent of the vote, it nevertheless won a majority of the parliamentary seats and thus was able to form the new government. The victory represented the triumph of Afrikaner nationalism. A small minority caught between the overwhelmingly more numerous blacks and the wealthier and better-educated English-speaking population, Afrikaners were nonetheless determined to impose their control over the country they considered theirs. They succeeded. The 1948 election marked the beginning of four decades of National Party rule. It also ushered in the apartheid system.

Apartheid has since undergone continuous change and evolution as the government tried to maintain the viability of an ever-threatened system of white domination that bucked historical trends and demographic realities. But the rule of the National Party itself was not threatened, so it was not modified. As long as apartheid remained in place and blacks were disenfranchised, the party could not be challenged. It was kept in power by the strength of Afrikaner nationalism and whites' fears of being swamped by the black majority, and also by the manipulation of the formal political system, the use of government jobs as patronage, reliance on the security apparatus to repress the opposition, and an extensive system of ideological control and propaganda.

The party gambled in 1990 that it could finally accede to demands to set aside the formal apartheid system without completely relinquishing power. It would share power with others, to be sure, but it would not be cast out alongside the system it had championed for forty years.

At first glance, the NP's contention seemed preposterous. In the 1989 parliamentary elections, the National Party had received only 48 percent of the white vote, and whites were probably no more than 12 percent of the total population of the country. But the National Party did not depend on votes alone. It was more than just a political party: it had become the state as well, a party-state, to borrow the term used by President Sekou Touré of Guinea in the 1970s. Despite the outward trappings of democracy, the NP had de facto consolidated the single-party system many African leaders had tried to erect, to little avail. Ironically, the South African government cited the attempts to create single-party regimes elsewhere on the continent as one reason the black majority could not be allowed to rule South Africa.

The party did not control just the cabinet and the majority of seats in the Parliament but all institutions. The civil service and the parastatals were used to provide jobs and advancement for the Afrikaner population, the party's main source of support. The educational system was used to inculcate the party's philosophy in the young, with radio and television to reinforce it. A secret organization, the Afrikaner Broederbond, helped tie together the National Party, civil service, educational system, and the three Afrikaner churches. Finally, particularly in the 1980s under the leadership of P. W. Botha, the security forces were brought into the very center of the power structure through the enhanced role of the State Security Council.

The existence of this cohesive network made the contention that the National Party could abandon apartheid without completely relinquishing power somewhat less preposterous. It also meant that the transition to a new political system entailed much more than simply electing a new Parliament and forming a new cabinet. All these institutions in the NP sphere would have to change; otherwise, the transition would be incomplete.

THE REFORMERS AT THE TOP

The initiative for reform in this tightly knit system came from the top. A small number of politicians at the highest levels of the National Party chose to respond to the challenge of the black movements by introducing reforms rather than by repression alone. There was no liberal groundswell from the ranks of the white population. On the contrary, popular sentiment had been moving in the opposite direction, in response to the modest, halting process of reform undertaken under P. W. Botha. In February 1982 the conservative wing of the National Party, led by Andries Treurnicht, leader of the party organization in the Transvaal, split off in protest against a proposed new constitution that provided for the formation of a tricameral Parliament in which Coloureds and Indians, but not Africans, gained some representation. The modest amount of "power-sharing" entailed in this reform was more than conservative members of the National Party could tolerate. The dissidents launched the new Conservative Party (CP), represented in Parliament by seventeen MPs (members of Parliament) who followed Treurnicht. In the 1987 parliamentary elections, the new party received 26.4 percent of the vote, and in 1989, 31.2 percent.[1] The conservative upsurge clearly was not limited to a handful of disgruntled MPs.

Loss of popular support did not pose an immediate threat to the National Party. By gerrymandering electoral districts under the existing system of single-member constituencies, the incumbent party did not need a majority of votes to control the Parliament. In the 1989 election, 48 percent of the vote received by the National Party translated into control of 93 out of 165 seats, with the rest divided between the Conservative and the Democratic parties.[2] Even signs of growing dissatisfaction with President de Klerk's policies in 1990 and 1991 did not immediately threaten the government, because the party did not have to stand for election until early 1995.[3] By that time a new constitution would be enacted, giving the vote to the entire population and creating a totally new political equation.

Backed up by a disciplined Parliament controlled by the National Party, and not having to face the electorate before a new constitution was in place, de Klerk and the members of his inner circle enjoyed a broad degree of autonomy in crafting reform.

The men leading white South Africa into the new era were not newcomers bursting on the scene with fresh ideas and a totally new agenda. Instead, they were all established, mainstream politicians who had made their careers in the heart of the Afrikaner establishment, which rewarded loyalty and discipline and equated dissent with treason. Even more important, none of them had a reputation for being particularly *verligte*, or "enlightened," in the National Party's limited definition of the term.[4]

When F. W. de Klerk was chosen by the party caucus to replace P. W. Botha, who resigned in February 1989, he was not the candidate of the reformers; rather, he was thought to be a conservative, or at best to fall squarely in the party's center. Liberals greeted his election with dismay. Willem de Klerk, F. W.'s brother and a leading *verligte*, admitted that F. W. was "a party man, a veritable Mr. National Party" determined to maintain the unity of the organization above all else.[5] Nonetheless, Hermann Giliomee had singled out de Klerk and Gerrit Viljoen, in 1990 minister for constitutional development and a member of de Klerk's inner circle, as the men who might be able to "effect some reconciliation in Afrikaner ranks" after Treurnicht's resignation.[6]

De Klerk fully agreed that he was the quintessential party man. "He denies allegations," wrote his brother, "that his policy reflects discontinuity in National Party policy."[7] The president rejected the idea that his decision to unban the antiapartheid political organizations and to embark on the road of negotiations was the result of a political conversion. That notion, he declared, was "exaggerated, even sensationalistic."[8] In the fall of 1990 when some Afrikaner church leaders confessed they might have sinned in supporting apartheid as a system in accordance with scriptural precepts, de Klerk dismissed the notion of confession and repentance, arguing instead that the authors of apartheid had done what they thought best for the country and all groups in it.[9] The system had failed, but that failure was not a sin.

As a party man, de Klerk fell exactly within the nationalists' tradition of apartheid. That tradition encompassed three major components: racism pure and simple; the Afrikaners' fear of being overrun not only by the black masses but initially also by the better-educated and wealthier English-speaking community; and the realization that in the age of decolonization the demands of blacks for political rights and socioeconomic advancement could no longer be ignored. This last point differentiated apartheid, or the doctrine of separate development, from a system of simple domination. Supporters of apartheid claimed that blacks would not be dominated by whites but would develop on their own, within their own culture and tradition, in separate homelands, while whites would do the same in white South Africa. Eventually, the homelands would become independent like all other African countries. Blacks would thus acquire full political rights, and whites would continue controlling their own country, without dominating blacks.

This third component, the realization that naked racial domination was no longer acceptable, turned apartheid into an essentially reformist doctrine, particularly after the wave of decolonization swept Africa beginning in the late 1950s. Apartheid was not an attempt to maintain the status quo. Its aim was to create a new social and political system to fit the ideal of separate development, even if it meant pulling apart population groups that shared territory and were economically interdependent. One would have to turn to the socialist world to find examples of social engineering comparable to apartheid.

The reality of separate development was quite different from the theory. The white economy depended on black labor. Blacks could not make a living in the homelands, which comprised barely 13 percent of the country's land, most of it stony and arid. And to obtain even a modicum of separation, more than three million blacks had to be "removed" from areas defined as white and resettled into "homelands" where they had never before set foot.[10]

But there was also a streak of realism, and thus of reformism, in apartheid. The *verligte*—or pragmatic—wing of the Afrikaner establishment knew that pure repression could not succeed forever, and knew also that whites could safeguard what they wanted only if blacks were given enough stake in the system to accept it. Since this never happened, the system underwent continuous reforms as successive leaders struggled with the task of making apartheid work. Reforms were a matter of "modernizing racial domination," as Heribert Adam put it, not of eliminating it.[11] Policies that proved unworkable were discarded, and the government searched for another formula that might work. This tradition of change raised the question whether the reforms of the 1990s were also a new attempt to reconfigure apartheid rather than to make a clean break with it.

The increased tempo of black protest, beginning with the Soweto uprising in 1976, convinced the *verligte* element in the National Party that change was once again necessary. Gerrit Viljoen spelled out the reformists' position in 1978. As rector of Rand Afrikaans University, head of the Broederbond, and later holder of a succession of ministerial portfolios, Viljoen embodied Afrikaner *verligte* thinking and demonstrated its very narrow limits. What was considered enlightened in the Broederbond and the National Party was quite conservative by any other standard. In 1978, Viljoen argued that the National Party was faced with the rejection of apartheid by South African blacks and the rest of the world, and that the "original formula" could not cope with the situation. A major reason for the failure was that the policy was imposed on blacks without consulting them, he said. The National Party therefore had to introduce the principle of "negotiations and consultation," but without introducing power-sharing between the races. At the same time, Afrikaners had to learn to distinguish between those measures vital to the maintenance of Afrikaner identity and those that only entrenched discrimination. Among the former he listed separate school education, separate living areas, and the "group basis of politics."[12]

In the 1980s P. W. Botha—known for both unprecedented reforms and a hard-line policy of repression—enacted some of Viljoen's ideas. In a new feat of political engineering, a constitution was enacted in 1983. It gave whites, Coloureds, and Indians representation in separate chambers of a tricameral Parliament and control over "own affairs," while an overwhelmingly white—and Afrikaner—cabinet presided over "general affairs." Some apartheid laws were repealed, including the Mixed Marriages Act and the section of the Immorality Act making sexual intercourse across color lines a crime. Reservation of certain jobs for whites was abolished, as was influx control, the pass system designed to keep Africans not needed in the urban work force back in the homelands. Importantly, dialogue began with the jailed Nelson Mandela. De Klerk would later claim that the reforms he undertook were simply a continuation of those initiated by P. W. Botha, although Botha rejected that assertion.[13]

P. W. Botha was an unlikely reformer, a conservative forced by circumstances to play a *verligte* role. The process he initiated was a start-and-stop one in which the reforms that split the Afrikaner establishment and led to the formation of the Conservative Party went hand in hand with the imposition of the state of emergency, and the rise of the "securocrats" accompanied the opening of a dialogue with Mandela. But by the time Botha retired, the concept of power-sharing rejected by Viljoen as "something which Afrikaners have always been promised will never happen" had become the policy of the party.[14]

As a party man, de Klerk inherited this confusing and ambiguous tradition. He did not have to undergo a political conversion to favor reform: in line with the party record, he could be a faithful follower and a reformist. "When those of us in the inner circles—courageously led by P. W. Botha—had reached the conclusion that our policy had to shift from separate development to power-sharing, I gave it my full support," claimed de Klerk.[15]

This made the president's real position on reform difficult to assess. Like all National Party reformists, he walked "a narrow and slippery ledge," trying to change the system enough to make it acceptable but not so much that essential principles were violated.[16] As late as 1986, de Klerk, then head of the Transvaal National Party, had emphatically asserted that the NP "stood by its policy of separate residential areas, separate schools, and separate institutions for different race groups."[17] By 1991, he was announcing the repeal of the Group Areas Act. But that same year, he also announced the introduction of legislation giving neighborhoods the power to enforce their own "norms and standards."[18] The line separating the abandonment of old goals from the use of new means to attain old goals was getting thinner and thinner.

THE NATIONAL PARTY

Some steps taken by de Klerk in 1990 and 1991 could only be considered a reversal of past policies, notwithstanding protestations to the contrary. The unbanning of the African National Congress (ANC) and the Pan Africanist Congress (PAC) after thirty years and that of the South African Communist Party after forty, the release of people previously denounced as terrorists, and the repeal of most of the legislation that undergirded apartheid represented a major policy shift, not continuity.

These changes were introduced without consulting the party apparatus. De Klerk acknowledged that the decisions to unban the ANC and release Mandela had been reached within the cabinet; the party caucus had not been consulted, let alone the membership at large.[19] An NP internal bulletin leaked to the press even admitted that the party did not have an explicit mandate to unban political organizations, although it was free to do so because it had not bound itself not to take such a step.[20] Nevertheless, the party remained willing to follow de Klerk, which gave the president an advantage in the negotiations over Mandela, who faced a membership that insisted on being consulted.

Delegates at the National Party's congresses of 1990 and 1991—the organization has a federal constitution and each of the four regions holds a separate meeting—were faced with momentous issues, but there was little discussion. In 1990 a proposal was put forth to open the party to all races. The rationale behind the proposal was that the well-being of the NP under universal suffrage would hinge on its ability to form alliances with black moderate political organizations, and an exclusively white party could not easily fashion such alliances. The proposal was approved unanimously without much debate.[21] Party members were not necessarily enthusiastic about the change— blacks were turned away from a public meeting of the supposedly integrated National Party not long after the proposal's adoption— but, as one commentator wrote, the delegates apparently concluded that "in today's fast changing political world, it seemed more appropriate to entrust the leadership to handle whatever came up, as it saw fit."[22]

In 1991 delegates were asked to consider a new constitutional proposal intended to safeguard as much power as possible for whites, while also recognizing the political rights of blacks and abolishing representation by population group.[23] Again, there was virtually no debate. The party organization seemed uninterested in playing an autonomous role, checking the activity of the leadership, or giving it a well-defined policy mandate.

THE BUREAUCRACY

South African civil servants and public sector employees had much to lose from the end of apartheid. The new system might well be as bureaucratic as the old one, but it was a foregone conclusion that bureaucrats would no longer be overwhelmingly white and Afrikaner. Consequently, civil servants were uneasy. The government did its best to assuage the uneasiness by issuing assurances that jobs and pensions would be safeguarded, but the threat remained, fueled by the inevitability of change and by ANC announcements that it was taking steps to train administrators.[24]

In the interim, however, these same threatened civil servants enjoyed a great deal of power because the government was not pressing the bureaucracy to implement the reforms it was introducing. While the government announced momentous decision after momentous decision, the wheels of the apartheid bureaucracy were still turning in the old grooves.

Since 1948, the National Party had used the government bureaucracy not only to establish tight control over the country but to provide jobs for the Afrikaner population, which in the first half of the century had suffered dire poverty, caught as they were between a richer, better-educated, and enterprising English-speaking population and a cheaper black labor force. The problem of the poor whites elicited much concern even outside South Africa during this period.[25] The National Party was very successful in tackling the problem, to a large extent because it concentrated its efforts on the Afrikaners, ignoring, and often adding to, the much worse plight of blacks.

In 1946, just before the National Party came to power, only 29 percent of Afrikaners were in white-collar occupations; 30 percent were farmers, many of them impoverished; and 40 percent had blue-collar jobs. By 1977, the proportion of Afrikaners in white-collar jobs had risen to 65 percent.[26] Similarly, in 1946 per capita income among Afrikaners was less than half that of English speakers; by 1976 it had increased to over two-thirds.[27] Public employment had been the key to this transformation. By 1988, one-third of the white economically active population was employed in the public sector; the proportion was much higher among Afrikaners, who constituted the bulk of public employees.[28]

South African civil servants thus had much to lose and could be expected to resist change, at least through inertia if not openly. The bureaucracy had all the worst possible characteristics from the point of view of reform. Far from being a neutral apparatus used to working with whatever government was in power, it was the creature of the National Party. Far from being a meritocracy, it was the refuge of a specific population group. Far from accepting the inevitability of change, it had turned toward the Right in the 1980s, according to some studies.[29]

Moreover, the power of this essentially conservative, Afrikaner bureaucracy, whose members had a vested interest in the perpetuation of the old system that provided them with jobs and security, was likely to increase in the short run. The government's new stated policy was to devolve power and to decentralize as much as possible. This meant giving lower-level bureaucrats wider latitude in implementing reforms. Defended in the name of greater democracy, decentralization was likely to slow down the process of change and perpetuate the status quo.

An example will clarify this point. In April 1990, Rina Venter, the minister for national health and population development, announced the abolition of segregation in all hospitals, even before the Separate Amenities Act was repealed. The decision was presented as proof that the new South Africa was indeed around the corner, and the minister reassured skeptics that desegregation would be complete down to the level of the wards. However, the fourteen health departments existing in South Africa would not be abolished yet, and money would not be available to reopen the wards in white hospitals that had been closed for lack of patients.[30] Furthermore, hospital administrators would not be subject to authoritarian, bureaucratic directives but instead should implement the new policy in the way that best suited the specific problems of each hospital.

A year later, most hospital administrators, except for those in major hospitals in large cities, had decided that what best suited their hospitals' specific problems was no change at all. Most hospitals remained segregated, with patients piled two to a bed or sleeping on floors in wards still openly posted as "black," while "white" beds next door remained empty.[31] Bureaucrats imaginatively explained that the situation had nothing to do with discrimination: black patients were not psychologically ready to be in white wards, for example; or, desegregation would cause overcrowding in all wards, so transferring black patients to empty white beds would be pointless.[32]

The bureaucracy's resistance to change was hardly surprising: for forty years its duty had been to enforce apartheid regulations, and its members feared losing their jobs. What raised questions about the government's intentions was the decision to maximize the power of that conservative institution through decentralization.

THE SECURITY APPARATUS

Among the various components of the governmental coalition, the security establishment represented the greatest unknown, particularly after the end of the Botha presidency. The security establishment included "the SADF [South African Defence Force] and the noncivilian Department of Defence; the various intelligence services, consisting of Military Intelligence, the National Intelligence Service, and the Security Police; the armaments and related industries . . .; the South African Police (SAP); certain individuals and segments within universities and 'think-tank' institutions; and the State Security Council."[33]

The security establishment's main task for several decades had not been to defend the country against external aggression but to protect the minority regime against the threat posed by organizations seeking to obtain political rights for the majority. In pursuit of this goal, the security forces had been involved in a wide array of activities inside and outside South Africa, including covert military operations designed to destabilize radical regimes in neighboring countries, above all in Mozambique and Angola. Accordingly, the security forces played a deeply political role. At the same time, the SADF upheld a reputation for professionalism and accepted the authority of the civilian government. What made it possible for the security forces to be political and apolitical at the same time was interpenetration of the civilian and the military leadership, both of which were rooted in the tradition of Afrikaner nationalism and shared the same goals. "Civil-military interpenetration in South Africa," concluded one study, "is of the structural . . . kind," rather than purely conjunctural.[34]

But there was no assurance that the security forces would remain apolitical during the transition. The new goal of the civilians in the government was to reach agreement with the black political movements, not to crush them. Such agreement would inevitably mean the end of white control over the security forces. If it remained apolitical, the security establishment would thus implicitly renounce the old goals and accept its own demise. Under the circumstances, the possibility that the security forces might try to play an independent political role could not be dismissed lightly. In its most extreme manifestation, the refusal to submit to a new civilian leadership would lead to a coup d'état, yet this was not a likely danger in the South African transition. The most immediate concern was whether the security forces were still carrying out covert operations to undermine the ANC and other black movements and thereby contributing to the violence raging in the townships.

In the early 1990s, the relationship between the president and the security apparatus was delicate. The role of the latter had expanded considerably under P. W. Botha. Botha had been minister of defense from 1966 to 1980, and he kept that portfolio in his own hands for two years after becoming prime minister in 1978.[35] During this time he developed close working relations and bonds of trust with men in the South African Defence Force and the security agencies, and he continued to rely on them during his presidency. The securocrats, as they were dubbed, came to play a central role in government. Botha also created new institutions, notably the State Security Committee, which were attached to the presidency. Consequently the power of the executive increased, and that of the party apparatus and the Parliament correspondingly decreased. Within the executive, members of the security establishment became prominent.

President de Klerk inherited this situation, but with a major difference. The securocrats were not his men—his roots were in the party. For a long time he did not challenge them, either because he did not have the power to do so or because he found it convenient to let them take the blame for actions that belied the liberal image of his government.

The ambiguities of the relationship between de Klerk and the securocrats were highlighted first by the unfolding of the tortuous and shadowy scandal involving the police death squads and the SADF's Civil Cooperation Bureau (CCB), and later by a showdown with the ANC that eventually led to the firing of Defence Minister Magnus Malan and Law and Order Minister Adriaan Vlok, both holdovers from the Botha years.[36] Facts surrounding the CCB scandal remained obscure despite investigations by several commissions, a court case involving a South African police force general, and reams of investigations by newspapers and other groups. The Harms Commission, set up by de Klerk to investigate the matter, concluded in November 1990 that the police death squads suspected of assassinating anti-apartheid activists simply did not exist.[37] That conclusion was squarely contradicted in January 1991 by a court that concluded that a SAP general had indeed supplied poison to members of such a squad.[38] And while the existence of the CCB was never denied by Malan, he refused to take responsibility for it, claiming ignorance of its existence until 1989.[39]

Although the investigation failed to provide definitive answers, enough evidence came to light to show that Malan and Vlok—Malan in particular—were at the very least in poor control of what was happening in their departments and were possibly directly responsible for many shady dealings. Calls for Malan's resignation rang repeatedly in Parliament from the opposition parties, which invoked the "Westminster tradition" that holds a minister ultimately responsible for what his department does. Within the National Party itself, there was considerable discontent about Malan's position and worry about the repercussions of the lingering scandal.[40]

The government chose to accept the findings of the Harms Commission, hoping the matter would end there. It did not. The ANC was convinced that the death squads continued to operate, and even that a "third force" with links to the security apparatus was acting to stir up violence in the townships. The government dismissed those allegations, attributing the violence to tribal animosity between Zulus and Xhosas and to the competition for power between the ANC and the Inkatha movement led by KwaZulu Chief Minister Mangosuthu Buthelezi.

In April the ANC issued an ultimatum to the government, stating that unless certain steps were taken to put an end to the violence by May 9, the ANC would withdraw from all talks. One of the demands was that de Klerk dismiss ministers Vlok and Malan. After initially declaring that it would never surrender to an ultimatum, the government made several concessions and the breakdown in talks was averted. Malan and Vlok retained their positions, but not for long. In late July, a leak to the press provided proof that the police had secretly funded two major rallies held by Inkatha.[41] The revelations concerning what became known as Inkathagate both threatened de Klerk's carefully cultivated image as a man of integrity and strengthened the ANC's conviction that the security forces were involved in stirring up violence and undermining antiapartheid organizations.

Trying to salvage his reputation and the negotiating process, de Klerk pledged that all secret operations would be reviewed and curtailed. He also announced a major cabinet reshuffle, which included the demotion of Vlok and Malan to less important ministerial posts and their replacement with two members of his inner circle.[42] Roelf Meyer, who as deputy minister for constitutional development was closely involved in the process of reform and negotiations, became minister of defense. Hermanus Kriel, formerly minister of local government and housing, took over the law and order portfolio.

The reshuffle, coupled with de Klerk's assurance that secret funding to Inkatha had ended and other covert operations had been greatly curtailed, solved the immediate problem of keeping the negotiations alive. But the issue of the security forces' role was not settled. Instead, it reemerged in November 1992 as a result of information gathered by the Commission of Inquiry Regarding the Prevention of Public Violence and Intimidation (Goldstone Commission), by the investigators into the 1990 assassination of antiapartheid activist David Webester, and by the press. This information showed that the security forces were still involved in covert operations to discredit Umkhonto we Sizwe and, through it, the ANC, despite de Klerk's assurances that all such operations had ceased.

The president initially stonewalled, then in mid-December fired twenty-five officers, including six generals. Yet the move did not answer the fundamental questions about civil-military relations. Had de Klerk been aware of the operation, and was he using the military as a convenient scapegoat? Or had the security forces acted on their own, outside civilian control?

THE AFRIKANER BROEDERBOND AND THE CHURCHES

The ideological underpinnings of the apartheid system were provided over the years by a number of organizations, the most important of which were the Afrikaner Broederbond and the three Dutch Reformed churches. Together they supplied a strong element of ideological homogeneity among Afrikaners, helping prevent expressions of dissent and making it easier for the National Party to consolidate its rule. But these institutions were already greatly weakened as South Africa entered the process of transition. After the split between the National and the Conservative parties, the Broederbond could no longer hope to maintain a commonality of ideology and purpose among influential Afrikaners. The churches were divided and confused, finding it as difficult to continue justifying apartheid as to admit that they had been wrong. As a result, they provided little effective guidance to their members.

The Broederbond was at first a cultural organization, set up in 1918 "to prevent the disappearance of the Afrikaner volk as a separate political, language, social and cultural entity."[43] It became much more: a secret think tank designing policies for the National Party and a tentacular organization linking prominent Afrikaners from all fields in a powerful network that made it very difficult for dissent to spread.

What made the organization controversial over the years was not its promotion of Afrikanerdom or even its power but its secrecy. It recruited members by co-optation, choosing individuals in important positions or likely to rise to such posts. Members supported each other's advancement, making sure that in the end the Afrikaner political, educational, religious, and business elite would be tied by membership in the Broederbond.

The rise of the National Party magnified the role of the organization. The party established the Afrikaners' hold on the government, the bureaucracy, and the army and police; through state control, it also increased Afrikaner economic power, which had hitherto run a distant second to that of the English-speaking community. The Broederbond had members in all these sectors—even at the very top of the political establishment. Whether the National Party was dictated to by the Broederbond, or whether the Broederbond enhanced its power through its ties to the National Party, is a question an outsider cannot hope to answer. To a large extent, the question is moot: the two simply complemented and strengthened each other.

The influence of the Broederbond varied from period to period. It increased during the 1960s, leading to considerable criticism, particularly on the part of the English-language press, which resented the power and policymaking role of a secret organization accountable only to itself.[44] Later the Broederbond's direct political influence apparently declined somewhat, as Prime Minister John Vorster and P. W. Botha—both members—distanced themselves from it.[45]

The decline in the organization's importance was sealed by the open split in the Afrikaner ranks that led to the formation of the Conservative Party. Although the CP failed to become a major institutional player, the existence of two political organizations claiming to represent the interests of the Afrikaners dashed any hope of maintaining unity across the major institutions. Within government circles, the Broederbond retained some importance under de Klerk, particularly since it was controlled by the same *verligte* element that was leading the process of political reform. The president and many key ministers were prominent members of the Broederbond—Gerrit Viljoen was a former chairman.[46] The organization still prepared studies on major issues, including a new constitution. But the days were gone when one organization could unite in one ideological framework and for a common political purpose government ministers, principals of small-town schools, bureaucrats, and businessmen.

The Dutch Reformed churches, historically a powerful element of cohesion and conformity among Afrikaners, had also lost the ability to give their members firm political guidance. The three main groups—the Nederduitse Gereformeerde Kerk (NGK), the Nederduitsch Hervormede Kerk (NHK), and the Gereformeerde Kerk in Suidlike Afrika, commonly known as the Dopper, or conservative, church—differed from each other on subtle points of theology but had been united until recently in their support of apartheid, for which they found justification in the Bible. The position taken by these churches led to their estrangement from the World Council of Churches and other international religious organizations.

The difficulty the Afrikaner churches experienced in trying to adapt to changing circumstances was illustrated by the tribulations of the Dutch Reformed Church. While strictly segregated, it was part of a broader family that included the Coloured Nederduitse Gereformeerde Sendingkerk and the African Nederduitse Gereformeerde Kerk in Afrika. These two churches belonged to the South African Council of Churches (SACC). The moderator of the Sendingkerk, Allan Boesak, was a leader not only in the SACC but also in the United Democratic Front; in late 1991 he also became the head of the ANC Western Cape region. These nonwhite affiliates made the NGK more open to pressure for change than the other Dutch Reformed churches, but even here the process was slow and subject to backtracking. White members ended up divided among themselves and confused about the position of their church on apartheid, while blacks became even more suspicious about the NGK's willingness to change its stance, as the following example shows.

In 1986 the NGK issued a document called "Church and Society," which, in a major departure from previous doctrine, stated that the Scriptures did not provide a justification for apartheid and that racism was "a grievous sin." But the document also declared that "the church has a close relationship with the nation" and "will display characteristics that are typical of the culture of that particular nation." Thus, "in the structuring of the church, provisions may be made for linguistic and cultural differences related to the diversity of peoples."[47] In other words, the three separate churches could be maintained. Even this limited change was sufficient to create a split, and a conservative group broke off to create a new church.[48]

In 1990 the NGK's synod approved a new version of "Church and Society," going further than in 1986 but still falling far short of satisfying the demand of the black affiliates that apartheid be declared a sin.[49] The new document rejected racism and declared that any system that impairs human dignity is "sinful." It then equivocated, admitting that the church had "erred," but not sinned, by arguing that the Bible imposed separateness. It further confessed to "neglect" in not rejecting that argument earlier.[50] Nevertheless, the synod postponed deciding whether all NGK churches should be unified, irrespective of color. The black churches were not impressed.

A further act of this church drama was played out in November 1990 at an ecumenical church conference held at Rustenburg. During the course of the proceedings, in a highly emotional moment, the moderator of the NGK church declared "not only my own sin and guilt, and my personal responsibility for the political, social, economical and structural wrongs . . . but vicariously I dare also to do that in the name of the NGK . . . and for the Afrikaner people as a whole."[51] In an equally emotional response, Anglican Archbishop Desmond Tutu accepted the confession not only in his own name but in that of all participants. In the following days, everyone backed off. Tutu admitted that he had no authority to speak for the entire conference. The NGK delegation declared that the moderator had not spoken in an official capacity and therefore could not confess for the church as a whole. The conference closed on a note of discord and ambiguity. The other Dutch Reformed churches, it should be added, had not even begun to discuss these issues. In fact, the General Synod of the Dopper church, to which President de Klerk belongs, even raised questions about the propriety of the presence of a Dopper delegation at the Rustenburg meeting.[52]

These theological debates are important because they illustrate the ideological confusion and dissension pervading the white establishment in this period. The interpretations of the Bible that had been used for decades to back up the policies of the National Party had been rejected. They had not been replaced by a new orthodoxy but by division and uncertainty.

CONCLUSIONS

The South African political establishment was large and complex, a conglomerate that emerged in the long period of National Party domination and maintained its cohesion for a long time despite some problems and dissensions.

In the transition period, de Klerk still appeared capable of maintaining the unity of the governing coalition, although its ideological underpinnings had been eroded. Not only was he a party man, he was trying to be a man for the entire political establishment. Supported and counseled by a small group of close associates, he was also a leader, ahead of the pack, and he tried to move further down the road of apartheid reform.

The establishment did not openly resist. The party was willing to accept the leadership's proposals without discussion. The bureaucrats were worried about their future, but they still looked to the government for protection rather than turned against it. Speculations to the contrary notwithstanding, the security forces had given no indication that they were ready to step out of line. Institutionally, de Klerk entered the transition process in a strong position.

De Klerk's weakness, however, was the uncertainty of popular support. The white electorate was more divided than at any point since 1948, and this at a crucial time when the National Party would soon face a universal suffrage election. In a period of transition, dissension was not surprising. In addition, major institutions that had provided the ideological underpinnings for the government could not provide the same support for its abolition—the churches could not even decide what their position was, let alone influence the population at large.

None of this would impair de Klerk's ability to negotiate, particularly after the overwhelming victory in the March 3, 1992, referendum. But his capacity to put together a coalition strong enough to make the pact stick after an election could be jeopardized. De Klerk needed the unity of the establishment that had controlled the country for forty years in order to forge a political coalition capable of making a creditable showing in an election under universal suffrage. White support would not ensure a continuing major political role for the National Party, but it was indispensable to the success of de Klerk's policy. He simply could not lose white support and still win the gamble that the end of apartheid would not necessarily mean the end of a political role for whites and for the National Party.

Accordingly, de Klerk had to pursue two goals simultaneously, and they were probably mutually exclusive. He had to minimize conflict among whites and at the same time resolve the conflict with the antiapartheid movement. Attaining the former goal required a slow and cautious process of minimal reform, keeping together party, bureaucracy, security apparatus, and the public in general by accepting a minimum common denominator as the basis of reform. Solving the conflict with the antiapartheid movement meant finding a very different common denominator. Most likely, unity on the government side could be maintained only at the cost of perpetuating the conflict with the antiapartheid groups; solving that conflict would no doubt split the whites. There was no easy resolution.

Chapter 3

The Liberation Establishment

The African National Congress (ANC) and its allies in the mass democratic movement constituted the liberation establishment. While other groups had also been fighting apartheid, it was the ANC and its affiliates that had come to be recognized as *the* liberation movement both in and outside South Africa. This liberation establishment was composed of two sections.

The first was the ANC proper, an organization that had operated legally in South Africa from 1912 to 1960, had been exiled from 1960 until 1990, and had reorganized in South Africa since that time. In this book the term *ANC* will be used to refer only to this organization.

The second component of the liberation establishment, termed here the *mass democratic movement*, was less clearly defined. This was not a specific organization, although a more structured group officially called the Mass Democratic Movement had existed briefly before February 1990. Rather, it was a set of organizations that had sprung up inside South Africa during the 1980s while the ANC was still banned. Most of them were loosely structured internally and even more loosely connected to one another, but they shared determination to get rid of apartheid, broad acceptance of the principles set forth in the 1955 Freedom Charter—they were sometimes referred to as charterist organizations—and support for the ANC.

There were important differences between the government and the liberation establishments. The former was made up mostly of institutions with a clear identity and strong resources of personnel, finance, and experience, but with very limited popular support outside the white community. The latter consisted of loosely structured organizations, often with extremely unclear boundaries, weak financial resources, and very little technical expertise, but commanding a high degree of support at least among the African population. Thus the government establishment would have many advantages in formal negotiations, but the ANC would be much better placed in an election.

Before February 1990, the strength of the liberation establishment depended both on the reputation and image of the ANC, the symbol of the liberation struggle, and on the ability of the mass democratic movement to mobilize people in the townships. The two depended on each other. Until the mass democratic movement developed, the ANC had remained an ineffectual exiled organization, planning an armed struggle it did not have the resources to carry out. But the groups that constituted the mass democratic movement might never have been able to coalesce and bring pressure on the government had the exiled ANC not provided them with a common identity, sense of purpose, and international recognition.

The major components of the mass democratic movement were the township organizations, particularly civic associations and youth groups that after 1983 had been clustered under the umbrella of the United Democratic Front (UDF), and the majority of black labor unions, which in 1985 had come together to form the Congress of South African Trade Unions. Many church organizations, particularly those represented in the South African Council of Churches, sympathized with the mass democratic movement and the ANC, although they remained formally independent.

Until the unbanning, the exiled ANC and the mass democratic movement complemented each other, each drawing strength from the other's existence. There was no conflict between them because they operated in distinct geographic areas. As the ANC reorganized in South Africa, however, it inevitably drew into its ranks the militants of the mass democratic movement, threatening many of the township organizations with loss of leadership or, worse, loss of autonomy. The relationship between the ANC and the mass democratic movement thus became much more complicated.

THE AFRICAN NATIONAL CONGRESS

The ANC in the early 1990s was not a political party but a liberation movement that had worked above and underground, inside the country and in exile, through political means and through violence. As a liberation movement, it historically aspired to represent the entire downtrodden population of the country. In 1912 it "emerged as an organization to play the role of mouthpiece and leader" of the struggle against oppression, and its mission was "the forging of unity among the African people."[1] When it was unbanned in 1990, it still was a liberation movement, and although it started the process of transformation into a political party, progress in this direction was slow and halting, involving much conflict.

Transforming the ANC into a political party, that is, an organization fighting not for the absolute liberation of an entire population from an evil system but for a share of the political power in a democratic system in which power would be reallocated periodically, was a step with far-reaching implications. At a minimum, it meant abandoning the idea of the armed struggle and giving up Umkhonto we Sizwe (MK), the military wing. In the long run, it meant relying less often on mass action—marches and demonstrations, boycotts, and stayaways (politically motivated strikes)—for putting pressure on the government, and eventually accepting the verdict of the ballot box. The transformation also threatened the organization's financing, because foreign governments and organizations willing to support a liberation movement might find it less justifiable to fund one of many political parties; in any event, South African laws prevented a party from receiving such funds. Not surprisingly, the ANC was not willing to take such a step while blacks remained disenfranchised and the National Party remained a party-state.[2]

The transformation from liberation movement to democratic political party promised to be difficult. To become a political party the ANC had to lower its expectations of what its role would be in the future South Africa; it had to accept being one party among many rather than the symbol of liberation and the representative of the entire oppressed people. The difficulty of such a transition is demonstrated by the fact that no African liberation movement ever successfully turned into a political party. Dominant liberation movements went on to become political parties in nondemocratic systems, perpetuating the fiction that they embodied the aspirations of the entire population. South Africa itself offered a clear example of how difficult the transformation was. The National Party was in many respects an Afrikaner liberation movement that had made a very imperfect transition to political party after coming to power. The bundle of institutions discussed in the previous chapter blurred the distinction between party and government, between military and civilian authority, and between politics and administration.[3] Churches and cultural organizations provided the justification for the entire edifice.

The African National Congress was not unlike the National Party in this respect. The ANC was developing some traits of a political party, but it still maintained many characteristics of a liberation movement. It was possible to distinguish in the ANC a dynamics of "government" and party, of bureaucrats and political decisionmakers, of military and civilian authority. The National Party had its Broederbond, and the ANC had its own hidden intelligentsia in the South African Communist Party. It even had its own supporters among the churches. To be sure, these analogies can be overdrawn. Nevertheless, it is important to note that many of the problems of the liberation establishment were more structural than idiosyncratic, affecting the ANC as they had the National Party.

National Executive Committee

Unlike many liberation movements, the ANC never officially set up a formal government in exile. Its National Executive Committee (NEC) was nevertheless the equivalent of such a government, presiding not over a country but over an exiled organization with about twenty thousand members. Geographically dispersed among Zambia, Angola, Tanzania, and Britain—to mention only the most important countries—the ANC was centralized in terms of power, with the NEC acting as a cabinet and bureaucratic departments implementing policy. Until 1990 the Congress did not have an effective organization inside South Africa. An ANC underground did exist, but over the years the security forces successfully kept it from developing into a strong organization, as ANC leaders themselves admitted.[4] Organizations within South Africa, such as the UDF and its affiliates, provided much internal support for the ANC, but they did not take orders from the NEC.

The exiled ANC consisted of an informal government—the National Executive Committee—a military wing in the form of Umkhonto we Sizwe, and a bureaucracy manning the various departments. In Zambia and Tanzania, the ANC's bureaucracy ran farms, schools, and workshops; and in Angola, Umkhonto ran training camps. The Congress had diplomatic offices in London and representatives in many capitals around the world. What the external organization did not have on a significant scale was a membership, that is, people belonging to the ANC and supporting its political goals but not directly working for it or being supported by it. Many ANC members in exile, particularly those in African countries, depended on the organization for their survival. They were employees of a government bureaucracy, personnel of an army, or clients of a welfare state, not members of a political party.

The precise size of the ANC apparatus in exile was unknown. The exiled community numbered only about 1,000 before the 1976 Soweto student uprising swelled its ranks by sending a steady stream of youths out of the townships.[5] By 1985 the number had increased to 14,000, of whom 60 percent belonged to Umkhonto we Sizwe.[6] Other sources put the number of guerrillas trained by MK between 1967 and 1987 at 12,000, but did not provide any estimate of how many were still active—or alive—by 1990.[7] When preparations first began in South Africa for the return of the exiles, numbers as high as 40,000 were mentioned—probably reflecting the total number of South African exiles, many of whom had built lives for themselves abroad. A consensus finally developed that the ANC would be responsible for organizing the return of some 20,000 people.

The National Executive Committee, responsible at once for administering this complex establishment and trying to liberate South Africa, became a very undemocratic institution during the years of exile. In theory, it was democratically elected by the delegates to a party congress, and it was thus responsible to the party as a whole. A congress was held in 1969, electing a nine-member NEC. The next full-fledged congress was held in Durban in July 1991. In the interim, the size and composition of the NEC changed repeatedly, but mostly by co-optation, although a rather controversial election took place at the Kabwe consultative conference in 1985, bringing the NEC membership up from twenty-two to thirty members. By the time of the 1991 congress, the NEC, after more co-options and several deaths, appeared to have thirty-five members.[8] Until the Durban congress, the National Executive Committee of the ANC was a group de facto beholden to nobody but itself. For over twenty years it had not had to submit its actions to the scrutiny of a broad membership.

The initial negotiations between the imprisoned Nelson Mandela and the government took place in this situation of nonaccountability.

Mandela was able to consult with the exiled leadership and he had their approval in the negotiations, but the NEC was not in touch with the rank and file. Like the government, it had no explicit mandate for the new policy of negotiation, but that made little difference as long as the ANC remained a banned organization. Once it started reorganizing legally inside South Africa, however, the situation changed. Neither the new members nor the mass democratic movement would give the NEC carte blanche to pursue a negotiated end to apartheid.

The consultative conference of the ANC held in December 1990, in lieu of the postponed national conference that would elect the new NEC, brought the issue of accountability into the open. Delegates complained loudly about the lack of consultation and reporting back.[9] Two organizational and leadership styles clashed at the conference: that of the NEC, which assumed that the role of leaders was to lead and make decisions on their own, and that of the mass democratic movement, which upheld an ideal of participatory democracy requiring consultation of the rank and file before decisions were made and reporting back afterward. Unlike the government, the NEC by late 1990 no longer had complete freedom to act as it saw fit. "Accountability" had become a concept the leadership ignored at its peril, particularly since it would have to stand for reelection in June 1991.

The NEC in place in February 1990, to which fell the task of rebuilding the ANC inside the country and initiating negotiations with the government, was a very mixed group in terms of its members' history and ideological persuasion. Tom Lodge distinguished four groups.[10] The first comprised the veterans of the ANC Youth League of the prebanning period; President Oliver Tambo and Deputy President Nelson Mandela belonged to this group of well-known, popular, but also aging leaders. The second group dated back to the same period but had arisen from the labor unions and the South African Communist Party (SACP); SACP General Secretary Joe Slovo, the first white in the NEC, was the most popular member of this group. Of the two younger groups—from which the new top leadership would presumably emerge—one included people who had earned their spurs in Umkhonto, and the other those who had risen through the exiled bureaucracy. MK Chief of Staff Chris Hani and NEC Director of International Relations Thabo Mbeki were the best-known representatives of these two groups.

Ideologically, NEC members were extremely diverse. Mandela admitted after his release that the organization could not have a precise ideological orientation without splitting apart—what kept the ANC together was not a single vision of the future but unity in the struggle against apartheid.[11] The Freedom Charter, the 1955 manifesto to which all ANC members subscribed, carried the strong imprint of ideas prevalent in the early period of Africa's anticolonial struggle, later formalized in some countries as doctrines of African socialism—an ideal of justice, equality, and economic development brought about through the intervention of a benevolent state acting in the best interest of the entire population. But there were also many members of the SACP in the National Executive Committee, and Marxist terminology pervaded the political discourse of the ANC as it had that of other liberation movements. Finally, the conventional wisdom of the 1990s about the virtues of democracy and the free market was also leaving an imprint on the ANC. Less prevalent at this time were Africanist and black consciousness influences, which had been important in two periods: in the late 1950s before the split that led to the formation of the Pan Africanist Congress and in the late 1970s when young blacks imbued with Steve Biko's black consciousness ideas had joined the exiled ANC.[12]

Nelson Mandela

Nelson Mandela occupies a special place in a discussion of the ANC's top leadership. A major figure in the ANC in the 1950s, he was one of the leaders responsible for the upsurge in the organization's militancy, for the alliance with the Communist Party, and for the founding of Umkhonto we Sizwe. He was already influential when arrested in 1962, but by the time he was released twenty-seven years later he had been transformed into a heroic, almost mythical figure. This was the result of a successful campaign by the ANC to make him the symbol of the antiapartheid struggle. But he was more than a symbol. While still jailed, he became the major contact between the ANC and the government. The dialogue led to his release and, most important, to both sides' acceptance of the concept of a negotiated solution.

The special relationship Mandela initially enjoyed with F. W. de

Klerk enhanced his role even more. In the difficult last months of 1990, after the euphoria attending the unbanning had died down and as the enormous obstacles to be surmounted loomed threateningly, meetings and telephone calls between Mandela and de Klerk repeatedly smoothed the way. They also caused friction within the ANC. Although Mandela always proclaimed himself to be a faithful member of the National Executive Committee, bound by its policy and decisions, many in the ANC saw him as a rather autocratic figure, prone to making decisions without consulting the organization. At the December 1990 consultative conference, Mandela was forced to acknowledge this criticism, but he also insisted that his bilateral discussions with de Klerk would continue.[13]

As the enthusiasm generated by his release died down, he became a controversial figure. There was never any challenge to his leadership—it was unthinkable that anyone might run against him for the presidency of the ANC at the 1991 conference. But questions were raised about both the style and the substance of his leadership. In style, Mandela was out of step with the times. He was a courteous elderly statesman or, with more traditional audiences, a traditional chief exuding authority; to youths, he was a benevolent but stern grandfather. Crowds listened in reverent silence when he spoke, but rarely applauded. The cheering was reserved for Chris Hani or Joe Slovo, or anyone else who put more emphasis on the possible resumption of the armed struggle than on the fact that it had been suspended. As for the substance of his position, questions were raised about whether he was so anxious to reach an agreement that he would not bargain hard enough; whether in order to increase support for the ANC he would compromise its integrity by embracing discredited traditional authorities and homeland leaders; and whether he understood and accepted the principles of accountability and participation.

Another problem that generated uneasiness and resentment was Mandela's initial determination to ensure that his wife be given a high position in the ANC hierarchy. An admired figure for many years, Winnie Mandela had been ostracized in January 1989 by the mass democratic movement because of her alleged involvement in the kidnapping and killing of a fourteen-year-old activist, "Stompie" Moeketsi Seipei, accused of being a police spy. She was eventually tried and found guilty of kidnapping and being an accessory after the fact to assault in May 1991; she was given a six-year sentence, suspended pending appeal.

Despite the mass democratic movement's suspicions and the legal charges against her, Winnie Mandela staged a comeback with the support of her husband. She was named head of the ANC's social welfare department in August 1990, and a few months later she was elected to the regional executive of the important PWV (Pretoria, Witwatersrand, and Vaal) region; all objections against her were drowned out as thunderous applause greeted Nelson's carefully timed arrival. For a long time, there appeared to be no end to the promotion of Winnie Mandela. In September 1991 she lost her welfare portfolio when she failed to be elected to the new Working Committee, the inner circle of the NEC. However, she was reinstated to her welfare position without an explanation as soon as her husband returned from a visit abroad.

In May 1992 personal problems between the Mandelas and mounting opposition to Winnie within the ANC convinced Nelson to withdraw his support as well as to move into a separate house. Without his backing, Winnie's position in the organization plummeted rapidly, and she lost all but her elected position within the NEC. Nevertheless, the saga had already done considerable damage to the ANC and to Mandela personally. Winnie Mandela undoubtedly had her supporters, particularly among radical youths. But the real reason for her rise after 1990 was neither her popularity nor her ability but her husband's support and the unwillingness of others in the NEC to thwart him. The episode revealed an element of nepotism and corruption in the ANC that did nothing to enhance its image.

Umkhonto we Sizwe

The ANC's military wing was an integral component of the liberation movement, a burden in the process of transformation from liberation movement to political party, and a complicating factor in the negotiating process—eventually, MK elements would have to be integrated with the South African Defence Force to form the army of the new South Africa. But Umkhonto was not a particularly effective fighting force. If the government had concluded that repression would not reestablish even a semblance of normality in the country, it was because the internal movement had proved impossible to suppress and because trade sanctions and lack of new foreign investment were hurting the economy. Umkhonto's military operations had very little to do with the government's decision to negotiate, although they contributed to creating a climate of insecurity that made white South Africans more willing to accept the new policy. Yet MK remained a powerful symbol of the liberation struggle among the youth of the townships. Rent and consumer boycotts had proved to be effective weapons, but they did not provide a heroic symbol attractive to the young comrades. The appeal of the victorious armed struggle was no less powerful for being largely a myth.

MK was launched in 1961 as the liberation army that would allow the ANC to move the struggle from the purely political to the military level, thereby accelerating the process and increasing the chances of success. However, MK was able to operate for only about two years inside the country before its leadership was captured and its networks destroyed. From 1963 to the 1976 Soweto uprising, it was an exiled organization that could boast of no significant achievements. It had trouble both infiltrating cadres into South Africa and smuggling recruits out for training. Nevertheless, the ANC looked to MK as the key to the struggle, but in the absence of a political underground, military cadres never survived long enough inside South Africa to be effective. By the time of the 1976 Soweto uprising, "more than a decade had passed without MK registering a shot or a bomb blast inside South Africa."[14]

The student uprising provided MK with fresh opportunities. Refugees started streaming out of the country in large numbers, and in the following ten years MK, according to one estimate, was able to provide at least basic training for some 1,200 recruits a year, mostly in its camps in Angola.[15] Umkhonto was thus able to resume armed action, although the continued weakness of the ANC underground inside the country limited it to cross-border hit-and-run attacks.

Problems continued for MK. One, of its own making, was the apparently perpetual indecision of its leadership about the respective role of military action and political organization, which led to a constant uniting and separating of the two structures.[16] Another was the effectiveness of South Africa's destabilization policy toward the neighboring countries, which deprived MK of external bases close to the borders. The 1984 signing of the Nkomati accord between South Africa and Mozambique was particularly damaging to MK, which lost access to what had been considered its most promising staging area. MK continued carrying out attacks, but it neither posed a military threat the government could not handle nor acted as a catalyst for political agitation.

Umkhonto scored few successes, yet it would be a serious mistake to undervalue its importance either within the ANC's external organization or in the mythology of the antiapartheid struggle. Many of the top figures in the ANC were involved at one time or another with Umkhonto. SACP members appear to have been particularly active in the military organization, and for a long time the ANC in exile saw itself waging primarily a military rather than a political battle.

The beginning of negotiations raised the issue of the future of MK. Its days as a guerrilla army were numbered, but its cadres could not simply be repatriated, minus their guns, alongside other exiles. Umkhonto remained both a force within the ANC and a bargaining asset vis-à-vis the government. The possibility of a successful armed struggle was remote, particularly after the crisis in the socialist world deprived MK of its most important source of support—ANC Secretary General Alfred Nzo had openly admitted in January 1990 that the ANC lacked the capacity to intensify military activity.[17] But the war talk was attractive to the young comrades, providing a catalyst around which the radical wing of the movement could coalesce. As a political force, MK had to be taken seriously.

MK was also an important asset in the negotiating process and the key to breaking down white control of the military. The ANC openly acknowledged that this was the role it envisaged for MK in the future, announcing that officers were already being trained in conventional warfare in a number of countries so they would be ready when the time came to form the new South African forces.

South African Communist Party

The South African Communist Party was much more than an ANC ally. Ever since it had been outlawed in 1950, it had existed inside the ANC in a symbiotic relation that had served both organizations well over the years but was becoming problematic in the early 1990s. The relationship had brought to the ANC the assistance of the Soviet bloc, including funds, training for MK, and scholarships for students, while allowing the SACP to benefit from Western, particularly Scandinavian, aid to the ANC and the broader attraction of a movement that defined itself in opposition to apartheid rather than in favor of communism.

The symbiotic relation between Congress and party made it easy for the South African government to claim that the ANC was a communist front, controlled by Moscow for its own evil purposes. Counting communists within the ANC was a game played by both supporters and detractors of the Congress—with different results, needless to say. Recent information shows the presence of a very large number of communists in the pre–1990 NEC.

It is more difficult to determine to what extent the communist presence affected ANC policies. The SACP was rigidly aligned with Moscow, but during the 1980s it had been unwilling to follow Gorbachev's reformism, particularly since the Soviet new thinking about South Africa dismissed the possibility of revolution there and opened the door to a much more accommodating policy toward the South African government. The SACP's resistance to reform was symbolized by its choice of Havana as the venue for the 1989 congress. However, the party did accept a two-stage approach to revolution, and claimed that in the first its goals would be purely nationalistic, thus coinciding with those of the ANC. The issue of socialism would arise only in the second stage, and at that point the ANC and the SACP would go in different directions. With a striking lack of confidence in their ally, the communists were convinced that the ANC would inevitably fail to stand up to the ruses of "monopoly capital," because it was not a working class organization.

The beginning of the transition process in South Africa came at an awkward time for the SACP. Just as the second, socialist phase of the revolution should have been near, the party was becoming more dependent than ever on the ANC. The communist world was disintegrating with bewildering speed, and socialism had few supporters left. Moscow certainly had no aid to give, even if it had wanted to do so. At the same time, the unbanning of political organizations made it imperative for the party to develop a separate organization, or lose its identity.

The first step in the uncertain process toward reorganization and redefinition was taken in early 1990 with the publication of a paper by General Secretary Joe Slovo, entitled "Has Socialism Failed?"[18] He admitted the failure of the Stalinist interpretation of socialism that had prevailed in the past, but reaffirmed his faith in the possibility of a democratic socialism he did not clearly define. He also argued that the SACP had long been moving away from Stalinism, a claim contradicted by all that was known about the organization.[19] This belated conversion triggered considerable debate within the party, but it was by no means accepted by all members.

A second step was the launching of an above-ground organization in July 1990. The names of the interim leaders were made public, but it was also announced that other party members would remain incognito, for fear of police repression. The question of who in the ANC belonged to the Communist Party thus remained unanswered.

The relaunching of the party did not mean the end of its symbiotic relation with the ANC. On the contrary, SACP members and, more important, SACP leaders remained inside the ANC. The strong communist presence was reconfirmed by the elections to the National Executive Committee in July 1991. Over twenty of the eighty-eight members of the new NEC belonged to the SACP.[20] Later, when the twenty-six–member Working Committee was elected, at least seven communists were included.

The SACP congress held in December 1991 marked a setback for the reformists. While the leadership, through the proposed constitution and political manifesto, tried to steer the party away from Marxism-Leninism and toward democratic socialism, the delegates refused. The working documents had mentioned only Marx and Engels among the thinkers whose ideas inspired the party. The delegates insisted that Lenin be reinstated. The manifesto called for democratic socialism. The delegates erased the word *democratic*, arguing that it was redundant because true socialism is always democratic. Although the delegates accepted the need for multiparty democracy and extolled the virtues of people's power, the congress confirmed the SACP as a communist party of the pre-Gorbachev era, a rare phenomenon indeed in 1991. This unreformed party continued to overlap with the ANC. Eleven of the twenty-five newly elected Central Committee members also belonged to the NEC, and five of them were in the Working Committee. Chris Hani, elected general secretary to replace the ailing Joe Slovo, held top positions in the ANC, MK, and the SACP, although he admitted that he could probably not continue as MK's chief of staff.

The hard line taken by the delegates at the congress showed the continuing appeal of the communist message in its original, radical form among South African blacks. The ideas might be outmoded and discredited elsewhere, as the South African government incessantly repeated, but they still made sense to people for whom the existing system held little joy. This was not the long arm of Moscow but indigenous anger.

The party had only 23,000 members when the congress met, however, and its potential for growth was unknown. The sources of financial support were shrinking rapidly, as shown by the thin ranks of the representatives of "fraternal organizations" present at the congress. Only the Chinese and Cuban delegations represented government parties; most of the others belonged to obscure organizations of negligible political significance and even more negligible financial assets—for example, three different British communist parties sent representatives.

Its own small membership and financial base gave the party an incentive to continue operating inside the ANC, an organization with an undoubtedly brighter future. Indeed, a number of prominent communists decided to devote more time to ANC than to SACP business. Slovo, suffering from cancer, committed whatever time and energy he had left to the ANC. Chris Hani had originally chosen to devote himself to the ANC and MK, and agreed to run for SACP general secretary only when he was nominated at the congress without opposition. Some younger members with promising political careers were keeping their distance from the party. The relationship that President de Klerk once felicitously described as "a scrambled egg" was not likely to become unscrambled soon.

The new militancy and anger that the delegates expressed at the congress was thus likely to affect the ANC at a time when it also needed to attract moderate constituencies as it sought a negotiated solution and prepared to face an election. The faithful ally of many years could conceivably turn into a burden.

THE MASS DEMOCRATIC MOVEMENT

The ANC discussed so far was largely a head without a body, the outcome of decades of exile. Even after it started organizing branches and regional offices, it remained relatively small. The optimistic predictions of mid–1990 that membership would soon reach 6 million had given way by the time of the consultative conference to an estimate of 200,000 card-carrying members. When the congress met in July 1991, membership was put at 500,000, and that was probably an exaggeration, since records were poor and many people who had joined in 1990 had not paid their fees again the following year.[21] But the strength of the ANC was much greater than membership in the formal structures suggested. The real body of the ANC was the mass democratic movement, but that was not controlled by the NEC.

Beginning with the 1976 Soweto uprising, the townships had become increasingly organized—the student and youth groups of the 1970s were soon followed by others that mobilized older constituencies around issues of housing, rents, services, and transport—the problems of daily life aggravated by the apartheid regime. As Mark Swilling described it, "A common combination of organizations in each community is a civic, youth congress, students' organization (a branch of the Congress of South African Students [COSAS] until its banning in 1985), women's organization, and, in the metropolitan areas, a trade union local that acts more independently. There is no doubt that although church and youth groups predominate on the UDF's [United Democratic Front's] list of affiliates, it is the civics, youth congresses and student organizations respectively that are the UDF's most important bases."[22]

The United Democratic Front was formed in 1983 in response to the government's new constitutional proposal to give limited representation to Indians and Coloureds in a tricameral parliament, from which Africans were excluded. From the early 1970s on, the black trade union movement had also revived, culminating in the launching of the Congress of South African Trade Unions (COSATU) in 1985. In 1987, the UDF, COSATU, and sixteen other organizations joined in the Mass Democratic Movement (MDM), which was able to continue operating, though subject to much harassment, after the UDF was banned in February 1988.

When the ANC in 1990 started reorganizing inside the country, it had to find a way of relating to all these groups, which literally and figuratively carried the ANC flag but were also independent organizations, with their own officials, style of leadership, and vested interests. In theory, the answer was easy. The ANC would not try to absorb the township organizations in its own structures but would only recruit individuals. The civics in particular would be encouraged to continue operating independently of the ANC, opening their doors to members and sympathizers of all political parties. Labor unions also should preserve their autonomy—the mistake made elsewhere in Africa by liberation movements that tried to subordinate the labor organizations must not be repeated.

The practice was much more complicated. COSATU was a labor federation involved in organizing workers and in collective bargaining, and in this role it could easily act autonomously. But it was also part of the ANC-SACP-COSATU alliance, which had the goal of bringing down apartheid, and in this role it could not act independently of the other two groups. The civics did not formally take orders from the ANC, but they were certainly aligned with it, as members of other parties complained. The more subtle of the civics were careful not to display ANC symbols at their meetings, but others earnestly protested their nonpartisanship and invited members of all parties to join, while standing in front of ANC and SACP banners.

Problems in the relationship between the ANC and the mass democratic movement soon manifested themselves. After February 2, 1990, the MDM disappeared without a formal decision being taken, and the UDF entered a period of crisis. Many UDF leaders became ANC organizers, but they were reluctant to disband the front completely. In the end, the UDF could not find a raison d'être, despite desultory talk that it might turn into a watchdog organization. In August 1991 the front officially ceased to exist. Yet the ANC was not a substitute for the UDF. The two organizations shared basic political ideals, but they functioned along very different lines.

Historically, the ANC was a top-heavy organization whose leadership took the initiative. The UDF believed in participatory democracy, or people's power. Leaders were not supposed to act as bosses but to receive a mandate from their organizations and report back to the members on the results.

Theory and reality always differ, and UDF affiliates did not necessarily live up to their participatory ideals. Undoubtedly more decisions were taken from the top down than the organizations cared to admit. Furthermore, even groups that observed participatory principles within acted extremely undemocratically toward their opponents. Township residents usually had no choice but to share the political affiliation of local bosses, much as European peasants had at one time been forced to share the religious beliefs of their prince. In the worst cases, people's power degenerated to criminality. The phenomenon even gave rise to a new word, *com-tsotsis*, denoting comrades turned into *tsotsis*, or thugs. But despite these shortcomings, the UDF and the township organizations saw themselves as the embodiment of participatory democracy and bridled against the ANC bureaucracy.

COSATU was less affected than the UDF by the unbanning of the ANC. Since the late 1980s, it had succeeded in putting to rest an internal conflict between the supporters of "political unionism" and "collective bargaining unionism," or "populism" and "workerism," as the two trends were also labeled, by pursuing them simultaneously.[23] The workerist side of COSATU was not affected by the reappearance of the ANC inside the country. The struggle for workers' rights was seen by all as part of the liberation process, and the ANC was not yet in a position to worry about the impact of salary increases on overall economic performance. The populist side of COSATU was affected immediately, however.

On the one hand, the alliance with the ANC and the SACP increased COSATU's effectiveness in mobilizing workers for political action—a two-day stay-away in November 1991, nominally called to protest the imposition of a value-added tax, was a resounding success for the organizers. On the other hand, the priorities of the ANC and those of COSATU were not identical. For the ANC, political power was the major goal, and economic policy was something the new government would consider in due course. For COSATU, economic issues were paramount and, far from being left to the discretion of a future government, they should be the object of negotiations, separate from and equally important as political ones. COSATU would represent the liberation movement in these negotiations. The issue will be discussed later in greater detail.

THE ANTIAPARTHEID CHURCHES

The South African Council of Churches (SACC) lent considerable moral weight to antiapartheid organizations, particularly during the 1980s. Also, church groups had been among the most numerous affiliates of the United Democratic Front. The Reverend Desmond

Tutu, 1984 Nobel prize winner and Archbishop of Cape Town in the Church of the Province of South Africa (Anglican) since 1986, was a well-known spokesman overseas for the antiapartheid cause. So was the Reverend Allan Boesak, moderator of the Nederduitse Gereformeerde Sendingkerk, the Coloured affiliate of the NGK (Nederduitse Gereformeerde Kerk), president of the World Alliance of Reformed Churches, and a prominent UDF leader. The Reverend Frank Chikane, president of the South African Council of Churches, completed this trio of internationally known church activists. But in the 1990s the antiapartheid churches were struggling to redefine their position. As in the case of the Dutch Reformed churches, the old moral certainties were fast dissipating in the face of a new situation. Apartheid undoubtedly remained evil and sinful, but not everything that happened in the antiapartheid movement was good or could be condoned.

Even earlier, support for the liberation movement had posed an ethical dilemma for the churches, particularly as militancy and violence increased during the 1980s. The SACC compromised, accepting in May 1987 the "Lusaka document," which reaffirmed the churches' commitment to peaceful change but recognized "that the nature of the South African regime which wages war against its own inhabitants and neighbors compels the liberation movements to the use of force along with other means to end oppression."[24]

After 1990 this position became less defensible. The unbanning of political organizations appeared to make peaceful resistance a viable option again, and the spread of violence in the townships horrified the church leaders.[25] Whatever or whoever was ultimately behind the violence, blacks were killing blacks in large numbers, and often indiscriminately—squatters sleeping in their camps, commuters riding trains to work, mourners at funeral vigils. Condoning violence was becoming more difficult, and church leaders were striving to redefine their role and their position.

Archbishop Desmond Tutu spoke for many when he took a strong stand on the issue. While recognizing that the violence was in part a legacy of apartheid, that the country had no political culture of tolerance, and that the police had on the whole exhibited "disgraceful . . . behavior," he finally pointed the finger at the black community. "A lot of the violence is due to political rivalry. Political groups in the black community are fighting for turf and they do not seem to know, or certainly some of their followers do not seem to know, that a cardinal tenet of democracy is that people must be free to choose freely whom they want to support." "Something," he added, "has gone desperately wrong in the black community."[26] Many other church and non-church organizations concerned with human rights shared this feeling. The conviction became increasingly common that the apartheid regime was not the only enemy of human rights—the liberation movements were just as capable of violations and would have to be watched just as closely in the future.

The new attitude of church leaders created a challenge for the ANC. Churches were important in the black community, and it was not in the interest of the liberation organizations to test whether loyalty to the church was stronger than resentment of apartheid. The National Party was deliberately courting church organizations, particularly the African and Zionist churches, which had a huge membership and in the past had kept their distance from all political organizations. No one really knew whether any church could deliver its members' vote to a particular political party, or even whether it would be interested in trying, but the question could not be dismissed lightly.[27]

During its 1991 congress, the ANC took note of the problem. In his report, the outgoing secretary general, Alfred Nzo, mentioned among the difficulties encountered in setting up branches the fact that "the alliance with the SACP is perceived as a problem by some communities," and the lack of success in recruiting among minority groups.[28] The leadership took the problem seriously.

One response was the promotion of Allan Boesak, both a religious leader and a Coloured, to a new career within the ANC. Boesak had been sidelined for months by the demise of the UDF, the hostility of communists within the ANC Western Cape leadership, and personal problems—a highly publicized love affair with a white TV reporter had put an end to his marriage and to his position as moderator of the Sendingkerk. Mandela personally pulled him back into the ANC, promoting his election as president of the Western Cape region in late 1991, a position that entailed ex officio membership in the NEC. By so doing, Mandela was trying to establish a link both to the moderate, church-going constituencies that all political parties were courting by this time and to the Coloured community, which the National Party also was trying to attract. "Look around you," he told the overwhelmingly black delegates to the regional congress of the Western Cape, the region where the Coloured population is concentrated, "Coloured communities would like to see Coloured representatives. That is not racism, that is how nature works."[29] The simplicity of a movement united against the evil of apartheid was beginning to give way to the nuances of the different expectations of diverse constituencies.

CONCLUSIONS

The liberation establishment was an amalgam of groups with different histories and contradictory traditions. One of the questions in the transition period was whether these different groups and traditions would coalesce to build up a strong ANC as a political party or find separate roles for themselves in the new political system. In 1991, both trends were discernible. The labor unions and the civics still envisaged an independent role for themselves, and there was no reason to expect they would change their view. But the ANC congress held in Durban in July 1991 saw a major effort to bring the mass democratic movement into the ANC: the general secretary of the National Union of Mineworkers, Cyril Ramaphosa, became secretary general of the ANC. Various important UDF leaders, including Popo Molefe and Patrick "Terror" Lekota, were elected to the NEC. A few months later, Allan Boesak was also absorbed in the organization. By the end of 1991, the ANC was no longer controlled exclusively by the exiles; it had gone a long way toward integrating members of the mass democratic movement.

This had two repercussions. The first, already mentioned, was the conflict thus created between the stated intention of the mass democratic movement organizations to maintain their autonomy and the reality of overlapping membership and even leadership with the ANC. The other was the transformation of the ANC into an organization whose members increasingly questioned the right of leaders to make decisions without consultation. Going into negotiations, Mandela was therefore in a situation very different from de Klerk's. The state president was backed by a compliant and homogeneous establishment that did not appear inclined to challenge the leadership's decisions, but he would have to fight very hard to retain white support and to gain some among blacks. The ANC leader could count on a high degree of popular support, although predominantly among Africans, but he also had to deal with a complex and not necessarily compliant liberation establishment.

Chapter 4

The Second Tier

In February 1990 the government and the African National Congress (ANC), with its affiliates, were undoubtedly the two most important actors in the process leading to the new South Africa. But unless other organizations were pulled into the negotiations, the chances that any agreement would hold and violence could be averted were not good. These organizations fell into three major categories. The first comprised parties with main-player political ambitions, namely the Inkatha Freedom Party (IFP) and the Pan Africanist Congress of Azania (PAC). In the second category were the rejectionist parties of the Right and the Left, which knew that they could not influence the outcome of negotiations and therefore refused to participate in any initiative: on the Right were the Conservative Party (CP) and the extraparliamentary white extremist groups; on the Left were the Azanian People's Organization (AZAPO) and a few other small groups. Finally, there was a third group of parties and institutions that were guaranteed a role in the process regardless of the support they could muster, because, as official cogs in the existing apartheid machinery, they were facts on the ground that simply could not be wished out of existence. These included the Coloured and Indian parties in the tricameral Parliament, the governing parties of the six self-governing homelands, and the governments of the four independent homelands.

THE WOULD-BE MAJOR PLAYERS

The Inkatha Freedom Party and the Pan Africanist Congress of Azania were the two major political organizations competing with the ANC for black support. Inkatha portrayed itself as a moderate, democratic party offering an alternative to ANC extremism. The Pan Africanist

Congress saw itself as the representative of blacks' deep-seated aspirations for a reassertion of their African identity. Both experienced a great deal of difficulty carving out their role in the transition process, however.

Inkatha Freedom Party

The Inkatha Freedom Party was the most important of the second-tier political organizations in the early 1990s, the most controversial, and certainly the most dangerous in the short run. It was led by an extremely ambitious politician, KwaZulu Chief Minister Mangosuthu Gatsha Buthelezi, who demanded to be recognized as a leader of the same stature as de Klerk and Mandela, although the organization he headed had a mostly regional and ethnic base and limited assets.

Inkatha's importance depended in part on a carefully cultivated image as a moderate organization, and thus an alternative to the radical ANC. Above all, Inkatha was an organization whose support the National Party would need in order to put together a viable anti-ANC coalition and whose existence might be crucial in preventing the transformation of the ANC into a virtual single party dominating the country's political life. But there was another, much less moderate, side to Inkatha. The organization also appealed openly to Zulu nationalism, and such appeals always contained a veiled threat of violence: "Do not allow anybody to trample on our glorious past. Do not allow anybody to destroy that inner Zulu unity which has always stood the test of time," Buthelezi exhorted his followers.[1] The two facets of Inkatha—a moderate national movement and a fervent Zulu nationalist movement—clashed with each other.

The controversy surrounding Inkatha was based on its existence within the apartheid structure, the suspicion that it was being used by the government or—even worse—that it was knowingly allowing itself to be used by the government as part of a strategy to undermine the ANC, and the strident personality and ambiguous political stance of its founder and leader, Chief Buthelezi. Described in an official curriculum vitae as Chief Minister, KwaZulu Legislative Assembly, Ulundi; President, Inkatha YeNkululeko YeSizwe (National Cultural Liberation Movement); Chairman, the South African Black Alliance; Traditional Prime Minister of the Zulu People and adviser to the Zulu

King, Buthelezi played on a combination of traditional and modern identities in the pursuit of his political goals and personal ambition.

The use of violence against other movements, particularly the ANC, and the injection of ethnic strife in the politics of South Africa made Inkatha dangerous, and so did the possibility that Buthelezi, whose ambition exceeded his assets, would allow himself to be used as a destructive and destabilizing force in order to enhance his own position.

Inkatha YeNkululeko YeSizwe was formed in 1975, taking its name from an organization that had existed in the 1920s.[2] At the time, Buthelezi described the organization as a "national cultural liberation movement," because the government would not have tolerated the formation of a political party. As a cultural organization, Inkatha had a definite ethnic character. "All members of the Zulu nation are automatically members of Inkatha," Buthelezi explained.[3] As president of the organization, in accordance with its constitution, which specified that the position had to be occupied by the chief minister of KwaZulu, he could claim to be the leader of seven million Zulus.

Membership in Inkatha became virtually compulsory for people living in the rural areas of KwaZulu under the authority of chiefs and homeland bureaucrats. It was impossible to obtain any service—enrolling children in school, visiting a clinic, receiving a civil service salary or an old age pension—without an Inkatha card. By 1990, the organization claimed to have 1.8 million members, a figure that would have made it by far the largest political organization in South Africa.[4] The true figure was almost certainly much smaller, but still large, since membership in rural areas was compulsory.

Although working within the apartheid system and running an autocratic, single-party system as head of Inkatha and chief minister of KwaZulu, Buthelezi had played a part in frustrating the government's apartheid policy by refusing independence for his homeland, one of the most important because of its large population. Nevertheless, he always remained suspect to the antiapartheid groups, and by the end of the 1970s he had fallen out with the ANC. From then on, relations between Inkatha and the liberation movement went from bad to worse. The growth of the United Democratic Front (UDF) and the labor unions broke Inkatha's monopoly, at least in the fast-growing peri-urban areas of Natal.[5] Buthelezi's response to the launching of the Congress of South African Trade Unions was the founding of a rival labor organization, the United Workers' Union of South Africa

(UWUSA), but UWUSA never became a viable independent labor union. It lost what little credibility it had when the government admitted in July 1991 that it had funded it from the beginning.[6]

The release of Mandela further challenged Buthelezi's political standing and also threatened his ego. Mandela was a hero at home and abroad, and initially only the ANC held talks with the government, to the exclusion of all other groups. Compounding the problem, the ANC leadership in Natal was determined to isolate Buthelezi, insisting that Mandela should not meet with him and even calling for the disbanding of KwaZulu.

Fighting between supporters of the ANC-UDF and those of Inkatha broke out in Natal in March 1990. To an extent, it was the continuation of the strife of the previous three years, which had left more than sixteen hundred people dead by the end of 1989 in a struggle for political control over the townships in the Durban-Pietermaritzburg area of Natal.[7] The majority of the victims had apparently been UDF supporters.[8] In March 1990 the violence flared up again, with greater intensity. In just one week at the end of March, more than eighty people were killed, while hundreds of refugees streamed out of the embattled townships. Once again, most of the victims appeared to have been on the ANC-UDF side.

The violence was rooted in both sides' attempts to control the townships. Neither accepted the idea that individuals had the right to choose their political allegiance. Rather, Inkatha warlords and ANC comrades strived to establish their dominion in specific areas, driving out anyone unwilling to accept their control. Disastrous socioeconomic conditions, which provided a mass of unemployed young men ready to join the fray, certainly facilitated the violence, but they did not cause it. Conditions were terrible all over the country, but the violence was limited to certain areas.[9] Finally, ethnic conflict played no role in the fighting in Natal, since the population was overwhelmingly Zulu.

By the summer, violence in Natal had subsided somewhat, but the townships of the Witwatersrand were exploding. Inkatha and the ANC were again at the center of the problem, but their roles were reversed. In Natal, the ANC had been trying to strengthen its presence in areas originally dominated by Inkatha. On the Rand, Inkatha was trying to break into an area where the ANC, or more precisely the civics, were much better implanted. In the different circumstances, the conflict acquired some new dimensions. First, it took on ethnic overtones as a Zulu versus Xhosa problem.[10] Second, it pitted migrant workers against township residents. Third, it saw Inkatha offering its support to, and in turn winning the allegiance of, many of the black town councillors the ANC had scorned and tried to force to resign. Finally, it raised a major controversy about the involvement of the security forces, and thus about the responsibility of the government.

The question whether the violence was rooted in ethnic conflict gave rise to heated debate, which appeared to have a lot to do with ideology and very little with facts. The government, the press, and white public opinion in general chose to define the violence as black-on-black, and more specifically Zulu on Xhosa, claiming that the ANC was dominated by the latter group. In this portrayal, members of other groups simply ceased to exist. Improbably, in the ethnically mixed townships of the Witwatersrand only Zulus and Xhosas died in violent clashes—members of other groups were never affected. To the ANC and to white liberals, an ethnic explanation of the conflict was ideologically unacceptable, and even the description of the conflict as black-on-black was objectionable. Inkatha, on the other hand, readily accepted the ethnic explanation—Zulus were simply reacting to the insults by ANC supporters against Buthelezi, the Zulu king, and all Zulus.

The largest concentration of Zulus open to the Inkatha appeal was in the migrant workers' hostels. Zulu migrants shared the plight of all hostel inmates: they were looked down upon as unsophisticated and ignorant by the more urbanized township residents and generally were blamed for the high crime rate, particularly rape. The hostel inhabitants had also been neglected by the civic organizations, which had focused their efforts on issues such as rent boycotts, a concern that did not touch those living in the hostels. Finally, hostels housing in squalor and dilapidation hundreds of men without families inevitably provided a large reservoir of frustrated and socially isolated individuals who might easily turn to violence.

The social isolation of the participants in the violence was brought home vividly and gruesomely by the large number of unidentified and unclaimed bodies that remained for weeks on end in the mortuaries after every outbreak of violence—this in a country where attendance to funerals is an important social obligation.[11] Groups of Inkatha supporters from the hostels, wearing red headbands and carrying what came to be euphemistically called cultural or traditional weapons—which in reality included not only spears and shields but axes, sharpened metal rods, guns, and the occasional AK-47—became major participants in the violence and in all political rallies called by Inkatha.

Inkatha sought also to enlist the embattled black town councillors, long targeted by the civics as collaborators with the apartheid regime. The councillors' resentment of the ANC and the civic associations was high, since many had lost property, and some their lives, at the hands of the comrades. They were thus open to joining Inkatha, but for that organization the victory was hollow. The councillors were a doomed species—for example, between February 1990 and March 1991 alone, 404 councillors had quit and 6 had been killed. The power of Inkatha was hardly enhanced by the support of the councillors.[12]

The most controversial question concerning the violence was whether it was being orchestrated by the government or by a nebulous "third force" for its own purposes. As in the controversy about the ethnic element in the violence, the answers different groups gave to the question were based as much on ideology as on evidence. Beginning in September 1990, the ANC claimed that the violence stemmed at least in part from a deliberate policy of destabilization undertaken by a mysterious third force hoping to sidetrack the negotiation process by creating chaos. The ANC did not exculpate Inkatha, but argued simply that the organization was not acting on its own. The government dismissed the accusation as meaningless, a sign of the ANC's unwillingness to face up to the reality of ethnic strife and the antagonism its own extremism had created. The idea of the third force nonetheless persisted.

The third force was supposedly a group other than the government and Inkatha, but vaguely connected to both through uncontrolled elements in the security forces. The idea that such a force existed grew from unconfirmed reports that whites were participating in the violence on the Witwatersrand in September 1990. Thereafter, carloads of whites with blackened faces, and mysterious figures clad in gloves and balaclavas, were being spotted all over the strife-torn townships. ANC leader Walter Sisulu reported that "certain forces, who were not necessarily Inkatha, were killing Black people at random."[13] Others were less reticent, identifying those responsible for the violence as a combination of elements from the police, the army, and

Inkatha, therefore not a "third force independent of the government and Inkatha."[14] Parallels began to be drawn between this third force and RENAMO (Mozambique National Resistance), the opposition group South Africa had unleashed on Mozambique in the 1980s to destabilize the country and force FRELIMO (Front for the Liberation of Mozambique) to expel the ANC. Stung by the accusation of police involvement, Minister of Law and Order Adriaan Vlok turned the accusation against the ANC, claiming that the third force behind the violence might be a dissident radical group within the ANC over which the moderates, identified as Mandela, President Oliver Tambo, and Director of International Affairs Thabo Mbeki, had lost control.[15]

The allegations concerning the existence of a third force were neither proved nor convincingly set to rest by late 1992, and possibly they never will be. Some court cases and investigations by the Commission of Inquiry Regarding the Prevention of Public Violence and Intimidation (Goldstone Commission) provided proof of cooperation between the KwaZulu police and the South African police in specific incidents, and also highlighted the thin line that separated the KwaZulu police and Inkatha—both headed by Buthelezi. However, the Goldstone Commission's second report, released to the public on May 27, 1992, concluded that the "primary cause of the violence . . . is the political battle between supporters of the African National Congress and of the Inkatha Freedom Party."[16] The statement caused an outbreak of outrage on the part of ANC and human rights groups, who claimed the conclusion came "perilously close to conveying the impression of the State and its security forces standing like a knight in shining armour between two warring black factions in order to keep the peace," and thus played the game of the apartheid regime.[17] Justice Goldstone replied that, while no evidence had been presented to the commission that a third force operated in the country, investigations would continue.[18] The matter of the third force, and of the government's and security forces' link to Inkatha, remained open.

Overtly, relations between the government and Inkatha appeared to be both difficult and in a state of flux during the transition period. The government needed Inkatha and Inkatha needed the government, but Buthelezi was not an easy person to work with. When the government came to accept the inevitability of black political participation, as shown at the NP congress of 1986 (discussed later), it started counting Inkatha as a possible ally against the ANC. Evidence of this policy was the government's funding of UWUSA and the provision of training for Inkatha or KwaZulu security personnel, apparently to be used against the ANC.[19] After the violence broke out, the police usually appeared to favor Inkatha, being in many instances slow to intervene and, above all, allowing Inkatha supporters to carry in public the so-called cultural weapons. (In theory, these objects were carried by Zulus on special ceremonial occasions; they were nevertheless lethal instruments, displayed with impunity at political rallies.)

During 1990 Buthelezi indeed seemed to be a promising ally for the government. His hold on KwaZulu was strong, he was willing to challenge the ANC, and he advocated policies virtually identical to those of the National Party. He supported negotiations and rejected not only armed struggle but any form of political mass action—demonstrations, marches, boycotts—directed at putting pressure on the government. He rejected a constitution based on "simplistic majoritarianism" and defended the rights of groups—Zulus, of course, but by implication also whites—to be represented in the political system. He defended untrammeled free enterprise, condemned any form of economic redistribution, argued against the formation of an interim government, and depicted the ANC's demand for the election of a constituent assembly as a sinister plot to grab all power, creating a Soviet-style system.[20]

The government therefore offered Buthelezi what he wanted, public recognition as a leader as important as de Klerk and Mandela. When the chief minister, after finally realizing his ambition of meeting with Mandela, suggested that the best way of handling the problem of violence would be to form a troika consisting of de Klerk, Mandela, and himself, the government agreed with alacrity, although nothing came of the idea in the end.

But in July 1991 the relationship between the government and the IFP started falling apart. On the eve of the party's annual congress, the *Weekly Mail* published irrefutable information that the government, through the police, had secretly funded Inkatha activities. The published documents provided proof concerning only the funding of two rallies in late 1989 and early 1990, as well as of continuing support for UWUSA, but they inevitably strengthened suspicions that government aid was much more extensive.[21]

It was the beginning of what came to be known as "Inkathagate," which caused the government much embarrassment and led de Klerk to carry out a major cabinet reshuffle, including the already-mentioned demotion of ministers Adriaan Vlok and Magnus Malan. More important for Buthelezi, it dealt another blow to his already low credibility as a genuine antiapartheid leader, caused the government to distance itself from him, and possibly created financial difficulties for Inkatha. Following Inkathagate, the constant flow of press releases—a hallmark of Buthelezi—dried up almost completely, suggesting either a decision to keep a low profile or a lack of funds.

A second blow to Buthelezi's relationship with the government came in late September 1991, when a National Peace Conference brought all South African political organizations together to devise a code of conduct for reducing violence as well as to set up formal mechanisms for promoting reconciliation and investigating incidents. Participants were greeted by a band of several hundred Zulus armed with traditional weapons waiting to "honor" Buthelezi and the Zulu king. The demonstration put the government in an embarrassing position. By tolerating it, the government could be accused of collusion with Inkatha. Breaking it up would most likely lead to a violent confrontation between police and well-armed demonstrators just as the Peace Conference was about to open. In the eyes of the government, Buthelezi had gone too far.

Increasingly, Inkatha appeared to be in limbo. Already estranged from the liberation movement—it had been excluded from the creation of the patriotic front of antiapartheid organizations—it was also becoming antagonistic to the government and shunned by it. As an independent force, it was too weak. Its efforts to reorganize as a multiethnic party had been virtually abandoned in favor of a renewed appeal to Zulu nationalism. Opinion polls concurred that support for Inkatha was slight, only about 5 percent in urban areas.[22] Acceptance of Inkatha was undoubtedly much higher in rural KwaZulu, but it was probably nonexistent in the rural areas of other homelands.

But Buthelezi remained determined that Inkatha would be recognized as a major political party and prominently included in all aspects of the negotiations. This made it a dangerous organization, with a potential for disrupting negotiations as well as for contributing to the continuation of violence. It also left Inkatha open to a renewed alliance with the government, should de Klerk decide that the benefits of such a policy would be substantial enough to justify the difficulty of dealing with Buthelezi.

Pan Africanist Congress of Azania

If Inkatha under the leadership of Buthelezi had become an organization whose political role was larger than its numerical support, the opposite was true of the Pan Africanist Congress. It had a potentially large following, but no apparent capacity to translate that potential into reality. As a result, it seemed condemned to remain an unimportant actor in the final stages of the antiapartheid struggle. Aware of that danger, as the negotiations started the PAC was desperately trying to get back into the process without losing its radical image or splitting the organization.

The Pan Africanist Congress was formed in 1959 as the result of a schism within the ANC. The issue that divided the Congress then was that of black power, or the differences between the supporters of a narrow African nationalism and those willing to embrace everyone, no matter their color, who supported the antiapartheid cause.[23] The PAC, though strongly socialist in its thinking, also rejected cooperation with the Communist Party, which it saw as influenced by a foreign ideology and dominated by whites. Finally, the PAC strongly believed in the power of spontaneous mass action, in contrast to the ANC, which had a long history of elite politics.

It was the mass action promoted by the Pan Africanist Congress in March 1960 that led to the banning of all major antiapartheid organizations. The PAC launched a campaign to defy the pass laws (which required blacks to obtain special permits to live and work in the cities), hoping it would turn into "a massive campaign of defiance which would ultimately erupt into a full-scale popular uprising."[24] But response was poor almost everywhere. The newly formed PAC did not have the organization necessary to reach people and convince them to participate, and its belief in the possibility of a spontaneous uprising was proved totally unfounded. But in the Vaal triangle, the industrial area south of Johannesburg, the PAC was better organized, and crowds turned out in substantial numbers. In the township of Sharpeville, the police panicked and opened fire on the demonstrators, killing sixty-seven people, most of them shot in the back while running away.

Massive demonstrations and an outbreak of violence in other cities in the following days shook up the white community. The government declared a state of emergency and on April 8 announced the banning of the ANC and the PAC.

It was difficult enough for the ANC to survive these measures, but it was worse for the PAC, a new political group that had not put much effort into creating an organization. The PAC remained little more than a name for a long time, finally reviving during the overall increase in political mobilization in the 1980s.

The distant episode of Sharpeville reflected well the basic problem that the PAC still faced in 1990. Its uncompromising stance, call for defiance, and rejection of politics as the art of the possible and thus of compromise gave the PAC a potential constituency among "the relatively politicized and aggressive elements among urban youth" in 1990, as it had in 1960.[25] The language of UDF- and ANC-affiliated student and youth organizations, such as the Congress of South African Students or the South African Youth Congress and its successor, the revived ANC Youth League, often resembled that of the PAC more than that of the ANC. The position of the Pan Africanist Congress best embodied the anger and impatience rife in the country, as well as the desire for absolute solutions and for a liberating catharsis that found expression in the imagery of the armed struggle. The PAC's "non-negotiables," declared President Zeph Mothopeng in 1990, included "restoration of the land to the indigenous people, the redistribution of all resources in order that the majority benefit, and one-person one-vote in a unitary state."[26] Such a position was not an auspicious starting point for dealing with the government, but it did reflect a widespread sentiment. Nevertheless, the PAC's potential support was not captured.

Two factors, closely interrelated, were probably responsible for this failure: lack of organization and lack of resources. In 1990 the unbanned PAC was a shoestring operation plagued by a shortage of financing and lack of organization. The slogan chosen by the PAC, "one settler, one bullet," was hardly designed to attract the support of liberal foreign donors like those who helped to keep the ANC afloat financially. No matter how hard PAC officials tried to explain away the slogan, they failed to be convincing, least of all to whites. The word *settler* had nothing to do with race, but with mentality, they argued. "Europeans who have made their homes in Africa and who identify with the aspirations of Africans are Africans."[27] And Moth-openg explained that "one cannot be expected to abandon the bullet until the ballot is secured to contest power."[28]

But the explanations did not dispel doubts or bring in financial support. In July 1990 PAC officials in Britain complained that they could not get any funding because all aid to South Africa was channeled through the Anti-Apartheid Movement, which gave only to the ANC.[29] And Barney Desai, explaining why the PAC could not expand its membership faster despite the enormous potential, argued that "we don't have the resources of the ANC, so we will have to depend on what we get from our own people."[30] By the end of 1990 funds for the PAC had dried up to the point that the organization resolved at its December congress that all working members should donate to the organization 3.3 percent of their salaries.[31]

The PAC also had trouble mobilizing supporters. Despite recurrent rumors that it was winning support away from the ANC, it never succeeded in bringing out crowds for a show of strength, nor was its presence particularly visible in the townships. The demonstrations it called usually attracted hundreds of supporters, when tens of thousands were turning out for the ANC. Possibly the most blatant demonstration of the PAC's problem was the funeral of President Zeph Mothopeng on October 23, 1990. While representatives of the ANC and even Inkatha turned out to honor the old antiapartheid activist, who had devoted his entire life to the cause and spent many years in jail as a result, PAC supporters did not. The ceremony, held in a large stadium, attracted only a few thousand people.

But the most difficult problem for the PAC was to find a place in the political system. It had chosen "an outbidding position," an analyst explained, trying to get support away from the ANC by telling people what they wanted to hear.[32] But that policy could work only up until negotiations between the government and other organizations started, because at that point the PAC would simply find itself cut off from the political game. One part of the PAC leadership was aware of the danger, but getting the organization as a whole to formulate a coherent policy toward the negotiations proved an insurmountable problem, for the PAC wanted neither to participate nor to allow the talks to go on without its presence.

At its December 1990 congress, the organization concluded that there was only one solution to South Africa's problems, namely, the election of a constituent assembly on a one-person, one-vote basis. The PAC would take part in talks to define the modalities of such an election, but would not consider negotiating on any other issue.

The ANC also supported the election of a constituent assembly, and on the basis of this common position the two organizations by December 1990 were discussing the possibility of creating a "patriotic front" of antiapartheid groups, similar to that formed by ZANU and ZAPU (Zimbabwe African National Union and Zimbabwe African People's Union) more than ten years earlier.

An alliance of the two groups seemed logical. The ANC had begun to discover its own weaknesses. Membership was growing slowly, and opinion polls suggested that the organization would receive far more votes than any other party, but might not be strong enough to govern on its own. The National Party was at this stage courting Inkatha. The ANC thus needed allies, and the PAC for its part needed a means of emerging from the political isolation to which it had been condemning itself.

The deterioration of relations between the government and the ANC and the consequent hardening of the ANC's position in the spring of 1991 also facilitated the formation of an alliance. Since the signing of the Pretoria Minute the previous August, the ANC had been feeling outwitted and manipulated. There was grumbling in the ranks that the leaders had given too much and obtained too little. Political prisoners were being released very slowly, and exiles were only beginning to return, their applications for indemnity bogged down in lengthy bureaucratic procedures. Adding to the frustration, the violence in the townships was not abating, and the conviction was widespread at all levels of the ANC that the government was deliberately allowing the violence to continue, if not fomenting it.

This prompted the Congress to issue an ultimatum in April 1991 that it would suspend negotiations unless a number of conditions were met. Most important were the demands that Defence Minister Magnus Malan and Law and Order Minister Adriaan Vlok be dismissed and that the carrying of so-called cultural weapons—the hallmark of Inkatha supporters—be forbidden. Issuing the ultimatum brought down upon the ANC the scorn of virtually all white political organizations, including those normally sympathetic to it, but it did facilitate relations between the ANC and the PAC. It also forced the government to give in on some issues.

Nevertheless, it took many more months of preliminary encounters, acrimony, and postponed meetings before the patriotic front was launched. Designed to bring together all organizations supporting the election of a constituent assembly, the Patriotic United Front, as it was officially named, not only failed to attract AZAPO but did not even produce a permanent improvement in the relationship between the PAC and the ANC, its principal members. Having agreed to attend what it called "preconstituent assembly talks" (later officially called the Convention for a Democratic South Africa [CODESA]), the PAC proceeded to create complications.[33] Plagued by internal dissension on the issue of participation, it started accusing the ANC of negotiating secretly with the government, breaching the patriotic front agreement. The ANC reacted disdainfully, denying that it had violated any agreement, but also making it clear that CODESA would meet as scheduled, with or without the PAC.

Once again, the PAC had sidelined itself. Its ambitions remained considerable, its potential support important, but its capacity to carve a viable political role for itself was reconfirmed as minimal. Although with the suspension of the negotiations in June 1992 the almost-forgotten patriotic front was again being talked about, the PAC did not appear capable of taking advantage of new opportunities.

THE REJECTIONIST PARTIES

Not all political organizations in South Africa accepted the idea that negotiations and an election should be the means to usher in a new political system. On the Right and Left, some groups barricaded themselves behind absolute principles, refusing all dialogue.

Conservative Party

Dr. Andries Treurnicht, the leader of the Conservative Party, was nicknamed Dr. No by the South African press, and for good reason. Rejection of everything being proposed was the stance of the CP in this period. It rejected the reforms introduced by de Klerk, it rejected negotiations, and it rejected the inexorable drift toward political rights for blacks. However, the party was incapable of setting forth viable proposals of its own. Its growing support among whites thus did not appear likely to be translated into a growing influence on the transition process.

Philosophically, the Conservative Party remained a staunch defender of the doctrine of separate development. In its simplistic form just a hankering for a return to the good old days, the defense of apartheid was portrayed in the more sophisticated version as an expression of the right of Afrikaners to self-determination. Stressing self-determination was an attempt to cloak apartheid in respectable language, embodied in the charter of the United Nations and in the ideology of the anticolonial struggle, and increasingly in the politics of the 1990s in Eastern Europe and many parts of Africa.

Afrikaners did not have a territorial base and were a minority everywhere. Nevertheless, in the CP's conception, self-determination meant the right to have a separate homeland. Conservatives, however, were divided about the geography of this homeland, with suggestions ranging from the existing white South Africa to the old Boer republics of the Transvaal and the Orange Free State, and even, in a proposal set forth at the 1992 congress, to those constituencies where the Conservative Party had won elections. Whatever the territory chosen, self-determination was looking much like the old apartheid, involving massive relocations of people in order to create ethnically homogeneous homelands where none existed.

Support for the Conservative Party had grown steadily throughout the 1980s, and it appeared to increase faster after February 1990, as shown by results of several by-elections. In November 1991, a by-election in Virginia, in the Orange Free State, saw a 15 percent swing in favor of the Conservative Party. Another vote in Potchefstrom on February 19, 1992, also resulted in a substantial gain for the Conservative Party, despite de Klerk's confident prediction that the result there would be much more favorable to the government, and a better indicator of public opinion, than that in Virginia, a town particularly hard hit by the recession.

This loss of support posed a serious problem for de Klerk. He was negotiating without a mandate from the white electorate—negotiations were not explicitly part of the National Party's 1989 program, and at any rate he had not received the majority of the white vote. Public opinion was apparently turning against him. He had promised whites that he would call a referendum on the new constitution, but he could no longer be sure of their approval. Paradoxically, his perceived weakness threatened the ANC as well. The conundrum was clearly expressed by Mandela:

> If de Klerk made the mistake of either calling for a white election . . . or if he asked for a referendum from the whites only, he might be outvoted. Once he is outvoted, there is the moral question whether he should continue on an issue where he has on countless occasions promised the country that the whites will be consulted. . . . We are also concerned because whatever reservations we have about Mr. de Klerk, however much we condemn him for the perception, right or wrongly, that he is playing a double game, he is the only person with whom we can negotiate a new constitution for the country.[34]

Daringly, de Klerk reacted to the crisis not by retreating but by challenging the white electorate to decide immediately whether it trusted him to continue negotiating with the ANC, or, implicitly, whether it preferred the rejectionist position of the Conservative Party. He called for a referendum on March 17, asking voters, "Do you support continuation of the reform process which the State President began on February 2, 1990, and which is aimed at a new constitution through negotiations?" The referendum campaign revealed a high degree of fear and anger among conservatives. Not only activists in uniform but entire families complete with grandmothers and babies turned out for rallies to express their rejection of a future in which, a participant explained to the author, "whites would be ruled by natives." In the end, 68.7 percent of the white public unexpectedly voted yes. Nevertheless, the referendum was less a manifestation of confident support for de Klerk and his policies than an acknowledgment that the Conservative Party ultimately offered no alternative.

White Extremists

Support for the Conservative Party was only one expression of white discontent. Another was the proliferation of white extremist organizations, all dreaming of a renewal of apartheid and of an Afrikaner homeland and theoretically willing to use force to achieve their goal. The importance of these groups was extremely difficult to evaluate. Their talk was fierce, and their display of khaki uniforms and weapons impressive, but it remained to be seen whether they would be willing in the end to resort to violence or whether it was all bluster.

No matter what they did, the white extremists were unlikely to stop the transition from apartheid. With much greater resources at its disposal, the government had already tried to crush the liberation organizations, and it had failed. Nevertheless, the extremists did represent a threat. Even a small number of well-armed and determined men could cause a lot of damage, as the experience of some African countries proved. Most important, an outbreak of white violence would create bitterness and resentment among blacks and fear of reprisals among whites, thus complicating the transition.

Some episodes of white violence had taken place during 1990, but they were few in number and limited in scope. Some bombs were placed in political parties' offices as an expression of displeasure, a vacant school building that was being readied to house pupils returning from an ANC school in Tanzania was destroyed, and a few other acts of petty sabotage were committed. The police intervened quickly and the problem did not escalate.

The groups discussed thus far were militaristic organizations threatening violence to stop the negotiating process. An attempt to catalog and list all these groups would be futile, not only because their importance was limited but also because, like the pieces of a kaleidoscope, they tended to endlessly split and reassemble in new combinations. The best known of these organizations was the Afrikaner Weerstandsbeweging. Its fame was based more on the fierce oratory of its leader, Eugene Terre' Blanche, and on its display of uniforms and weapons than on its actions.

Afrikaner fundamentalism took a more idealistic and less violent form as well. The Afrikaner Volkswag, led by Carel Boshoff, also advocated the creation of a homeland reserved exclusively for whites, but it chose a remote and sparsely inhabited area of the Northern Cape to build its dream republic. Realistic enough to know that Afrikaners would never be able to remove millions of blacks from the old Boer republics, Boshoff nevertheless believed that large numbers of Afrikaners would be willing to leave their government jobs and established farms and trek to a pioneering life in distant, inhospitable areas, to be developed without the help of black laborers. Orania, the newly established capital of the yet unborn republic of Orandia, was a forlorn settlement of some ninety houses built originally for whites working on a nearby dam and later purchased by the organization. Orania's tiny population, dilapidated conditions, and lack of economic prospects strongly suggested that few Afrikaners saw a new trek as the answer to their problem.

Azanian People's Organization

Rejectionism was not an exclusively white attitude. The Azanian People's Organization and some very small, radical groups from the Western Cape shared the attitude.[35] Like the PAC, AZAPO was an organization unable to realize its potential. Founded in April 1978, it picked up the flag of Steve Biko's black-consciousness ideology after other organizations were banned.[36] Given the enormous importance of the ideology in mobilizing blacks anew in South Africa in the 1970s, AZAPO might have been expected to become a major organization, but it failed to transform the acceptance of the ideology into organizational strength. By the time of Mandela's release, it had limited support and could not define its strategy, locking itself by default into a rejectionist tradition.

The organization existed countrywide, but with very uneven strength. It claimed 60,000 to 70,000 members in the Northern Transvaal, where it had a following among the agricultural workers of that stronghold of conservatism and Afrikaner nationalism. But it admitted having only 500 members in Natal, and "quite a few more" in the Cape; it did not even mention the Orange Free State.[37] Besides being unevenly distributed, AZAPO's membership was very diverse, with a highly intellectual leadership prone to abstruse debates and with a following among uneducated farm laborers.

After February 1990 AZAPO tried to cast itself as the group that would unite all black organizations. It proposed setting up a consultative network among antiapartheid organizations of all ideological persuasions, but it did not have the authority or command enough respect among other groups for its calls to be heeded.[38] After the first major outbreak of black-on-black violence on the Witwatersrand in August and September 1990, it called for a peace meeting of all organizations—except Inkatha, which it did not consider a bona fide component of the liberation movement—but it was spurned by both the ANC and the PAC. During 1991 it considered joining the patriotic front and agreed to become a convener of the first meeting together with the ANC and the PAC. At the last moment, after sending out on its own initiative a letter to all prospective participants establishing new conditions for attendance, it was ousted from the convener role by its partners. AZAPO therefore did not attend the conference and join the front. The black-consciousness tradition, which had played a crucial role in the history of the antiapartheid movement, was grinding to a halt as AZAPO floundered in a morass of intransigence and petty posturing.

THE DE JURE PARTICIPANTS

The parties in the tricameral Parliament, those of the self-governing homelands, and the governments of the so-called independent homelands were assured a place in the transition process by virtue of their legal existence, not of their political weight. Most of these organizations sided openly with the government, and even the few that did not had more interest in supporting the reforms proposed by the government than those favored by the ANC, since the government sought a political system that would enhance the power of minority organizations.

The two major parties in the Parliament, the NP and the CP, have been discussed. Of those remaining, only the Democratic Party (DP) in the white House of Assembly could conceivably find a meaningful independent place in a process dominated by the ANC and the National Party. Formed only in 1989, the DP was the heir to a long line of relatively liberal political organizations. The most important of these, the Progressive Federal Party, had advocated universal suffrage, the abolition of the apartheid laws, and a consociational, power-sharing constitution—all ideas the NP adopted and began implementing in 1990. Morally, the NP's acceptance of these ideas could be viewed as a vindication of the Democrats' stance; politically, it was nonetheless a heavy blow because it deprived the party of its separate identity.

For almost two years the DP was in disarray. Some members favored an alliance with the ANC and even claimed the right to maintain membership in both parties; others wanted to join the National Party; the embattled center, represented by Chairman Zach de Beer, sought to develop a distinctive image for the party as a liberal, centrist organization that could help mediate between the ANC and the NP.

At its congress of December 1991, the party appeared to consolidate around the centrist position. The new identity of the DP was strengthened shortly thereafter, when Zach de Beer was chosen to head the working group of parties preparing the long-awaited Convention for a Democratic South Africa. This new role was important for the DP's survival. Given the weakness of the party, it was more doubtful that it would have a significant impact on the negotiations.

With the exception of Inkatha, the parties of the self-governing homelands and the Coloured and Indian ones in the tricameral Parliament could hope to survive only by tying their fortunes to those of the major rivals.[39] The homeland organizations were new, the result mostly of a hasty, probably government-inspired attempt to transform the homeland cultural movements into political parties that could participate in the negotiations.[40] Invariably headed by the homelands' chief ministers, and almost certainly funded from their budgets— hence by the South African government—they had by definition no autonomy. The Coloured and Indian parties had little support in their own communities, which had overwhelmingly rejected the 1983 constitution and boycotted elections.[41]

The ANC made an attempt to attract these organizations to its side—to the dismay of radicals who thought that such "puppets of apartheid" did not deserve recognition—but with scant success. Only the Transkei, and to some extent KaNgwane and Venda, openly supported the ANC's position. Bophuthatswana, KwaZulu, and increasingly the Ciskei remained openly hostile. The remaining homelands were leery of the ANC's views of the transition process and a unitary state because they offered little to small parties with a regional power base. The government's advocacy of a constitution entrenching strong regional and local governments, on the other hand, was attractive to politicians who both recognized that the homeland system was doomed and aspired to a continuing political role (see chapter 5).

The so-called independent homelands, the pseudo-ministates created by Pretoria in an attempt to make apartheid work, could not survive the abolition of the system.[42] Heavily subsidized by the South African government, and not recognized by any foreign country, they would have to be reincorporated into South Africa as part of the transition. This was a foregone conclusion. But they could not simply be made to disappear. Their reincorporation was a process to be negotiated, and this offered political opportunities for the more ambitious leaders. Major General Bantu Holomisa of the Transkei appeared especially determined to translate his control of the homeland into a political or military career in the new South Africa. He was close to the ANC, and in particular to Chris Hani, MK's chief of staff. While he favored reincorporation of the homelands into South Africa, Holomisa was also building up his military, according to some reports by incorporating MK personnel. His political career would probably not end with the demise of an independent Transkei.

Bophuthatswana presented a different challenge: President Lucas Mangope refused reincorporation into South Africa, although his homeland was a particularly absurd one, not only fragmented but scattered over a vast expanse stretching from the Northern Transvaal to the middle of the Orange Free State. However, it was the only homeland with a degree of financial viability, thanks to the royalties it received from platinum mines. Its population was as poor as those of other homelands, and the prospects for development just as dim, but the government could finance almost three-quarters of expenditures from its own revenue.[43] This greater financial autonomy gave the president the confidence to oppose reincorporation and to refuse cooperating in any other way during the transition process. When the government was releasing political prisoners as part of the process leading to negotiations, Mangope refused to do the same. Organizations unbanned in South Africa continued to be curbed in the homeland. In the transition period, Mangope was becoming an apprentice sorcerer's nightmare, a political figure the government had conjured up in its pursuit of apartheid but could no longer force to disappear.

CONCLUSIONS

The organizations of the second tier presented a challenge for both the ANC and the government. Inkatha, the PAC, and the Conservative Party were powerful enough, although for different reasons, to influence the process directly. Inkatha had shown both the willingness and the capacity to challenge the ANC openly, with violence if necessary. It probably could not win votes away from the Congress, but it certainly could make it more difficult for the ANC and the civic associations to organize in the townships. But Inkatha was not a compliant government ally, either. Buthelezi played his own game;

he would travel with the government only when he thought it in his own interest to do so. While it was unlikely that the government and the ANC would side together openly against Inkatha, the organization was a problem they both had to face.

The PAC remained a dark horse. Too disorganized to challenge the government except verbally, it could not be dismissed by the ANC, because its militancy reflected attitudes that were common in the townships, particularly among the youth. Nevertheless, the PAC remained unable to realize its potential. The danger was that, like Inkatha, it would try to make up for its weakness as a political organization by resorting to violence and disruption.

The Conservative Party was more of a problem for the government than for the ANC. Its importance, however, was greatly reduced by the March 17 referendum, which showed that most voters did not believe it offered a concrete alternative to the government's approach. Like the PAC, the Conservative Party represented an apparently widespread way of thinking, but it was unable to formulate a program and thereby take advantage of potential support.

The smaller organizations, powerless in themselves, were important in the initial phase of the transition process. Until an election was held, providing a true measure of the support enjoyed by various parties, they had to be offered a seat at the table. This provided the government an incentive to push for broad agreements during the initial, preelection phase of the process, when it could play the numerous small parties against the ANC. Conversely, it was in the interest of the Congress to leave most decisions in the hands of an elected body it hoped to dominate.

PART 2
The Arenas of Struggle

The political parties and organizations discussed in the preceding chapters were engaged in a many-faceted struggle for power. The main division pitted the government against the liberation establishment, with the second-tier organizations trying to find a place in the contest in order to influence the outcome or at least survive. The key issue was the transfer of power from the apartheid regime to a new government.

But this change was only one aspect of the process. Dismantling apartheid was not simply a question of abrogating some legislation and replacing one government with another—only the National Party took such a narrow view. All components of the liberation establishment as well as other antiapartheid organizations agreed that much more was needed: dismantling the segregated apartheid city, redressing economic grievances, restructuring black education, addressing the land issue, implementing a massive program of affirmative action—the list had virtually no end. But different issues had different saliency to each group. For this reason, in the transition phase three major arenas of conflict emerged, at the central government level, at the local level, and in the economic realm.

In the tradition of the earlier African liberation movements, the African National Congress (ANC) appeared intent on following Kwame Nkrumah's advice to seek first the political kingdom. Transfer of power at the center was the only issue that really mattered in the short run. Other problems would be tackled in due time by the new government. Like the National Party, the ANC had a state-centered view of politics. Control over formal institutions was what counted most. For both organizations, the major struggle was over the writing of a new constitution, the exercise of power in the interim period, and final control over the state. It is true that the National Party, after relying for forty years on the development of strong state structures to attain both political and economic goals, had become in the 1990s a champion of decentralization of power in what it called a participatory democracy. But the NP favored decentralization only because it considered the state all-important, and thus sought to minimize its scope before surrendering control.

85

The priorities of the mass democratic movement were different, in part for ideological reasons but to a large extent because of self-interest. To the civic associations, local issues were paramount. Transfer of power at the center would not be enough unless the apartheid cities were dismantled, government revenue redistributed within the metropolitan areas, and services redirected from the white suburbs to the townships. Furthermore, transfer at the center could even be dangerous if the new government attempted to solve local problems from the top down, pushing aside the organizations of civil society. For the Congress of South African Trade Unions (COSATU), economic restructuring was an intrinsic part of the transition process, which should be discussed immediately and implemented as part of the political settlement. It simply could not be put aside until the new government formulated an economic policy. Moreover, economic reforms could not be discussed only among political parties; labor unions and business must also be involved.

The civic associations demanded that negotiations start immediately in each city and town, with a view to replacing the existing mosaic of white and black councils and Coloured or Indian management committees with integrated local governments embracing the entire area. Paradoxically, the government concurred, because local negotiations fit in with its new strategy of decentralization. During 1991, as a result, all major metropolitan areas and some smaller towns saw the halting beginning of negotiations aimed at solving immediate critical problems and also at restructuring local institutions.

The economic arena experienced the least progress toward negotiations. To be sure, unions and employers continued to bargain on the workerist issues of wages and working conditions. But the populist issue of a new economic order, which COSATU insisted must be discussed as part of the overall settlement, had not been tackled. COSATU demanded the establishment of an economic forum of equal status with the political one and running concurrently with it, but the response from government and the business community was slow and unenthusiastic. Free enterprise, not negotiations, was the answer to South Africa's economic problems, they argued.

The local and economic arenas received much less attention than the national one, but they were far from insignificant. For better or for worse, they broadened the scope of the negotiating process, making it more difficult for the ANC and the National Party to settle for a narrow political agreement and possibly preventing them from reaching any agreement at all. They also provided a measure of pluralism to the political process, no matter what happened at the center. Although there was no shortage of political parties in South Africa— nineteen were present at the first meeting of the Convention for a Democratic South Africa (CODESA)—the ANC and the National Party dominated the national negotiations, narrowing the political spectrum and creating the danger of polarization or, at the opposite extreme, of collusion. Parties with a history of centralization, bureaucratization, and a strong statist orientation, the two risked mutually reinforcing these tendencies, particularly if they agreed to a form of power-sharing, as the National Party wanted.

Launching local negotiations and, if it became a reality, an economic forum ensured that other groups would participate. It is true that many of the political parties participating in CODESA were as unimportant in these processes as they were at the national level. Even the would-be major players, like Inkatha and the PAC, had very little to say on local and economic issues. But the ANC and the National Party were less dominant in this realm. The ANC had to contend with the members of the mass democratic movement. The National Party was less powerful in the local councils, some of which were controlled by the Conservative Party or the Democratic Party, than it was at the national level. The business community, a silent partner since 1990, would be forced to become an active participant in an economic forum. Local and economic issues changed the process from a contest between two political parties to one in which a variety of stakeholders participated.

Chapter 5

Toward a New Constitution

In the history of most African countries, the attainment of independence was the turning point between the colonial and postcolonial eras. Symbolically the transition was marked by an emotional ceremony in which the old flag was lowered and the new one raised, the colonial government stepped down and the new one took office. How the new government was formed and what constitution regulated its functioning were issues that received relatively little attention. Constitution making was a task often entrusted to foreign experts, and it did not excite much interest.

In the South African transition, however, the enactment of a new constitution was the central issue. Symbolically it would mark the transition from the old to the new order, because the 1983 constitution had kept apartheid alive despite government claims that the system had been abolished with the repeal of the Group Areas Act, the Population Registration Act, and the Land Acts during the 1991 parliamentary session. But the new constitution was much more than a symbol: all sides considered it the major instrument for shaping the character of the country for years to come. The writing of the constitution was thus not just a technical exercise to be entrusted to experts; it was the main issue to be negotiated by the political parties.

There were reasons to be skeptical about the contention that the right constitution could make the difference between peace and civil war in South Africa, or between a prosperous future and one that would sink the country in the morass of economic decline and political decay that afflicted the rest of the continent. Constitutions are easy to ignore, particularly if they try to create a political system far removed from the existing balance of power. But the concept that the right formal institutions could neutralize political forces was well entrenched in South Africa, where whites had for forty years tried to devise a system that would safeguard their position. The writing of the new charter thus remained at the center of an intense debate and of a great deal of political maneuvering.

Both the debate and the maneuvering centered on two issues, the content of the constitution and the process through which it would be enacted. It was a foregone conclusion that process would determine content. While the debate centered on the constitution itself, the political maneuvering thus focused on the process.

The debate was characterized by the absoluteness of the positions taken by all sides. There was little open-minded discussion of the respective advantages and shortcomings of different systems but many gloomy predictions about the future of South Africa if the other side got its way. Even political systems normally considered to fall well within the realm of democracy were condemned in strong terms by one or the other party. For example, the government and Inkatha rejected as "simplistic majoritarianism" and a step toward dictatorship the idea that the party receiving the majority of votes should form the government. The African National Congress (ANC) looked at federalism as a plot to perpetuate separate development.

THE CONSTITUTIONAL MODELS

The conflicting goals of the major parties were reflected in the constitutional models they favored. The government sought to perform the seemingly impossible feat of extending the franchise to the entire population and maintaining an appearance of democracy while preventing majority rule. As a result, it outlined a very convoluted constitution. The ANC expected to win the majority of votes in an election, so it favored a straightforward charter that would give the majority party the right to form the government.

Evolution of the National Party's Approach

The constitutional proposal the government would take to the negotiating table had a long history, being the latest in a series of attempts to avoid the dreaded possibility of a black-controlled government. In retrospect it is clear that the National Party (NP) had fought a losing battle from the start, although it had succeeded in postponing the inevitable for several decades. Even in 1991, it had not given up. Resigned to the fact that blacks would soon have full political rights, the National Party was still looking for ways of avoiding majority rule.

The National Party's obsessive fear of majority rule was based on its own experience. In its South African version, the system had not meant democracy. Members of Parliament were elected in single-member constituencies, with the candidate receiving the greatest number of votes taking everything. Gerrymandering made it possible for the party to win the majority of seats even if it did not receive the majority of votes, as happened in both 1948 and 1989. Since there was no separate presidential election—the state president was elected by Parliament—the majority party was guaranteed unchallenged control of both the executive and the legislature. Separation of powers became meaningless. Parliamentary debates were occasions for MPs to display their skills or vent their frustrations rather than means to influence political choices. The government almost never lost a vote.

Nevertheless, absolute control over the formal institutions did not help the National Party quell black demands for political rights. The homeland system, devised to eventually enfranchise blacks in their own independent territories, was not working. First, Coloureds and Indians had no political rights, even by the system's fictional standards, because they had no homeland—hence the provision in the 1983 constitution for their representation. Second, the independent homelands had failed to win international recognition, making it difficult for the government to coax the remaining ones toward independence.

Consequently, while still formally pursuing the homeland policy, the party in 1976 started a long search for a political system that would preserve white power yet also satisfy black demands. Although the National Party had come a very long way by 1991, there was a great deal of continuity in its thinking and certainly no clean break with the past. Furthermore, members of the cabinet and party caucus, let alone the voters, were strung all along the road traveled by the NP over the previous fifteen years—those who refused to move past the original apartheid doctrine had by this time crossed over to the Conservative Party.

In 1977 a cabinet committee headed by P. W. Botha, who was to become prime minister two years later and state president under the 1983 constitution, presented a proposal to give Coloureds and Indians representation in the Parliament through the device of a consociational, or power-sharing, constitution.[1] The committee clung to the position that there was no reason to give political rights to Africans within the Republic, however, because they would eventually be citizens of their own independent homelands.

Consociationalism was a fashionable idea in South Africa, penetrating both academic and political circles. In brief, consociationalism was based on the assumption that in ethnically and culturally plural societies like South Africa the political system had to allow group representation. However, proponents of consociationalism argued, groups could not be predetermined. The statutory groups established by the Population Registration Act were unacceptable, because they imposed an artificial identity on individuals. Rather, people should be allowed to define their group membership by voting freely—proponents of consociationalism assumed that parties would represent cultural and ethnic groups, not ideological tendencies. The group-parties thus freely defined would all be guaranteed a voice in decisionmaking through a system of proportional representation in the Parliament and also in the cabinet. But the power of these group-parties created by the voters' choice would go further: each of them would have control over those issues most directly affecting that group— education and culture in the first place.[2]

It is worth pointing out that in the late 1970s proposals for a consociational system, embracing all South Africans in a country reincorporating the homelands, represented the most liberal form of white thinking. The idea that groups would not be formally represented in the political system was inconceivable to all but a handful of radical whites. The constitutional guidelines adopted in late 1978 by the Progressive Federal Party, the most liberal organization in the Parliament, outlined a consociational system.[3]

When the government started elaborating a constitutional proposal following the Botha committee's report, it included some consociational principles, mixed with a heavy dose of old apartheid. Africans were still excluded. The government clung to a statutory definition of groups instead of accepting their self-definition. Whites, Coloureds, and Indians—as defined under the Population Registration Act—would elect their respective parliaments on separate voters' rolls.

Each parliament in turn would elect a prime minister and cabinet, while separate provincial and local authorities would operate for each group, taking care of "own affairs." "General affairs" would be dealt with by a joint council of ministers, drawing on members of the separate cabinets and chaired by a president elected by all parliaments. The council of ministers would make decisions only by consensus, thus giving each group veto power.[4]

The proposal left intact many apartheid concepts, but it did contain an element of power-sharing. Decisionmaking by consensus would not allow Coloureds and Indians to reverse apartheid laws, but it would provide a safeguard of sorts against further impositions.

But the National Party was not willing to accept even this limited form of power-sharing. The constitution that was finally approved in 1983 contained all the most conservative features of the 1977 document and none of the more progressive ones. It maintained statutory group definition, the exclusion of Africans, and the distinction between own and general affairs, but it did not require representation of all groups in the central cabinet and thus eliminated veto power. General affairs remained firmly in white hands. In 1983 the National Party had not been ready for power-sharing.

By 1986 the leadership was. The more pragmatic, if not necessarily liberal, NP officials had come to recognize that the 1983 constitution had not created a system acceptable to all South Africans and to the outside world. If anything, the introduction of the new system had made things worse. The 1984 Coloured and Indian elections were boycotted by more than 80 percent of potential voters.[5] Opposition to the tricameral Parliament also provided the catalyst for the organization of the United Democratic Front, which gave the ANC at least an indirect above-ground presence in the country for the first time in twenty years. The imposition of the state of emergency in July 1985 and then again in June 1986 failed to reestablish any semblance of normality, but it led the international community to tighten sanctions, with the U.S. Congress approving the Comprehensive Anti-Apartheid Act in October 1986.

In the midst of the turmoil, the National Party held a congress in August 1986 and formally endorsed the idea of power-sharing it had rejected three years earlier, even extending it to the African population. The meaning of power-sharing was spelled out in an official NP position paper written by Stoffel van der Merwe, who would later become a member of the cabinet and of F. W. de Klerk's inner circle: all South Africans must participate fully in the process of government at all levels; participation must not entail domination by one group over another; each group must have self-determination over own affairs, while sharing in the decisionmaking concerning general affairs; the envisaged system must guarantee the rights of individuals, but also afford protection to minority groups; and, finally, the new political system must be created through negotiations among the leaders of all groups.[6]

The limits of the concept of power-sharing accepted at this time become clearer in light of a few points. First, the National Party denied vehemently that by accepting the idea it was reversing its position; on the contrary, power-sharing was the logical outcome of separate development because each group would have control over own affairs but share responsibility for those decisions that unavoidably affected all. What the National Party had rejected in the past was merely a distorted idea of power-sharing that allowed domination of one group by another.[7]

Second, the party also approved a resolution on "group security," formally proposed by F. W. de Klerk, then minister of national education and by reputation a conservative member of the cabinet. Power-sharing and cooperation among groups, he told the congress, required the satisfaction of their basic demands. These included the preservation of "own community life within which an own dispensation and character can be preserved"; self-determination on "matters of intimate concern to the group"; "effective protection for each group against domination by others"; and recognition of "collective rights of the group as a group."[8]

Third, the party insisted that the new power-sharing system be negotiated among members of statutorily defined groups. The full implications of the insistence on negotiations were easy to overlook. Acceptance of negotiations did not mean just that the government was prepared to talk to members of the extraparliamentary opposition, rather than to jail them. It also meant the government wanted each group to have equal weight in the process, thus overrepresenting whites and grossly underrepresenting Africans, in effect making them a minority. In other words, negotiations were seen by the government as an alternative to elections and a means to keep whites from being swamped by blacks in the transition process. Negotiations for power-sharing without domination were thus a denial of majority rule, a point that became a major bone of contention in 1991.

The limits of the National Party's new reformism were tested and found quite narrow a few months after the 1986 congress, when the KwaZulu-Natal Indaba, or council, concluded its deliberations and submitted its proposal for power-sharing in Natal province to the National Party. It was rejected in its entirety within forty-eight hours.

It is necessary at this point to consider briefly the background to the Indaba. The roots of the idea lay in the realization of Natal businessmen and politicians that the policy would not work in their region, given the fragmentation of KwaZulu and Buthelezi's refusal to accept independence for it, at least if the borders were not modified. Fragmentation was not a problem unique to KwaZulu, but it was more extreme there. It was also less justifiable even in apartheid terms, since it was dictated purely by economic interests, not by the geographic distribution of different ethnic groups. Good agricultural land, particularly that suitable for growing sugar cane, and areas along the main roads were kept in Natal, while the hilly and eroded residue was given to KwaZulu. Consolidating KwaZulu in the hope of making its independence acceptable to Buthelezi would mean taking good land away from white farmers and from the sugar estates in particular, and thus it was not a solution the business community was willing to consider.

Whether Buthelezi would have accepted independence for the homeland under any degree of consolidation is open to debate.[9] The question is in any case moot, because no such offer was made. Instead, by the early 1980s attempts were under way in Natal to work out a solution to the province's problems based not on the strict separation of Natal and KwaZulu but on a form of consociational cooperation. Business, particularly sugar growers, saw this as the least threatening approach.[10]

In 1980 the Lombard Commission, set up by the Durban Chamber of Commerce and the South African Sugar Association, sketched a sort of federal solution for KwaZulu-Natal, with a single government for the province and three separate regional administrations controlling KwaZulu, the white farming areas, and the Durban metropolitan region.[11] Two years later the Buthelezi Commission, appointed by the KwaZulu legislature and representing major political parties and business groups in Natal, also recommended a consociational solution

for the region, with a legislature elected by proportional representation and a cabinet in which all parties and cultural groups would
be represented.[12]

Two critics of the Buthelezi Commission's recommendations called
it a "major compromise away from majority rule."[13] Buthelezi agreed
that this was the case, warning, in what would become a refrain by
1991, that majority rule would lead only to a winner-take-all outcome,
hence to violence and civil war.[14] The National Party nevertheless
rejected the recommendations of both the Lombard and Buthelezi
commissions. The major problem was the proposal for a single authority for KwaZulu-Natal, which contradicted the principle of separate development.[15]

Neither Buthelezi nor the Natal businessmen gave up; instead, they
convoked the KwaZulu-Natal Indaba. The Indaba brought together
representatives of political parties, businessmen, and scholars from
April to November 1986 to prepare a constitution for the region,
implicitly setting a model that could be followed in the entire country.

The Indaba proposal was a mixture of old and new.[16] The most
important change was that it would extend political rights to the entire
population of the region, probably leading to the formation of a regional executive in which blacks would be in the majority. But it also
gave recognition to statutory ethnic groups, guaranteeing that they
would have representation in the legislature. Specifically, it called for
a bicameral Parliament, with one chamber based on proportional representation, the other composed of ten representatives from each of
five groups—Africans, Afrikaners, English-speaking whites, Asians,
and "South Africans," the last a catchall category encompassing people who could not fit elsewhere, like the Coloureds, or who did not
want to be identified with a specific ethnic group for ideological reasons.

The party or coalition of parties receiving at least 50 percent of votes
would choose the prime minister and appoint half the cabinet, while
the remaining half would be elected by the minority parties, with at
least one minister coming from each of the groups represented in the
second chamber. If no party obtained a majority of votes, the entire
cabinet would be elected by Parliament. The proposal also provided
for the formation and official recognition of cultural councils with veto
power over decisions concerning particular groups, similar to the
"own affairs" system created by the 1983 constitution.[17]

The Indaba proposal was thus based on the principle of power-sharing that the National Party had just embraced. It was also arrived at through negotiations among representatives of a wide variety of interest groups, rather than by an elected constituent assembly, precisely the process the National Party advocated. Yet the government declared the proposal unacceptable. What appeared to be missing were ironclad guarantees that no group would dominate another—blacks would simply acquire too much power both in the executive and in the chamber elected by proportional representation. Power-sharing was still a very narrow concept for the National Party, and even the maintenance of statutory ethnic groups failed to satisfy its stringent requirements.

But the National Party's political evolution continued, facilitated in part by a change in the top leadership that took place when President P. W. Botha suffered a stroke in January 1989. The younger, more dynamic F. W. de Klerk replaced him as head of the party in February and eventually as state president after the September election. The party under de Klerk did not depart radically from old positions, but simply moved a little further down the same road to reform it had been traveling for years.

The plan of action issued in preparation for the September election reiterated the NP's commitment to power-sharing without domination and to group protection.[18] However, the document also admitted that "the present basis in terms of which groups are defined for the purpose of political participation creates many problems," and suggested that in the process of negotiations provisions be made for a group open to all South African citizens.[19] In other words, statutorily defined groups still remained at the center of government thinking, but a safety valve was offered in the form of an open group. Much of the document was devoted to reassuring white voters of the party's commitment to group rights and protection, the protection of community life for each group, and the maintenance of "civilized norms."

A further step in the National Party's thinking was the publication of a new constitutional proposal in September 1991. This important document embodied the government's initial position in the forthcoming negotiations. Once again, the proposal did not represent a break with the past, although important changes were introduced. The NP still clung to the concept of power-sharing without domination it had first adopted in 1986. However, it no longer insisted on group representation, seeking instead to safeguard the position of whites through a mixture of extreme consociationalism and devolution of power to lower-tier governments. The new system, characterized by fragmentation and an extraordinarily weak executive, was dubbed a participatory democracy.[20]

Power-sharing at the center would be ensured by a bicameral system: the first house was to be elected by proportional representation, and the second engineered under a very complex system that would enormously enhance the power of the smaller parties. First, each region would be allocated the same number of seats in this second house. Second, for each region these seats would be divided evenly among all parties receiving a minimum, still unspecified number of votes. The system obviously aimed at watering down the power of the ANC, presumably the party that would receive the most votes, and at ensuring parliamentary representation for all small parties, including those of the homelands, which would draw only an insignificant number of votes in a nationwide election. This second house would not only approve normal bills by simple majority, in concurrence with the first house, but also vote by an unspecified weighted majority on bills affecting minorities or regions.

Executive power would reside in a collective body known as the presidency, consisting of the leaders of the three largest parties in the first house, with the chairmanship rotating annually among the three and all decisions reached by consensus. Such an executive was bound to be deadlocked by lack of consensus on any major reform affecting the status quo, particularly if the National Party was one of the three represented in the presidency.

The second aspect of power-sharing was devolution of power to regional and local governments. The proposal specified that these second- and third-tier governments would not simply be administrative entities, as they had been previously. Rather, they would have "original and entrenched authority with which the other tiers of government may not interfere."[21] To ensure autonomy, each second- and third-tier government would have an elected authority responsible to the voters, legislative and executive power, and an independent tax base.

For the second-tier government, the National Party apparently had in mind a replica of what it proposed at the center, with entrenched representation for subregions and a multiparty executive. At the local level, "the term participatory democracy gains a particular meaning."[22] Details of the proposal are considered in the following chapter, but suffice it to say here that the government envisaged a system in which each town would negotiate its own charter and in which some power would be devolved to neighborhood councils.

The 1991 constitutional guidelines revealed not a change in the basic goals of the government but a definite slippage in what it thought was attainable. The National Party remained opposed to a political system that would give rights and protection to all citizens but no recognition, protection, or a special place to groups. Such a system would have quickly eliminated the special privileges enjoyed by whites and reduced the National Party to an opposition role, with very scant possibility of ever being part of the government again. Majority rule remained unacceptable. Mechanisms were needed, Constitutional Development Minister Gerrit Viljoen declared, to "prevent an un-sophisticated majority vote from plunging the country into a one-party state or dictatorship, or abolishing human rights arbitrarily."[23] The government thus clung to the concept of power-sharing.

It was, however, in full retreat concerning the groups with which power should be shared. In 1986 the answer was "among the groups defined by the Population Registration Act." In 1989 it was "among the groups defined by the Population Registration Act, plus an open group in which membership is voluntary." In 1991 the Population Registration Act had been abrogated, although clauses would remain in force until the new constitution was approved, and the National Party had given up on the idea of maintaining a political system based on predefined ethnic groups. Instead, it was trying to entrench group protection by ensuring a political role for minority parties. "In the constitutional sphere, the political party is the most effective means of furthering the interests of such [socioeconomic and cultural] groups."[24] Further protection, it hoped, would be offered by a system of government in which power was so fragmented and the require-ment for consensus so stringent that introducing major change would be almost impossible.

The Proposal of the African National Congress

The ANC's thinking concerning the future political system was simplicity itself compared with the government's. It had not evolved greatly over time, and it was spelled out quite clearly in two documents well rooted in the tradition of Western democratic countries, one on the constitution and the other on a bill of rights.

Skeptics among white commentators and politicians argued that such proposals could not be taken at face value, because the ANC remained a profoundly illiberal movement, closely allied with the South African Communist Party (SACP), relying on coercive tactics such as boycotts and "stay-aways," and maintaining an armed wing. All these points were correct. But it is in the nature of all transitions to democracy that most of the participants do not have a democratic background—if they did, there would be no need for a transition. Furthermore, the ANC had good reasons to favor a democratic system, because it was very likely to win the majority or at least a plurality of the vote. Its proposals, which had been widely debated within the organization down to the branch level and discussed and approved at the July 1991 congress, therefore had to be taken seriously as the movement's initial negotiating position.

The ANC called for a nonracial democracy in a unitary state. Rejecting a federal solution outright, it nevertheless recognized the need for decentralization and thus for strong regional governments—the objection to federalism was apparently based on fear that it would be used as a device for entrenching the homelands. It did suggest a bicameral system, in which both chambers would be elected on the basis of proportional representation, but according to different, yet unspecified, rules. It emphatically rejected the notion that one chamber would represent regions, ethnic or cultural groups, or corporate groups.[25] The Congress remained uncertain whether it would be better to have a president elected directly by the voters or a prime minister responsible to the Parliament—the matter was left for future discussion. There was no doubt, in any case, that the cabinet would be formed by the elected president or by the party controlling the majority in the Parliament; there would not be a power-sharing executive. The ANC, in other words, had rejected the winner-take-all Westminster system prevailing in South Africa in favor of proportional representation, although it was the party most likely to benefit from the Westminster system. It had thus made a major concession to the smaller parties. However, it equated democracy with majority rule, not with consociationalism, rejecting proportional representation in the executive.

Protection of minority rights was to be guaranteed not by the inclusion of minority parties in the cabinet but by a strong bill of rights protecting individuals.[26] This proposed bill of rights was extremely inclusive; whether it would be enforceable was a different matter. It included "first generation" political and civil rights—those recognized by the U.S. Bill of Rights; "second generation" economic and social rights of the United Nations declaration; and "third generation" environmental rights.[27]

The constitutional guidelines set forth by the ANC were impeccably democratic and quite straightforward. From the point of view of white South Africa, however, they had a major shortcoming: they would put the ANC in the government seat, alone or as the strongest member of a coalition. This prompted the ANC's opponents to argue that a political system based on numbers was not democratic. "The conviction that race and numbers are the only decisive factors in a heterogeneous society is a fallacy," de Klerk declared in Parliament on May 2, 1991. "There is a majority in this country that rejects typical majority domination."[28]

The Democratic Party's Compromise

The constitutional proposals set forth by the Democratic Party are worth considering here because they were carefully thought out to provide the beginning of a compromise among the other parties. Fully realizing that it would never be able to win a large number of votes in an election, the DP sought to play the role of mediator, and in so doing moved away from its old position concerning the political system most suited for South Africa.

The DP proposed a federal system, a bicameral legislature with a house elected by proportional representation and a senate composed of representatives of both regions and towns, and an executive in which all parties receiving at least 10 percent of the vote would be represented proportionally.[29]

The DP had thus largely moved away from consociationalism, which had marked the thinking of its predecessor, the Progressive Federal Party. While proportional representation maximized the chances for all parties and the groups they might represent to gain seats in Parliament, the new proposal did not envisage the creation of cultural councils with powers comparable to those of the states and a veto over matters concerning a particular group. The Democratic Party also still insisted on a broadly representative cabinet, although not one that must reach decisions by consensus. A compromise along the lines of the DP proposals would require the ANC to accept federalism, a senate representing at least in part the regions, and a cabinet possibly including some opposition parties. The National Party would have to accept the fact that the minor parties could not enjoy the same power as the most important ones—and thus could not drastically curb the ANC—and that many of the organizations on whose support it counted would probably have very little representation in the legislature and none in the cabinet.

Inkatha and Ethnic Nationalism

Inkatha's constitutional proposal, issued in December 1991, also appeared straightforward and in line with existing democratic systems. Essentially, it called for a federal system, with a lower house elected by proportional representation and an upper house representing regions and "any special interests."[30] Executive power would be shared between a president and a prime minister, as in the French system, but there would be no mandated participation by opposition parties in the cabinet. In that sense, Inkatha's position was quite different from the government's, which it otherwise resembled.

The aspect of the proposal certain to be strongly opposed by the ANC was the composition of the upper house, which included representatives of regions and, above all, of special interests. The regions were to be drawn up according to economic, territorial, and cultural and linguistic criteria. Added to the possibility that special interests would also be represented, "cultural and linguistic criteria" raised the specter of group or ethnic representation in the new system. In the context of the increasingly nationalistic statements emanating from Buthelezi, such an interpretation was not farfetched.

While the government did not dare talk openly of homelands as constituent units of the system, Buthelezi did—thereby confirming the ANC's suspicions about federalism. KwaZulu in particular would have to be recognized, argued Buthelezi: "This is something that those who attack KwaZulu as KwaZulu and call for the disbanding of KwaZulu just do not understand. They do not understand the depth of the commitment that we have to each other as Zulu brothers born out of Zulu warrior stock."[31] The same idea was expressed by the *amakhosi* (chiefs): "We deplore the tendency to associate our Zulu traditions and the remnants of our once great Zulu domains with the structures of apartheid. We see Ulundi as the capital of KwaZulu and we see it as a black spearhead against apartheid."[32]

Here lay the major difference between the position of the government and that of Inkatha. The former had a commitment to decentralization as a way of curbing the power of the ANC, but not to the existing homelands as such. In fact, they had become an embarrassment. A federal system was defensible, but racially based homelands were not, particularly when designed by whites. Buthelezi also recognized that the homelands should be disbanded, but insisted that KwaZulu was different, thus putting himself against both the National Party and the ANC. He even implicitly threatened violence if KwaZulu rights were trampled. "We say that none should be left aggrieved in South Africa, lest what happens in this country emerges as so terrible and so destructive that the civil wars [in Mozambique and Angola] are child's play by comparison."[33]

Buthelezi underscored his point in December 1991 by insisting that both the Zulu king and the government of KwaZulu send their own delegations to CODESA, arguing that Zulus had to be represented at the conference and that Inkatha did not provide such representation because it was a multiethnic political party. But Buthelezi did not demand that all self-governing homelands, even less all traditional leaders, also be represented at CODESA—Zulus must be considered a special case, he said. A compromise suggestion that all kings and paramount chiefs be invited to attend the talks as observers was rejected by Buthelezi. Instead, he chose not to attend the conference, which had insulted the king, although an Inkatha delegation did participate. The issue had not been resolved by the time CODESA collapsed in June 1992.

There was a lot of bombast in Buthelezi's position, but his statements could not be dismissed as mere posturing. The possibility existed that he would succeed in stirring enough ethnic nationalism among Zulus and, as a reaction, among other groups to create an issue that could not be disregarded in drafting the new constitution. The spread of nationalism elsewhere in the world at this time was a reminder that this could happen in South Africa as well.

THE POLITICS OF CONSTITUTION MAKING

In the initial phase of the transition process, as much attention was focused on how the constitution would be written as on what its content should be. All parties assumed that the process would determine the content. By the time a constitution-making forum was set up, the balance of forces influencing the choice of a constitution would already have been determined.

Alongside this view of the constitution-making process as a political one, characterized by maneuvering and alliance building, a second trend still existed in South Africa, namely, the idea that constitution making and indeed policymaking in a divided society could not be left simply to political forces and the will of the majority. Rather, a solution had to be carefully crafted by experts to reduce the dangers of violence and domination. This trend was not likely to prevail in the end, but it is nevertheless worth mentioning because it shows the difficulty white South Africa experienced in accepting the fact that the days of social and constitutional engineering were coming to an end.

Constitutional and social engineering was an important part of the NP tradition, and it had left a lasting imprint on the political discourse of the country, above all among whites. The trend was accentuated in the 1990s by a new complacency brought about by the collapse of socialist regimes in Eastern Europe. To whites, the collapse proved that socialism was not a viable option, and that South Africa had no choice but to follow the route of free enterprise and political democracy. The choices to be made were thus not ideological but technical ones, intended to shape a political and economic system that enhanced the interests of all participants. Innumerable studies were published and ideas floated purporting to offer solutions to the country's constitutional problems.[34] The issue was not whether these ideas were viable in theory but whether they had the backing of political organizations required to make them viable in practice.

The Process

The politics of constitution making centered on two closely linked issues: the control of the process and the formation of alliances. Initially, the government and Inkatha favored a constitution negotiated among the participants at a multiparty conference and ratified afterward in a referendum, or possibly in a series of referenda in which the vote of each statutory group would be counted separately. The ANC, together with the Pan Africanist Congress of Azania (PAC) and the Azanian People's Organization (AZAPO), demanded that the constitution be approved by a constituent assembly elected by universal suffrage under a system of proportional representation. The government and Inkatha rejected such a constituent assembly, using the same arguments they mustered against majority rule: it was a winner-take-all system, whereby the party winning the majority of votes would impose its choice on everybody. Furthermore, holding elections for a constituent assembly would be divisive and inflammatory, locking the parties into extreme positions from which they would find it difficult to retreat later. Negotiations among representatives of all parties, on the other hand, would force reconciliation and compromise. After such compromise, elections could be held safely.[35]

In reality, it was unlikely that the ANC would be able simply to impose its constitution through an elected constituent assembly. It might have a majority of seats, but constituent assemblies normally do not reach decisions by simple majority. The real problem was that elections for a constituent assembly would create a precedent for proportional representation rather than power-sharing, and the government was not willing to accept this.

The second major issue concerning process was how the country would be governed in the interim period, while the new constitution was discussed and elections held. This was an important issue particularly if the government succeeded in stretching out the transition for years, as it seemed intent on doing. The National Party's initial position was that there was no need for interim arrangements. The incumbent government was duly formed under the existing constitution and accordingly would remain in place until a new charter was enacted. The contention was accurate from a strictly legal point of view, but it was politically untenable, since the legitimacy of the system was contested by the black population. Pragmatism eventually forced de Klerk to admit that it was necessary to create mechanisms for consulting with other political parties in the interim period.[36] The question remained nevertheless whether the National Party could eventually be forced really to share power with other organizations or would succeed in maintaining control, only involving other parties sufficiently to relieve the pressure for immediate change.

The ANC pressed hard for the formation of an interim government before elections for the constituent assembly were held, arguing that if the National Party continued to govern alone, it would be in the anomalous position of being both the referee in the negotiating process and one of the participants in it. Control over the police and the army, furthermore, offered the government ample opportunities to stifle the activities of other political organizations, to encourage or stop violence selectively, and to distort the process. Preparations for the constituent assembly elections also could not be entrusted to a single-party cabinet, since the government could manipulate the outcome. Finally, the National Party could not be allowed to continue introducing reforms unilaterally, thus creating new situations the next government would have to confront.

Not all antiapartheid groups shared the ANC's enthusiasm for an immediate interim government. The PAC in particular feared that such a cabinet could easily become a trap, allowing the National Party to force other organizations to share responsibility for any unpopular policy or decision, but without giving them sufficient authority to change it. For example, political parties represented in an interim government would immediately be held responsible for the disastrous condition of black education, but would be unable to tackle the problem. The major beneficiary would be the National Party. The PAC favored instead participation only in those activities that impinged directly on the transition, while the government would continue to take the responsibility and blame for other policies. In particular, the PAC wanted joint control over the security forces and the preparation of the elections.

By late 1991 the basic positions of the parties were unchanged, but at least consensus had developed on the first step of the process, which was to be a conference attended by all parties with proven constituencies. After much bickering about names—the government wanted a "multiparty conference" and the ANC an "all-party conference," the conciliators offered an unpronounceable "MPC/APC," and the PAC contributed the equally unwieldy "pre-constituent assembly talks"—it became known as Convention for a Democratic South Africa, or CODESA.

CODESA held its first meeting on December 20 and 21, 1991. Greeted as the formal beginning of negotiations, in contrast to the previous "talks about talks," the convention was seen mostly as a ceremonial occasion, not a working session that would tackle controversial issues. It did, however, set up five working groups that would report back to a second CODESA general meeting scheduled for March 1992. The working groups were charged with discussing the creation of a climate for free political participation; general constitutional principles; transitional arrangements/interim government/transitional authority; the future of the TBVC states (the independent homelands); and the time frame for and implementation of CODESA's decisions.[37]

The meeting created a clear division between the parties that accepted the principle of negotiations and the rejectionists. The Conservative Party and the Afrikaner Weerstandsbeweging refused to attend on the Right, the PAC and AZAPO on the Left. Thus the patriotic front was dead; even more consequential, parties that by this time probably had the support of at least one-third of the white population, as the March 1992 referendum would show, were staying out of the process. Inkatha attended, but Buthelezi personally abstained in protest over the refusal of the organizers to accept separate delegations for the Zulu king and the KwaZulu government. In the end, while nineteen delegations attended the conference, significant segments of the political spectrum were not represented.[38] The problem in the future would be not simply to reach an accord among participants but to prevent nonparticipants from destroying it. Since only parties or governmental delegations had been invited to attend CODESA, the organizations of the mass democratic movement, particularly unions and civics, were outside the negotiations. Indirectly, they were represented through the ANC, but to make their presence felt directly these groups would have to concentrate on local negotiations and the creation of an economic forum.

There were no surprises in the positions taken by the major parties. De Klerk hinted that the government was ready "to begin negotiating immediately on amending the Constitution of the Republic to make an interim power-sharing model possible on a democratic basis," and that even the Parliament should be changed "to include the total population in an equitable manner"; he provided no details, however, which made it impossible to judge to what extent, if any, the government had changed its position.[39]

The conference would have been uneventful if not for an outburst of anger by Nelson Mandela that left few doubts about the gulf separating the National Party and the ANC, as well as the deterioration of the personal relationship between himself and de Klerk. The outburst was triggered by de Klerk's speech, which included an attack on the ANC for not disbanding its armed wing: "The stipulation in the Peace Accord that no political party shall have a private army places a question mark over the ANC's participation in a Convention which, essentially, is taking place among political parties," de Klerk declared.[40]

Mandela's reaction was unexpectedly vehement. De Klerk, he declared, was taking advantage of his position as the last speaker to launch an accusation to which the ANC could not reply. But reply he did. "Even the head of an illegitimate, discredited minority regime has certain standards to uphold," he declared, but de Klerk had sunk even lower.[41] He then proceeded to vent a long series of grievances against the government. More than the content of the attack—Mandela did not raise any points the ANC had not complained about before—it was his tone that surprised the witnesses. The next day, de Klerk and Mandela showed great cordiality to each other, but the damage was done. Whites had seen their president humiliated in public by the ANC leader. The negotiations would be difficult and acrimonious.

Forging Alliances

Around the positions of the two major contenders, alliances began to emerge. The alliances were not formal, nor were the positions of the various groups clear-cut, because all remained uncertain about the best strategy to follow. The greatest ambiguity came from the National Party, which appeared to waver between two or even three positions, or perhaps to be following all simultaneously in order to keep its options open. The basic dilemma for the government was whether it should attempt to forge a broad-based anti-ANC coalition or whether it should seek an alliance with the moderates in the Congress, trying to separate them from the more radical elements and particularly from the SACP. As a variant of the first approach, the National Party was also trying to broaden its own power base, making the party multiracial. This attempt, however, undermined the very parties that could lend the government support.

Until the Inkathagate scandal broke, the government had been trying to create the impression that the NP could put together a coalition of parties capable of winning the majority of votes, relegating the ANC to the ranks of the opposition. The coalition the government had in mind included Inkatha and other homeland parties, the Coloured and Indian parties in the tricameral Parliament, and minor moderate parties, which the government surreptitiously funded, such as the Federal Independent Democratic Alliance.[42] The constituencies the NP hoped to reach through these organizations were the Indians and Coloureds afraid of black domination, the Zulus opposed to the supposedly Xhosa-dominated ANC, and the moderate, church-going Africans the National Party hoped would oppose the ANC because it was communist dominated. Undoubtedly, if the National Party had been able to forge a coalition comprising all whites, Coloureds and Indians, Zulus, and church-going Africans of all ethnic groups, it would have won an election handily. The problem was that not all Zulus supported Inkatha, many church-going Africans did not consider it problematic to side with the ANC, and Coloureds and Indians worried about the future did not necessarily look to the National Party for their deliverance. Whites themselves were defecting to the Conservative Party. The potential strength of the envisaged coalition remained unknown.

At any rate, this coalition strategy ran into difficulties because of the complicated relations that developed with Inkatha and to a lesser extent the Labour Party. The National Party was a natural ally for Inkatha, which had failed in its bid to be recognized by the ANC as a central component of the antiapartheid movement. For a while Buthelezi's views on the negotiations and the future political system appeared identical to the government's, although he expressed them with much greater stridency. Inkathagate abruptly ended this concordance by embarrassing both the government and Inkatha and causing them to distance themselves from each other. With a leader other than Buthelezi, the basic relationship might have been preserved despite the crisis, particularly since the government did not take drastic steps such as imposing a ban on traditional weapons. But Buthelezi felt betrayed and resorted to an independent position, falling back increasingly on Zulu nationalism and thus further decreasing the possibility of establishing close links with any other organization. In turn, this made it more difficult for the government to assemble a strong moderate alliance.

Relations between the Labour Party (LP) and the National Party also deteriorated. The break was determined by two factors, the Labour Party's criticism of government policy and the NP's attempt to transform itself into a multiracial party. During the debate on the bill that repealed the Group Areas Act, the Labour Party objected to a proposed clause allowing communities to set "standards," arguing that it would leave the door open to apartheid under a different guise. The response was swift. The National Party convinced almost half the Labour MPs to change their allegiance, becoming the second largest party and thus the official opposition in the House of Representatives during the 1991 parliamentary session. When Parliament reopened in January 1992, additional LP members crossed over to the National Party, giving it control over the House of Representatives.[43] What was left of the Labour Party had already joined the patriotic front and was leaning toward the ANC. This episode served to underline a basic problem in the National Party's strategy. It could not simultaneously form an alliance with moderate black parties and try to become a multiracial organization itself, because it would compete with potential allies for the same constituency. The fate of the Labour Party was a warning to others.

The ANC also appeared to pursue various options simultaneously. One was building an alliance with other liberation organizations, which culminated in the attempt to form a united patriotic front of over ninety organizations at a conference in Durban on October 25–27, 1991. But the patriotic front began to disintegrate even before it was formed. AZAPO, a convener of the conference together with the ANC and the PAC, angered the other two organizations by sending on its own initiative a letter to all participants, suggesting that those organizations involved in apartheid institutions, such as homeland political movements and parties in the tricameral Parliament, should resign their official positions before attending the launch of the patriotic front. No such decision—which would have prevented the front from ever being launched—had been taken by the organizers. The ANC and the PAC immediately dissociated themselves from the letter, announcing that AZAPO would no longer be considered a convener of the meeting, although it was free to attend it. Not surprisingly, AZAPO stayed away.

Nevertheless, the front was launched, and it appeared initially to be at least a partial success, pulling the hesitant PAC into the negotiations. But soon the PAC reversed its position, as it had done in the past, and it decided not to join CODESA. Most other patriotic front members did not attend either, because they were not political parties. The patriotic front was thus not represented at the talks.

Another strategy the ANC was pursuing was to court some of the moderate organizations and leaders to keep them from becoming government allies. Mandela in particular favored the idea of trying to win homeland leaders over to the ANC's side, but he often ran into opposition from the organization's rank and file. Shortly after his release, for example, he was forced by the ANC followers in Natal to abandon plans to meet with Buthelezi. At the 1991 congress, he was again criticized for holding talks with homeland authorities without consulting the local branches of the Congress.[44]

The uncertainty displayed by both the government and the ANC in their alliance policies was in part due to the fact that none of their strategies were particularly successful, although none were a complete failure either. The government's hopes of causing a break between moderates and radicals in the ANC were dashed repeatedly.[45] The ANC congress in July 1991 and the SACP congress in December of the same year saw both organizations proclaiming their undying alliance. Yet Mandela and others were beginning to realize that the relationship with the SACP would be a burden to the Congress in the long run, and they began to take some steps to minimize the problem. The reinstatement of Allan Boesak was part of this trend.

The ANC's attempts to attract the homeland leaders and the government's efforts to create a moderate alliance faltered because smaller groups were cautious, and did not want to antagonize either side until they knew which would prevail.[46] By and large, the government was offering more to the minor parties, because its constitutional proposals aimed at maximizing the power of all minority organizations to the detriment of the ANC. However, the National Party's efforts to broaden its constituency also put it in direct competition with the moderate black parties.

CONCLUSIONS

The convening of CODESA in December 1991 marked the beginning of the most important phase of the negotiating process. The preliminaries—the release of most political prisoners, the repeal of major apartheid laws, and the ANC's suspension of the armed struggle— were out of the way. The initial demands of the two main organizations were on the table. But the two sides were far apart, and there was still no consensus even on the process that should be followed in an attempt to resolve the differences.

The principal parties came to the negotiations with different strengths and weaknesses. The government controlled the institutions, particularly the security forces, and its financial power was infinitely superior to that of its opponents. It could draw on a large reservoir of experience and technical resources the other side did not possess. Nevertheless, it was the government, not the ANC, that would emerge from the negotiations with less power than it had at the beginning.

The ANC could not manipulate organizations and create facts on the ground as the government did, it had no control over the security forces, and its negotiators were learning on the job rather than entering the process with a long political experience. But no matter what happened, it would emerge at the end stronger than it had been at the beginning. Unlike the government, it was negotiating itself into power, not out of it.

Although the ANC and the National Party were still far apart in their demands, and a compromise would be difficult, they nevertheless represented by default the center of the political spectrum. There was no viable force between them. The Democratic Party was trying to reestablish itself as the ideological center, and its demands were clearly drawn up to offer a possible compromise solution, but politically the DP was not important enough to become the nucleus around which a moderate coalition could gather. It simply did not have anything to offer to attract other groups. Inkatha, which had in the past been viewed as a possible center, particularly abroad, had sidelined itself through its increasingly strident Zulu nationalism.

While the center was weak, the more radical organizations both on the Right and on the Left were strong and likely to get stronger as the major actors started making concessions to reach an agreement. The National Party was losing support, which drove de Klerk to fall back on the rhetoric of Afrikaner nationalism rather than to move forward with a vision of a better future for all in the new South Africa. The ANC ran the risk of strengthening the Africanist organizations, and possibly even losing some of the support of COSATU and the SACP, if its leaders were seen as too anxious to put their hands on the levers of power and too ready to make major concessions in order to do so.

The militancy of Right and Left led the two main protagonists to make hard-line statements and to put on a belligerent front. But they were also drawn together and forward by the conviction that there was no other solution except to negotiate. "We are on one boat, one ship, and the sharks to the left and the sharks to the right are not going to distinguish between us when we fall overboard," stated Pik Botha during the first, heady meeting at Groote Schuur in May 1990.[47] As CODESA opened, the ANC and the National Party, for all their differences, were still allies against the fundamentalists on both the Left and the Right.

Chapter 6

The Local Arena

While the end of apartheid was being discussed at the center, the system of local governance it had spawned had already collapsed. The problem was not how to negotiate its disappearance but how to put something else in place quickly. The crisis in the townships had reached dramatic proportions. The population was swelling rapidly because of the repeal of influx control legislation and the lack of economic opportunities in the homelands to which blacks had been relegated. But virtually no new houses were being built in the townships, and huge squatter camps were growing. Shacks of corrugated iron, plastic, and cardboard; piles of garbage in the streets; and inadequate water taps were eloquent signs of the growing emergency. There was no money under the apartheid system of financing to keep even existing services functioning, let alone to expand them to meet ever-increasing needs. Encouraged by the civics, residents were refusing to pay rent and electricity bills, reducing the already meager finances of the black councils and destroying any possibility that services might be improved. Attempts by the authorities to force local inhabitants to pay their bills by cutting off electricity and sometimes even water were not working—it was not possible to deprive entire townships of basic services for extended periods. There was a real emergency and no mechanisms to cope with it.

Even so, the population was organized. This was one of the most striking characteristics of South Africa in this period. No matter how small the township or remote the area, there were always structures of the mass democratic movement. During the 1980s these organizations had used local issues as part of the struggle against apartheid and the central government. When the African National Congress (ANC) was unbanned and resumed its historical role of leading the antiapartheid struggle at the center, the civic associations started devoting more attention to local issues as an end in themselves rather than as a means to a national struggle. In the 1980s they were trying to make the townships ungovernable, but in the early 1990s they were beginning to focus on how the postapartheid city should be governed in the future.

LOCAL GOVERNMENT IN SOUTH AFRICA

The South African system of local government was rooted in the same principles as the tricameral Parliament, and as a result it was extremely convoluted and idiosyncratic. The apartheid city had not one local government but many. Each population group was in theory responsible for local "own affairs." Whites had their municipal councils, Indians and Coloureds their management committees, and after 1982 Africans had their black local authorities, with elected councils. The white, Indian, and Coloured local units were supervised by the own affairs cabinets of the respective house in the tricameral Parliament. Black local authorities were ultimately controlled by the provincial administrations. This setup, declared the government, embodied "the overall policy of maximum devolution of administrative functions to the lowest level of government—municipal institutions—so that all communities, including Blacks, may themselves regulate and manage those matters which determine the immediate quality of their lives."[1]

But the black population saw the elected councils as a sham. Voter turnout in the 1988 election was officially put at 25.1 percent of the registered voters, themselves estimated at 78 percent of those eligible to vote. In Soweto, only 11.3 percent of registered voters participated.[2]

In addition to having little legitimacy, the system was basically unworkable, because the black councils had no financial resources. The white municipalities derived their revenue from the rates paid by the valuable business and industrial properties and by white homeowners. They derived additional revenue from the sale of electricity to white homeowners and to the black townships.[3] The black councils' major source of income was the rents and service charges imposed on the small houses built by the government for blacks. While these charges weighed heavily on the family budget, they did not provide much revenue for the townships. Furthermore, during the 1980s and particularly after the repeal of influx control in 1986, the townships found themselves saddled with a huge population of squatters that contributed to the councils' expenditures but not to their revenue. By the end of the decade, more people lived in backyard shacks and squatter camps than in formal housing.[4] Attempts by the councils to increase revenue by increasing rents and service fees backfired, since the civics responded by organizing boycotts. In April 1991 the arrears owed to black councils by residents withholding rent and service payments amounted to about R 1 billion in the Transvaal alone, and the Transvaal Provincial Administration was forced to allocate a grant of R 410 million to the black councils. A year later, despite much-publicized agreements reached in some townships, nationwide arrears had mounted to more than R 1.5 billion.[5] In other words, the system was bankrupt.

It was also politically unsustainable. The United Democratic Front's (UDF's) campaign against the black councillors had been effective. Violence against them and their properties, political pressure, and the realization that the councils in any case were powerless led growing numbers of councillors to resign. By April 1991, 48 percent of the black local authorities had crumbled and been replaced by white administrators appointed by the provincial authorities. Even in the remaining councils, many seats were vacant, and pressure on remaining councillors remained high.[6]

Finally, the fragmentation of local authorities made it difficult to tackle problems that were metropolitan in scope. Transport, communications, water and sewerage, electricity, all required areawide networks, not localized solutions respectful of different cultural traditions and community values. In 1985 this led to the creation of a new institution, the Regional Services Councils (RSCs), which were composed of representatives of the various local governments in an area, but were responsible to the provincial administrators appointed by the central government. Officially the "general affairs" branch of local government, the RSCs were essentially an admission that the existing fragmented system could not work.

The picture presented by local government thus was most confusing. It was marked by a proliferation of units, but it was not really decentralized. Both the black councils and the Regional Services Councils were responsible to the appointed provincial administrators, making a mockery of the idea of self-government. One study concluded that "local government restructuring has led to even greater centralization of powers by the government, and . . . the amount of space that is left for existing or new local authorities is negligible."[7] The system was also deeply marked by the principle of racial representation. Even the Regional Services Councils, which were multiracial in their composition, were ultimately based on racial representation, since they comprised representatives of the racially based local councils.

THE NATIONAL PARTY AND LOCAL GOVERNMENT IN THE 1990S

The already difficult position of local governments was made even more untenable by the changes of the early 1990s. The repeal of much apartheid legislation destroyed whatever semblance of rationality the system had.[8] In addition, for political reasons the government started stressing decentralization, shifting responsibility—and blame for the growing discontent—to local governments. Initially the reforms affected the white councils even more than the black ones.

The repeal in 1990 of the Reservation of Separate Amenities Act of 1953 left municipalities to take the blame for the continuation of petty apartheid, although in reality the central government was equally responsible. While the Separate Amenities Act was in effect, local governments had been given no choice but to segregate such public facilities as parks, swimming pools, and libraries. When the government abrogated the act, it took credit for having ended segregation. However, it had simply rescinded the obligation to keep facilities segregated, not mandated that they be open to all. Legal experts pointed this out, and the government implicitly admitted it when the minister for budget and local government, Amie Venter, announced that he would "ask the provincial administrators and the United Municipalities of South Africa to consider the principle of introducing legislation which would positively outlaw discrimination in municipal amenities."[9] But when blacks discovered that facilities in most small towns remained segregated, the local authorities were seen as responsible. This suited the National Party (NP) well, because most councils continuing to enforce segregation were controlled by the Conservative Party.

The repeal of the Group Areas Act also created absurd situations that local governments were not empowered to correct. It opened all parts of all cities and towns to members of all race groups, but it did not reform the system of government based on race. The result was that blacks moving into a previously white area still could not vote for the councils of the towns in which they were now legal residents, and their children could not automatically attend the local public schools, which were still classified as white.[10]

To some extent, these problems were an inevitable consequence of rapid change, with reforms reaching different parts of the system at different times. But in part they resulted from a deliberate decision to encourage an extremely decentralized system of local government, leaving each town, even each neighborhood, to work out its own solutions. Such extreme decentralization, the government apparently hoped, would provide scope for white communities to maintain their special character without recourse to openly discriminatory legislation. Neighborhood control was a much more respectable concept than enforced segregation, even though the effect might not be very different.

The National Party's proposals for local government reform emphasized devolution of power to the local level on the one hand, while limiting options on the other. The government was willing to let each town choose among various models, but it reserved the right of final approval.[11]

The NP's basic ideas were contained in a report of the Council for the Coordination of Local Government Affairs, made public in October 1990. The Thornhill Report (named after the council's chairman) was four years in the making. As with the constitutional models, there was no sudden change in the NP's thinking about local governance but only a slow process of change.[12]

The Thornhill Report proposed four alternative models of local government from which each town might choose. Two were based on de facto retention of the separate racially based authorities already in existence. The council defended these models with the argument that after the repeal of the Group Areas Act and the Population Registration Act existing authorities would no longer be racially based. This was sophistry—in the foreseeable future a Soweto council would continue to represent a black area, and the Johannesburg council a predominantly white one. In one model, the separate authorities could choose to govern their jurisdiction on their own—a solution that appeared to give white local authorities the prerogative to refuse merger with the black townships. In the other, they could join to form local services councils, modeled along the lines of the Regional Services Councils. Existing authorities would be represented on these service councils, with a number of votes proportional to their financial contribution. Under this arrangement, too, the wealthier white governments would remain disproportionately powerful.

The other two models envisaged the abolition of the existing racially based authorities. In one alternative, the election of a joint local council would be complemented by the formation of neighborhood committees to defend the interests of specific communities and "protect standards," a euphemism for the formulation of zoning and other regulations that would shelter predominantly white suburbs from the encroachment of low-cost—hence black—housing. The last option, referred to as the simple majority model, was to divide a city into wards, each of which would elect a representative to the council. However, the Thornhill Report specified that the size of the ward might be defined either by the number of residents or by financial criteria. The latter would give white voters disproportionate representation.

The theme underlying all the models, including the so-called simple majority one, was that there would not be forced massive redistribution of resources from wealthy white to poor black suburbs within each metropolitan area. One model the Thornhill Report did not envisage was the one demanded by the ANC and the civic associations: "one city, one tax base," with no further subdivisions and complications.

The principle of neighborhood control contained in the Thornhill Report reappeared in the Abolition of Racially Based Land Measures Act of June 1991. The bill repealed the Group Areas Act, but it also introduced controversial clauses giving homeowners in each neighborhood the power to establish "norms and standards"[13]—a barely disguised attempt to maintain racial segregation, in the view of many organizations.

The National Party's constitutional proposals issued in September 1991 carried the ideas concerning decentralization and local autonomy one step further. Clearly, the party had decided that local control, particularly if extended to the neighborhood level, would offer whites the best possible protection after the repeal of the Group Areas Act. But despite the emphasis on decentralization, the central government still had the final word concerning what kind of local solutions were permissible.

The NP document "Constitutional Rule in a Participatory Democracy" argued that third-tier, or local, governments were not "administrative extensions" of the central one, but should instead be responsible to the voters, enjoy legislative and executive power, and have the right to impose taxes.[14] The central government did not have the power to decide how localities should govern themselves. Rather, in each town or city negotiations should be held among all concerned groups to draft a local government charter.

Despite the new rhetoric about participatory democracy and decentralization, however, it was clear that the central government was not willing to allow localities to enact a charter on their own. The new constitution would lay down and entrench the principle of local government autonomy, but a national Local Government Act, agreed upon in the constitutional negotiations, would spell out "the broad principles and structural framework of local government." Any locally negotiated agreement would have to conform to the requirements of the act in order to win official recognition and to become "the 'local constitution' of the local authority concerned."[15]

The Local Government Act would thus be a crucial document. The National Party's constitutional guidelines were vague about what provisions would be incorporated in it, but the few indications given suggested that the government intended to prevent the establishment of municipal charters based on simple or unqualified majority rule.[16] The principle of universal suffrage would be considerably modified at the local level by the special rights of homeowners, and of minorities in general, in regard to unspecified "circumscribed sensitive matters."[17] Furthermore, in the election of city councils, property valuations and voter numbers might be accepted "in a fair proportion to one another as the basis for the delimitation of wards."[18] In other words, wealthy white homeowners would enjoy more representation than other voters. Another system envisaged by the National Party would have half the members of the city councils elected at universal suffrage, with the rest elected by homeowners, lessees, and ratepayers only, excluding an estimated seven million blacks (half the black urban population) living in backyard shacks and squatter camps.[19]

Despite its emphasis on decentralization, the government was not ready to give up control over the structure of local government. But it had introduced the idea that local groups should try to negotiate a solution suited to the needs of each locality. This idea was also upheld by organizations of the mass democratic movement. Although the ultimate goals of the National Party and the liberation establishment remained quite different, they at least converged concerning the desirability of local negotiations.

THE ANC AND THE CIVICS: STATE POWER AND PEOPLE'S POWER

The liberation establishment was somewhat divided in its concept of local government. The ANC's vision was once again very simple. It favored a single local government for each town or city, elected at universal suffrage on the basis of one person, one vote, with no additional qualifications. The slogan "one city, one tax base" summed up well the organization's main concern: ending the statutory division that put all the money in the white towns, leaving the townships without resources. Instead, each area should come under the jurisdiction of a single council, elected by all residents on a single roll.

The mass democratic movement certainly shared this concern of the ANC, and upheld the same view of local government. But it complicated matters by superimposing on this idea of representative democracy a concept of participatory democracy rooted both in the history of the civic associations as independent organizations and in the long-standing debates and concerns of the socialist camp.

The different political styles and traditions of the exiled ANC and of the mass democratic movement have been discussed in chapter 3. To some extent, the gap between the two had narrowed at the July 1991 ANC conference, when members of the mass democratic movement joined the exiled leaders in the new National Executive Committee. But this integration of the top ranks did not settle the entire issue. Fear of ANC domination remained strong among civic organizations; they often felt the Congress tried to take credit for the achievements of local groups that had fought and won their battles alone. Even within the ANC proper, one current emphasized the importance of the autonomy of the civic associations as a guarantee of democracy in the future South Africa.

Despite the ANC's commitment to democracy, many of its followers tended to see it not as one of many political parties but as a government-in-waiting. As the dominant liberation movement, the ANC would become the government. The danger would thus arise that the ANC might seek to impose a centralized and bureaucratic form of state control, depriving all other organizations of their autonomy, as other African liberation movements had done after attaining power. Other political parties were not seen as sufficient counterbalance to the domination of the ANC. It was only the organizations of civil society that could prevent this undemocratic outcome. People's power alone could curb state power.

Although this concept of a democracy based on the direct involvement of the organizations of civil society arose from the struggles of the 1970s and 1980s, it was not unique. Indeed, the theoretical formulation prevalent in South Africa was usually traced to the writing of Antonio Gramsci, whose vision of the tyrannical state was based on his own experience with the one-party fascist regime of Italy and the problem of how to maintain democracy under a vanguard party in a socialist state. But similar ideas had also surfaced, with different degrees of clarity, in most African countries experimenting with socialism.

In Algeria, the creation of worker-controlled management committees to counterbalance the power of appointed state managers was based on a similar assessment that state power is always authoritarian. In Ethiopia, early reforms set up organs of people's power in the form of peasant associations and urban neighborhood councils. In Angola, the idea of direct popular participation was embodied in the people's power committees, which secured the cities for the MPLA (Popular Movement for the Liberation of Angola) at the time of independence. In Mozambique, considerable tension developed between the power of the party, increasingly centralized and bureaucratic, and the tradition of mass participation that stemmed from the war of independence.

In all these examples, state power quickly triumphed over people's power. Self-management was dismantled, peasant and neighborhood associations were brought under central control, people's power committees were eliminated, and state administration and party cells were de facto merged in the Mozambican villages in a single bureaucratic structure. Civil society historically lost out to the state in Africa.

But the concept was still alive in South Africa. What people's power meant in practice and how the civics and other organizations of civil society should curb the state remained unclear. The mass democratic movement did not reject representative democracy at the local level, so it accepted elections for local councils contested by different political parties. However, it also demanded a continuing yet undefined role for civil society that went beyond participating in elections and even lobbying for policies.

For the ANC as a formal organization, the ideas concerning people's power and local government coming from the mass democratic movement posed a delicate problem. It could not reject them, but accepting them in their entirety was also difficult. No organization claiming to be even moderately democratic can reject the right of citizens to organize at the grass roots. Furthermore, the support of the mass democratic movement was crucial; without it, the ANC had no effective means to bring pressure on the government—the civics and the trade unions could mobilize people for mass action much more easily than the new ANC branches. But the ANC, its constitutional proposals made clear, also conceived of local governments as lower-tier structures whose powers were delegated from the center, not as entities with an inalienable right to their autonomy. Ultimate power resided with the national government, inevitably restricting the role of local grass-roots organizations.

To the ANC's adversaries, these subtleties in the relationship of the civics and the Congress were not particularly important. Rather, they saw the civics as simply part and parcel of the ANC, and they refused to join. The Pan Africanist Congress of Azania (PAC), Azanian People's Organization (AZAPO), and Inkatha all shunned the civics, in turn making them even more clearly aligned with the ANC. The reality of the situation belied the claim that the civics were not aligned to any political party but were resident associations open to all. Yet, ultimately, the ANC did not control the civics and could not force them to accept its own policies.

The confusing problems arising from the nature of the civics, their relationship with the ANC, and their future role in South Africa were reflected in many situations. For example, the civics as organizations of civil society were supposed to maintain their independence from local government, but some civics were getting ready to become local governments. In Cape Town, a course was organized for members of civic associations and the South African Municipal Workers' Union to learn more about local government. The reason for the course, according to one of the participants, was that "the civic associations have done away with 80 percent of all puppet structures in the country. Now we have to fill the vacuum we created."[20]

Other civic associations considered the possibility of forming a new political party, thus giving up their role as organizations operating in the sphere of civil society. Speculation to that effect arose when representatives of the civics, the UDF, and the Congress of South African Trade Unions met in May 1991 to discuss launching a national civics organization. Despite assertions by participants that the purpose of the new organization was simply to provide better coordination among civics after the disbanding of the UDF, rumors that it was being created to challenge the ANC were rife and died down only when the initiative faltered.[21] An official launch scheduled for August 1991 never took place. A South African National Civic Association was finally formed in March 1992, but it remained a low-profile organization that apparently had difficulty defining its role.

On some occasions, the distinction between the ANC and the civics was lost altogether. An example of this was provided in some Eastern Transvaal towns where the civics had called for rent and service boycotts in protest over perceived abuses by the local government and business community. Eventually the problem was settled in negotiations between the ANC and the local white authorities, and a final agreement to call off the boycott was signed by the ANC on behalf of a number of civics.[22]

By and large, however, the civic associations continued to operate independently, which created a different kind of problem. Like the government, the ANC did not care for the idea that local agreements could be reached before national negotiations were completed. Only a transfer of state power could provide the framework for building real people's power. Until that time, continuation of the struggle at the local level was crucial, but attempts to reach local solutions were highly dangerous, since they could undermine an overall solution. "Negotiations at the local level have implications for those at the national level. Any issue which requires redefinition of the constitutional arrangements has to be referred to negotiations at the national level," concluded the ANC's local government department.[23]

ANC and government representatives thus tried to establish a framework that would make local negotiations possible but also keep them in line with the national process. While they disagreed, at times strongly, about the details of how this should be done, they concurred on the necessity for some control from the center.[24]

NEGOTIATING THE POSTAPARTHEID CITY

As the government and the ANC tried to devise acceptable blueprints for local government, and intellectuals discussed the dynamics of state power and people's power, negotiations were already taking place in all major cities and some towns, although in a tentative, piecemeal fashion. These local initiatives stemmed more from sheer necessity than from theory, because the system of local government had already broken down and the consequences were felt all around—by township residents left without even basic services, by bankrupt black councils, by white municipalities unpaid for the bulk supplies they sold the townships, and by provincial administrations paying ever-increasing amounts in bridging finance to keep the system afloat. These problems could not wait until a new constitution was negotiated and new local administrations formed. But a solution required more than new local institutions. A major transfer of resources from the relatively wealthy white areas to the townships was also needed. The unspoken question underlying all negotiations was how significant this transfer would be.

Even though local negotiations aimed at establishing an interim solution rather than a new permanent system, they nevertheless revealed some of the tensions and problems surrounding local government issues. In particular, they showed that the civic associations were determined to have a major say in the future of local government; that local agreements were extremely fragile because none of the parties involved had the power to ensure compliance with the decisions; and that the National Party saw the future metropolitan government more as a federation of existing councils than as a new, nonracial, unitary structure.

Most of the local agreements negotiated in this period did not attempt to set up a new local government system, but simply tried to restore some flow of revenue to the black councils and to prevent white municipalities from cutting off water and electricity to the townships. Usually the civics agreed that township residents should stop the boycott and make a reduced monthly payment for services, while the provincial administration or white municipality agreed to cancel arrears—which were beyond the black councils' capacity to repay, in any case—and to continue providing services. Most of these agreements were ineffectual, because large numbers of residents did not resume payments, and neither the civic associations nor the black councils could do anything about it.

In major metropolitan areas, negotiations were much more ambitious. While the most immediate problem remained the financing and supplying of services to black residents, all participants were also consciously trying to shape the future local governance model. The most far-reaching of these attempts took place in the area around Johannesburg, leading to the creation of the Central Witwatersrand Metropolitan Chamber and to an ambitious plan to negotiate a new integrated local government structure ahead of a national settlement.

The process began with the signing of the Greater Soweto Accord in September 1990. One of the first attempts to tackle the crisis of the townships, the accord was heralded as a breakthrough, creating a model fit for replication. It was signed by the Soweto, Dobsonville, and Diepmeadow city councils (the three townships constitute Greater Soweto); the Soweto Civic Association; and the Transvaal Provincial Administration (TPA).[25] Under the agreement, the residents would terminate the boycott and would pay initially only a low, uniform flat rate for all services. Eventually they would have to pay for electricity according to metered consumption, but rates would be kept at subeconomic levels for low-consumption households. All arrears would be canceled.[26]

The agreement did not work. A major problem was that none of the signatories had the authority to convince the residents that they should pay their bills, or the power to force them to do so. The civic associations could only advise residents to pay. The councils and the TPA did not have the administrative capacity to keep track of who was paying and to discontinue services selectively to those who failed to comply. One year after the agreement was signed, gloom prevailed. "Soweto," wrote one reporter, was "sliding into dark."[27]

The signatories accused each other. The Transvaal Provincial Administration blamed the residents for failing to pay, but also pointed out that the accord did not provide a lasting solution in any case, because the agreed rate would cover only 20 percent of the cost of service delivery even if all residents paid. The Soweto Civic Association argued that the black councils and the TPA were responsible for the failure, since people could not be expected to pay as long as services remained dismal; nothing but a complete reorganization of the system, involving the dissolution of the black councils, would solve the problem.[28]

The failure of the Greater Soweto Accord provided the incentive for the organizations involved to go beyond the limited initial approach and attempt to negotiate a more comprehensive solution to the governance of the metropolitan area. The Central Witwatersrand Metropolitan Chamber was set up for this purpose in April 1991. The chamber was a body without an official position or real power—it was simply a forum for negotiating a new local government system for the area. It had its own formal constitution, signed by all participants, and a complex structure of committees and working groups, but it had no power to enforce any agreement it reached. The power to enforce decisions remained in the hands of the existing units of government. With the passage of the Interim Local Government Act, mechanisms were set up for giving an agreement official recognition, but the final decision resided at the center, not with the participants in the negotiations. The chamber thus remained a weak body. It was also a conflict-ridden one, bringing together a number of diverse and antagonistic groups, some of which had serious doubts about the wisdom of belonging to the chamber at all.

The metropolitan chamber included representatives of the Transvaal Provincial Administration as well as the Regional Services Council, the white municipalities, the black councils, and the civic associations for the Johannesburg metropolitan area. Political parties were not represented, although most had a presence in the chamber through the signatories of the agreement. The participation of the Transvaal Provincial Administration gave the National Party an indirect presence. The white liberal establishment was represented through some Democratic Party councillors, and most prominently through the chamber's chairman, former leader of the Progressive Federal Party Frederik van Zyl Slabbert. The ANC had a strong presence through the civics. But the PAC and AZAPO were not involved at all, and Inkatha—though theoretically present through the black councillors, most of whom had joined it by this time—was not playing a role either. Buthelezi admitted the weakness of Inkatha at the local level, declaring that it was unfortunate that the "Inkatha Freedom Party had been sidelined on many local government issues because of party-political games."[29]

The position of the civic associations toward the metropolitan chamber was ambiguous. Many were participating, but some refused to join. The Civic Association of the Southern Transvaal (CAST) had initially opposed the metropolitan chamber, although many of its members had joined. It justified its opposition on the ground that the chamber was based on racial representation—racially segregated local government bodies had joined—and that it included the illegitimate black councillors. Also, the formation of such a body was a process at odds with the concept that the solutions for a new South Africa would have to be devised by an elected constituent assembly.[30] CAST's alternative proposal was the election of local constituent assemblies, which would in turn elect representatives to the metropolitan chamber.[31] Eventually, however, CAST accepted the chamber as constituted.

Despite all these problems and the hostility that permeated the relations among its members, the metropolitan chamber continued to meet, driven by the urgency of the urban crisis and by the knowledge of the participants that if they did not work out their own solution, a new system would eventually be imposed from the center.

By early 1992 the chamber had made very little concrete progress. A new Greater Soweto Accord was reached, coupling rate increases with improvement in services and committing the TPA to help finance services on a regular basis. The new measures remained difficult to enforce, however. The real significance of the chamber was not that it devised a new, viable system of metropolitan government—it didn't— but that it made it de facto impossible for existing local structures to make decisions without consultation. Various chamber committees working on specific issues, and often able to draw on considerable technical expertise, subjected the decisions of the official bodies to close scrutiny. For example, a plan by the Transvaal Provincial Administration to develop a large new township in Rietfontein, about forty kilometers south of Johannesburg, was challenged by the civics as an attempt to perpetuate the structure of the apartheid city. The location of the new township was dictated by the apartheid criterion of keeping blacks as far away as possible from white residential areas, even if this meant dumping them a long distance from business and industrial centers, which increased the difficulty of finding jobs and imposed on those who did the added cost of long-distance commuting. In the midst of negotiations for a new metropolitan government, the provincial administration still clung to the old concept. In the absence of the metropolitan chamber, it would have been able to implement the plan without public scrutiny.[32]

A very complex agreement on "Interim Constitutional Arrangements" was also reached by the members of the chamber on December 4, 1991. The details were confusing, and there was no firm agreement yet on all the steps outlined in the document. It was possible that the plethora of local and joint negotiating forums to be set up would make the area even more ungovernable than it already was. The entire negotiating process remained extremely tentative, and indeed the chamber itself stopped meeting for a period in early 1992, caught in a bog of disagreement and recrimination. Members of the organization knew that the units of government they represented had to come together in a broader structure, but they could not agree on what was needed.

The decision reached by the metropolitan chamber to set up a series of negotiating forums was in agreement with the policy of the central government. An "Interim Measures for Local Government Act," approved in July 1991, made it legal for local units to set up such forums.[33] The bill also created mechanisms to give official recognition and thus binding value to locally agreed solutions. But the government wanted the provincial administrators to maintain strict control over the process. They would decide whether agreements were acceptable, and even whether civic associations could take part in the negotiations. The power given to the appointed provincial administrators had led the ANC to condemn the Interim Measures for Local Government Act as "fundamentally flawed because it contains no acceptable guiding principles on which new local government structures can be based," and "it may enable democratic structures to be established in one town, [while] racial structures can remain in another."[34]

An example of the local government structures favored by the National Party was offered by a preliminary agreement reached in Kimberley in June 1992. Acclaimed as a breakthrough in creating a nonracial local government based on power-sharing, the agreement provided for the election of a council composed of twelve whites, seven Africans, four Coloureds, and one Indian. The population of Kimberley comprised more than one hundred thousand Africans, fifty-two thousand Coloureds and Indians, and thirty-six thousand whites. Inevitably, the ANC reacted strongly against the proposal, because it entrenched racial representation and disproportionate power for whites.[35]

CONCLUSIONS

The reform of local government was an important part of the transition process in South Africa, much more so than in political transitions elsewhere. In most countries, a change of political regime does not require a restructuring of the entire system of local government, but needs only a change in personnel at the highest levels. This was not true in South Africa, where towns and cities had deliberately been structured to attain the goal of separate development.

That the system would have to reform was a foregone conclusion. That race could no longer figure openly as the major organizing principle was also accepted by all parties. But the government had not given up the hope yet that decentralization would make it possible to keep life in the white suburbs largely unchanged. The more power was devolved to the neighborhood level, the less life in white suburbs would be affected.

A very decentralized system created from the top down could conceivably attain such results, particularly since economic factors would also curb the scope of change in the white suburbs. But the decentralized process of local negotiations that was beginning in 1991 made it more difficult to achieve such results consistently. As the experience of the Central Witwatersrand Metropolitan Chamber indicated, local negotiations enhanced the importance of the civic associations, while the black councils were made to look like little more than an extension of the provincial administration that funded them. Civic associations, which focused exclusively on local issues, were not likely to back away from their demand for "one city, one tax base," that is, for a system spreading government resources equitably across metropolitan areas. Existing black and white councils could agree among themselves, but they were unlikely to implement any plan successfully if the civics opposed it. Indeed, the civics' and ANC's opposition to the Kimberley agreement threatened its implementation from the outset.

Both the ANC and the government wanted decentralized local government, but they were also leery of what unchecked local negotiations might produce. This gave the local arena an extraordinary degree of complexity. The byzantine system of local government ensured that a plethora of institutions would be involved. The political strength of the civics made it impossible to leave them out, although they alone among the participants had no institutional role. At the same time, the government and the ANC, as the two major partners at the national level, were bargaining with each other about how to coordinate and supervise local initiatives.

Conspicuously absent from the process were other political parties; even the ANC had a role more as a government-in-waiting, with the right and duty to supervise lower-tier authorities, than as a political party representing its members and supporters. This risked creating a backlash on the part of other political organizations, excluded from an arena where the future of local government was being shaped.

Chapter 7

The Economic Arena

Within hours of his release from prison in February 1990, Nelson Mandela horrified the South African government and the white business community by suggesting that the African National Congress (ANC) might find it necessary to nationalize major economic assets for the good of the entire society.

This simplistic statement, carelessly tossed out with no apparent regard for the shock it would create, triggered an equally simplistic and emotional response from the government and the business community. Mandela's speech reflected an outmoded vision of economic development, completely discredited by the collapse of the Eastern European communist regimes, they argued. Only the free market could ensure growth, and only growth, not redistribution, could solve South Africa's social and economic ills. Nobody bothered to explain what "free market" meant in the South African economy, where the public sector controlled more than 50 percent of fixed assets and a few conglomerates dominated the stock market.[1]

Mandela's speech and the reaction to it set the tone of most discussions of economic issues in South Africa for several years. It was on the whole a meaningless discussion, with the two sides exchanging volleys of general principles, seemingly without ever making contact with each other or with the reality of the South African economy.[2]

Yet economic issues would have to be tackled as part of the conflict-resolution process. A purely political transition appeared unlikely to bring a lasting settlement. Not only were the socioeconomic problems confronting the majority of the population enormous—so they were in other African countries where the transition to independence did not entail economic transformation—but large, mobilized constituencies existed that were determined to put economic problems on the agenda even before a settlement was reached.

Nonetheless, in the early 1990s progress in the economic domain lagged far behind that in the national or even local government arena. There, as already noted, the major participants had come to accept the fact that neither side would simply abandon its aspirations and surrender, and they had started to negotiate, although haltingly and with many setbacks. But on economic issues, the government and the business community still maintained the illusion that the liberation establishment could be prevailed upon to accept the status quo.

The ANC's position remained in flux, and divisions appeared in the organization. One part of the leadership became increasingly aware that commitment to redistribution had to be counterbalanced by pragmatic considerations concerning the impact of reforms on production, as well as on foreign loans and investment. But another segment of the organization remained deeply committed to the principles set forth in the Freedom Charter; its talk of nationalization had the flavor of the revolutionary takeover the ANC had abandoned in the political realm. In general, it was the politics of absolute principles rather than the politics of negotiations that continued to dominate the economic debate.

Despite the lack of progress, the general climate in the country suggested that economic issues, too, would eventually become the object of negotiations, and the identity of the actors who would eventually engage in the process was evident. The government and the major political organizations would take part in this as well as in all the other processes. In addition, labor unions and the business community were bound to be cast in a central role. Finally, the economic arena had the greatest potential for mobilizing white right-wing extremists into the process if the issue of land redistribution was seriously discussed.

THE SOUTH AFRICAN ECONOMY

White South Africans liked to talk of their country as one where a first world and a third world lived side by side. The first world, that of the white population, comprised the mining, industrial, and service sectors, and the large white commercial farms. The third world belonged to the black population, and it included the rural homelands and the urban informal sector.

This characterization of the South African economy conveyed well the extreme contrast between the world of whites and that of blacks— the California-style white suburbs versus the dusty townships and the miserable squatter camps, or the 12.9:1 ratio of white to African per capita income.[3] But it did not even begin to explain the relationship between the two. South Africa's third world was not a traditional enclave that would eventually be absorbed into the mainstream of late twentieth century economic activity, but a new entity deliberately created by apartheid policies and originally meant never to become integrated into the modern economic sector.[4] The attempt to relocate Africans not employed in the first world to homelands comprising barely 13 percent of the land started to shape South Africa's third world into a realm of refugee camps supported by remittances from migrant workers. The sudden abrogation in 1986 of the influx control policy attracted people from the impoverished homelands to urban areas that offered neither jobs nor housing, adding to the South African third world the sprawling squatter settlements surrounding the cities. Subsistence agriculture, however, virtually disappeared. Only 10 percent of the income of homeland residents came from agriculture.[5]

THE FUTURE OF THE ECONOMY

Such extreme contrast unsurprisingly led the liberation movements to include economic redress among their demands. "The people shall share in the country's wealth! . . . The land shall be shared among those who work it! . . . There shall be work and security!" proclaimed the Freedom Charter. For the Pan Africanist Congress of Azania (PAC) and other Africanist organizations, the return of the land was the very symbol of liberation. From the perspective of all antiapartheid movements, nationalizing economic assets did not mean taking away something that belonged to whites, but meant getting back what had been unjustly appropriated in the first place. Most whites saw it differently: blacks were simply trying to take away the first world whites had built over the years, and, to make matters worse, they would inevitably destroy it. The issue was highly emotional for all population groups.

The problem was compounded by the poor performance of the

South African economy. Economic growth, sluggish throughout the 1980s, was negative in the early 1990s, the result of low gold prices, a large debt problem, economic sanctions, lack of business confidence, and capital flight. Workers were being laid off in the thousands by mining companies whose production costs were higher than the international gold price, by the parastatals trying to become more efficient in preparation for privatization, and, in a ripple effect, by all other businesses facing a shrinking market for their goods. As a result, South Africa confronted in all its starkness the problem of how to promote economic equity. In a stagnant economy, the gap between blacks and whites could be narrowed only by taking away from whites.

The government and the ANC exchanged salvos on economic issues without making any progress in practice. Nevertheless, piecemeal economic reform was already taking place, as various groups tried to force change even ahead of negotiations. The Congress of South African Trade Unions (COSATU), the ANC, the government, the business community, and the white farmers were the groups most active in trying to create new facts on the ground in this period.

THE CONGRESS OF SOUTH AFRICAN TRADE UNIONS

The Congress of South African Trade Unions was by far the most important organization intent on making economic issues an integral part of the transition process, as well as on creating a new situation even while the process was taking place.

COSATU was the principal organization to emerge from the battle for union rights waged by black workers in the 1970s and 1980s. Formed only in 1985, COSATU was heir to all the conflicting trends in the history of black unionism in South Africa. One, derived from the 1950s and 1960s, entailed a close link of black trade unions and liberation movements. Following a pattern common in many African countries before independence, the South African Congress of Trade Unions (SACTU) was closely associated with the ANC, and it even subordinated its union goals to political ones. Formed in 1955, SACTU immediately joined the Congress alliance, attended the Congress of the People, signed the Freedom Charter, and devoted most of its efforts to organizing political stay-aways rather than strikes on economic issues. With the banning of the ANC, SACTU officials virtually abandoned union organizing to take up the political battle, eventually suffering the same fate of imprisonment or exile as the ANC leadership.[6]

The unionism that developed during the 1970s, by contrast, was a shop-floor movement. In the South African context, black unionism had by definition political implications, since it involved a struggle to win rights that the apartheid regime recognized for white but not for black workers. Nevertheless, the new struggling unions concentrated on issues that would later be called "workerist," as opposed to "populist": wages, working conditions, and the right to unionize, rather than the broader issue of the abolition of apartheid. This concentration on classic union issues was facilitated by the fact that, at the time black labor unionism revived in South Africa in the early 1970s, there was virtually no political activity in the country, thus no pressure on the new organizations to participate in a broader movement.

A wave of strikes in Durban in 1973 marked the revival of the black unions. From then on, the process never stopped. Slowly and with many setbacks, the labor organizations grew. Difficult as it was, the progress made by the unions worried the government, which was quick to perceive the possibility that the new organizations would eventually take up the political cause that had been dormant in the country for ten years.

The result was the appointment of the Wiehahn Commission in May 1977 to consider a series of labor issues, including recognition of black unions. Two years later the commission recommended that black unions be allowed to register, thus to participate officially in the bargaining process. However, the right was limited by many clauses—for example, foreign workers, including citizens of the so-called independent homelands, were initially excluded, as were agricultural laborers. The government hoped that registered unions, subject to a complex series of rules, could be kept from picking up the political banner anew. Recognition, in other words, formally extended workers' rights, but it was also seen as a way to control and depoliticize the unions. Fully aware of the implications of the decision, and with many qualms, unions nevertheless began to register.[7]

As the internal antiapartheid movement revived, the new unions were forced to decide whether to participate in the broader political efforts to bring about the end of apartheid—the populist option—or to concentrate strictly on labor issues—the workerist option. Township organizations were proliferating and workers came under pressure to join them, not only as individuals but with the full weight of their unions.

There was strong resistance to the demand. In part, it may have been fear that government repression would endanger the labor movement still struggling to get established. In part, it was the unions' jealousy of their autonomy and the fear that workers' interests would take second place to those of the liberation movement, as they had in the past. Finally, many unionists also disagreed with the organizing style of the township groups, which by the 1980s were carrying the banner of the antiapartheid movement. Civics, they argued, were top-down organizations, in which decisions were made by a few leaders. There was too little consultation, reporting back, and accountability in the civics.[8] It was the same accusation that both the unions and the civics would level against the ANC in the 1990s.

As township activism increased, however, it became more difficult for the unions to remain outside the political fray. With the launching of COSATU in 1985, the populist option, also characterized as "social-movement unionism," prevailed.[9] COSATU mobilized its members for political causes, eventually joining the United Democratic Front and other organizations in the formation of the Mass Democratic Movement and, after 1990, forging an alliance with the ANC and the South African Communist Party (SACP). The culmination of the process was the election of a prominent unionist, National Union of Mine Workers General Secretary Cyril Ramaphosa, as ANC secretary general in July 1991. But COSATU and its affiliates did not subordinate the workerist issues to the populist ones, as SACTU had done. Rather, they tried to pursue both at the same time.

The growth of COSATU, the launching of new affiliates, and the remarkable success unions encountered in wage negotiations in the major sectors showed that the strategy was successful. By the time of its 1991 congress, COSATU had 1.25 million members, of whom almost 290,000 belonged to the National Union of Metalworkers of South Africa and about 270,000 to the National Union of Mineworkers.[10] Despite the severe job losses resulting from the economic recession, membership was still growing. The National Council of Trade Unions (NACTU), which leaned toward the Africanist organizations, was also growing and claimed a membership of about

250,000.[11] Furthermore, unions were achieving results for their members, with the wages of black workers increasing much faster than those of whites.[12]

The integration of prominent COSATU officials in the ANC leadership was extremely important in the period of transition. It brought into the process people who had considerable experience in negotiations. It also made it less likely that the ANC would settle for a purely political solution without also insisting on the discussion of economic grievances. In fact, COSATU saw the attempt to separate political from economic issues as a tactic used by government and employers to reduce the power of the working class.[13] Finally, COSATU's determination to retain its autonomy increased the complexity of the liberation establishment.

The negotiating experience the unions brought into the process was extensive and multifaceted. During contract negotiations, the unions had learned to work out a compromise between two conflicting initial positions. It was an adversarial process, in which the two sides remained opposed to each other even after a new contract was signed. But the unions also had some experience with more cooperative undertakings. The 1991 contract negotiated by the National Union of Metalworkers provided for the creation of joint union-employer committees to devise new training programs and to investigate strategies for growth and job creation.[14] Another example was the cooperation between COSATU, NACTU, and the South African Employers' Consultative Conference on Labor Affairs from 1988 to mid–1990, which culminated in a joint proposal for amendments to the Labor Relations Act. The unions, in other words, had shown that they could negotiate with employers successfully in an adversarial process, but also that they knew how to operate in a more cooperative relationship when necessary, and that they were willing to share responsibility under certain conditions.

The strong presence of the unions both in the alliance and in the leadership of the ANC also brought economic issues into sharper focus. COSATU's agenda for the transition from apartheid included the discussion of a workers' charter to be included in the constitution, as well as the formulation of an economic policy.

COSATU's views were first aired in a discussion document prepared for its August 1991 congress. The proposed charter aimed at safeguarding the workers' right to organize and strike, as well as the labor unions' right to be independent of employers, government, and political parties.[15] The demand for union independence was directed not against the government of the day but against COSATU's own allies, the ANC and the SACP. A white government might try to suppress black unions, but it could not really hope to subordinate their goals to its own in the name of a broad political alliance. A government claiming to represent the interests of the entire black population, or a party claiming to represent the workers, however, might well attempt to curb the autonomy of the labor unions.

The discussion paper singled out structural deficiencies of the economy: lack of investment, excessive dependence on export of raw materials, reliance on the import of heavy machinery, poor quality of industrial goods, and only an ineffective agricultural policy. Future policy should promote growth and job creation, improve the standard of living of the working class, make the economy more competitive internationally, and address the inequalities created by apartheid. All this would be accomplished by democratic planning in a mixed economy. While still vague and couched in very general terms, COSATU's approach to economic problems was strikingly oriented to the urban and formal industrial economic sector. Agriculture and the informal sector, which provided a living for the majority of the black population, received no attention.

The issue of most immediate concern to COSATU was its own role in the negotiations. Initially, it demanded the right to participate fully in the process. The question was first raised after the Groote Schuur meeting of April 1990, at which the ANC was the sole representative of the antiapartheid forces. The ANC was criticized for leaving out other groups not only by the Africanist organizations but also by COSATU, which demanded that workers be allowed to send their own delegates to future talks.[16]

In the following year the leadership of COSATU changed its position. After the election of Ramaphosa and other unionists to top ANC positions, the danger that union interests would be neglected became slight.[17] Furthermore, COSATU supported the ANC's demand for an elected constituent assembly, and this precluded direct union representation in the process, since only political parties would participate in the elections.

By November 1991, COSATU had abandoned its demand for a direct role in the political process leading to the enactment of a new constitution. Emboldened by the success of a two-day stay-away called to protest the imposition of a value-added tax, COSATU instead demanded that a separate economic forum be convened to define future economic policy. This forum would be as important as the political negotiations, take place at the same time, and of course be attended by the unions.

THE AFRICAN NATIONAL CONGRESS

The ANC also put economic issues on its agenda, but much less emphatically. Not surprisingly, negotiations on a new political system had higher priority for the Congress, which also had difficulty in fashioning a coherent economic position. Not only were the issues extremely complex, but the leadership of the organization was caught among the conflicting pressures coming from different domestic constituencies, as well as from the international community. As a result, statements emanating from the Congress on economic matters were initially confused and contradictory. A more comprehensive policy document issued in May 1992 succeeded in balancing—on paper—the different demands for redistribution and growth, government intervention and free enterprise, and protection of domestic industries and regional integration. Whether they could be balanced in practice was a different matter.

It was possible to distinguish three positions within the ANC. One, initially set forth by Mandela, was simply a reiteration of the ideas expressed in the Freedom Charter: in a postapartheid South Africa, major economic assets should be placed under government control, to be used for the benefit of the entire community; the government should assume the major responsibility for directing the economy; and land should be given back to those who worked it. With the exception of the last point, this was the policy followed by the National Party when it first came to power—since the land laws preceded the triumph of Afrikaner nationalism, the NP did not have to worry about control over land. They were also the ideas about economic development that dominated the third world well into the 1970s and were generally accepted by industrialized countries and development agencies at the time. But during the 1980s state intervention had fallen into disrepute as a development strategy, making it easy for the National Party to attack the ANC for advocating policies similar to the ones it had implemented itself until recently.

The second position, best represented by Thabo Mbeki in discussions with foreign businessmen, was more in keeping with the dominant ideas of the 1980s. It stressed the importance of the private sector and the need for high levels of foreign investment and played down the possibility of nationalization. The problem with this view was that, while well accepted abroad, it failed to address the immediate concerns of most black South Africans.

A third view, reflected in the organization's economic documents, could be characterized as a modernized, updated version of the first. The "Discussion Document on Economic Policy," which emerged from a September 1990 economic workshop, and the resolution on economic policy prepared for the July 1991 congress still had a definitely statist flavor. They also represented a rejection of the economic advice African countries were then receiving from international agencies.[18]

Taking notice of the existing extremely skewed income distribution and of the economic stagnation of the preceding decade, the ANC prescribed a policy of "growth through redistribution." Economic growth, the ANC acknowledged, was essential if the standard of living of the population was to improve. But this did not mean that redistribution had to be postponed until some future date, or that the improvement in the general living standard could take place only through a "trickle down" to the poor of the benefits of growth. Rather, redistribution itself could become the engine of growth. Increased expenditure on housing and services, production of simple, mass-consumption manufactured goods, and job creation programs would redistribute wealth and stimulate growth. A land reform program "capable of simultaneously addressing a major national grievance, responding to the acute land hunger and increasing food production" would also be part of the strategy.[19]

While supporting a mixed economy and stressing the need to promote entrepreneurship, the discussion document also opposed the government's efforts to privatize public sector firms, and warned that any parastatal the government transferred to private ownership would immediately be renationalized by the ANC. It also raised the two specters that hung over all discussions of economic issues in South Africa—control over the mines and the domination of the private sector by a few conglomerates. Mineral wealth should be "husbanded in such a way that it benefits all the people," and the possibility of creating a state-controlled marketing agency for minerals should be investigated.[20] As for the concentration of economic control, the ANC "would investigate the existing concentrations of economic power with a view to promoting a more efficient and effective use of resources."[21] Although it would be better if the reforms were carried out in cooperation with business, "if such cooperation were not forthcoming a future democratic government could not shirk its clear duty in this regard."[22] Adding to the concern of the government and the business community, the ANC admitted that its economic strategy would require additional revenue, and that fiscal reform would therefore have to be taken into consideration.

The discussion paper was an extremely ambiguous document. It could be read as an elaboration of the principles contained in the Freedom Charter (as adjusted for 1990 concerns, such as environmental protection and women's rights) or as a more moderate document, displaying a greater degree of realism about the dangers of excessive state intervention and the need for foreign investment.

The ambiguity was not accidental. To some extent, it was a reflection of the intrinsic difficulty of crafting an economic policy that could redress the injustices of the apartheid system without wrecking an economy already hard hit by a prolonged recession. But to a larger extent, it was the result of continuing divisions within the organization. By May 1992, when the new policy guidelines were issued, the ANC appeared to have made much progress in defining its economic policy, but the differences had not been overcome.[23] The policy document was coherent, balanced, and thoughtful, consciously attempting to reconcile state intervention and private enterprise, public and private interests. But the debate at the conference convened to approve the guidelines, according to participants, confirmed the continuing disagreement in the organization. Delegates forced the leadership to retain in the document the concept of nationalization, which Mandela and others had by this time decided to drop because it was so controversial. Economic issues remained highly contentious.

One issue on which the ANC as a whole had an unequivocal position was that of land.[24] Repeal of the 1913 and 1936 land acts was not sufficient to settle the problem. Africans could not be expected to buy back at market prices land from which they had been forcibly evicted with no or only nominal compensation; the fact that many evictions had taken place in living memory, some as recently as the 1980s, made the idea even more ludicrous. The ANC unambiguously advocated a land reform program, including the imposition of ceilings on the amount of land or the number of farms an individual could own, changes in the land tax, and measures that would ensure that underutilized land would be transferred to the landless. But, like other black organizations, the ANC discussed the land issue in a more political than economic context. Land reform was a matter of righting past wrongs, but economic development would come from the industrial sector and the mines. The ANC, like COSATU, was essentially urban oriented.

THE GOVERNMENT AND ECONOMIC REFORM

During the 1980s the South African government converted from a policy of heavy state intervention in the economy to the new faith in private enterprise and the free market preached by all international development agencies and increasingly embraced by third world countries and formerly socialist ones. This newfound faith of the National Party was highly political. Whatever the economists might say, it was not self-evident to the average South African that state intervention was a bad thing. The policy had not led to an obvious economic catastrophe, as it had elsewhere. On the contrary, from the whites' point of view it had worked extremely well, solving the problem of the poor Afrikaners and providing them with a standard of living that was extraordinarily high in relation to the country's level of development. Second, economic problems were easy to blame on factors other than state intervention. Blacks saw apartheid, not the state's interference in the functioning of the free market, as the cause of their poverty. And whites, beginning to feel the pinch of a protracted recession, found it easier to fault international economic sanctions than domestic policies.

Whatever the truth of the matter, most South Africans saw a decrease in state intervention as a political ploy. To blacks, it was a sign that the National Party was seeking to reduce the sphere of government control before handing over power. For whites, it was a sign that the government was betraying its constituents, no longer providing them the protection and services to which they were entitled.

The economic reforms introduced by the government beginning in the late 1980s were inspired by the new development orthodoxy of the World Bank and the International Monetary Fund, but they were applied selectively. The government embarked on a program of strict monetary control, progressive elimination of food subsidies, and the privatization of parastatals.[25] But subsidies were maintained in other areas, including agriculture and housing for civil servants. Furthermore, while embracing in theory a strategy of export-led development, the government did not eliminate—even raised, in some cases— tariff protection for local industries. The government also increased social spending in the townships, channeling more money through the Regional Services Councils and other means. The positive impact of such increases was wiped out, however, by the mushrooming population growth and by increased unemployment as privatization, low gold prices, and economic recession in general led to the retrenchment of tens of thousands of workers. Government spending, which should have been curbed under the new approach, continued to expand, both because of the attempt to address some urgent social problems and because the apartheid structures, with their costly administrative duplications, remained in place.

The political rationale for the selective application of economic reform was clear enough. The government was trying at the same time to demonstrate to the West that its economic thinking was in line with the new orthodoxy; to maintain the allegiance of its old constituency among whites, particularly Afrikaners; to appease the discontent in the townships without radically reforming the apartheid system; and, at least in the eyes of the ANC and the more politicized blacks, to ensure that when political power was transferred the new government would not have as much control over the economy as the National Party had enjoyed.

Policies trying to attain so many conflicting goals were bound to be uncertain and contradictory. As a result, white discontent increased without black discontent being significantly reduced. The problem was that the government did not have the resources to solve the problems of blacks through increased government spending, as it had done for whites, because the numbers were too high. It had solved the problem of poverty among the five million whites by depressing the standard of living of more than thirty million blacks. A reversal of the policy would perhaps redress a past injustice, but it would not lift blacks out of poverty in the short run. Only years of sustained economic growth could do that.

The government failed to reap any political benefits from the measures it introduced, because of its paternalistic attitude that it was acting to "uplift" the black population and to eliminate "backlogs" while making sure that "standards" did not drop for whites. Black political organizations were demanding justice and a role in policy-making, not charity. But the government offered poverty alleviation programs without economic restructuring, and it lacked the resources to make those programs large enough to make a difference in the daily lives of most blacks. An Independent Development Trust set up in 1990 received R 2 billion from the government, and it was empowered to raise additional money by issuing bonds. The funds were devoted mostly to improving education and to developing "sites and services" schemes (that is, making available at subsidized prices plots of land serviced by roads, water, and sometimes sewer and electricity connections, on which individual families could build their own shelter).[26] In August 1991 the government earmarked for development projects an additional R 1 billion, obtained from the sale of oil from its strategic reserves. Most of the funds, it was announced, would go for urban sites and services schemes and rural water supplies.[27] In late 1991 it allocated more than R 220 million for food programs, its own studies having concluded that between 2.5 million and 16 million South Africans suffered from malnutrition.[28] All these efforts, however, remained piecemeal and divorced from an overall economic policy.

The government refused to launch any program to facilitate redistribution of assets between blacks and whites. This was particularly evident regarding the land issue. A White Paper on Land Reform was issued by the government in early 1991 to accompany the bill repealing "racially based land measures."[29] "The new policy," stated the White Paper, "has the definite objective of ensuring that existing security and existing patterns of community order will be maintained. The primary objective is to offer equal opportunities for the acquisition, use and enjoyment of land to all people within the social and economic realities of the country."[30] The paper stressed "the government's opposition to any form of redistribution of agricultural land, whether by confiscation, nationalization or expropriation."[31] Not surprisingly, the ANC reacted with "outrage and deep disappointment." The effect of the paper, argued the Congress, was "to codify the present state of dispossession under the cover of free market proposals."[32] Equally negative statements were issued by all organizations with an interest in land issues and human rights, including quite moderate ones.[33]

The government remained completely unwilling to take positive steps toward making land more accessible to blacks, even when that was possible without expropriating existing owners. For example, it disregarded a study prepared by the Development Bank of Southern Africa, a government-controlled institution not known for its radicalism, which argued that substantial amounts of land could be made available to small farmers without recourse to drastic expropriation measures.[34] As a first step, the government could have made available land already bought from white farmers under the Trust Land Consolidation program but not yet transferred to the homelands.[35] Additionally, the Department of Agricultural Development and the commercial banks together controlled about three million hectares repossessed from white farmers who had defaulted on their loans. Other land was held by churches in trust for blacks, and numerous black communities had legal claim historically to tracts of land from which they had been expelled as recently as the 1980s under the government "black spot" removal plan. (Under this plan, the government forced black communities living in areas reclassified as "white" to move to the homelands.) Finally, much land already zoned for agricultural small holdings around the major cities was not under cultivation. All together, the study concluded, some eight million hectares (twenty million acres) could be made available in a short period to give five hundred thousand black smallholders full title to their farms, without impinging on existing property rights or on communal tenure in the homelands. But the government was not interested in the idea.

The unwillingness to face up to the problem of redistribution was particularly striking in the government's handling of evicted communities trying to repossess their land. The repeal of the land and group areas acts had given renewed intensity to the efforts of these communities and the human rights organizations that supported them.[36] While the details of each case differed, many of these dispossessed populations had title to the land, having purchased it when it was still permissible to do so; in other cases, the land had been put in a trust for the community for a variety of reasons. Legal niceties had not prevented the government from forcing communities off their land and resettling them in homelands when this had been considered necessary for the elimination of "black spots."

With the repeal of the Group Areas Act, some of these communities tried to move back. In most cases the land still belonged to the government; only rarely had it been sold to white farmers. Restitution would have been relatively easy, but the government refused on principle to recognize that evicted communities had a right to return, choosing instead to deal with each case individually through the courts.

THE BUSINESS COMMUNITY

The issue of whether apartheid and capitalism are sides of the same coin or contradictory forms of socioeconomic organization has been the object of endless and highly ideological debate, and no attempt will be made to address it here.[37] Nonetheless, it should be stated that during the 1980s the representatives of the major corporations appeared to accept the inevitability of a radical change in the apartheid system faster than the government. The Botha cabinet wavered between the knowledge that reform was inevitable and the fear of what lay ahead, but the business community had fewer qualms. Faced with mounting problems as the migrant worker system failed to provide the skilled manpower required by evolving technologies, business had no trouble accepting the lifting of the occupational color bar and the reform of petty apartheid, and it even learned to live with the new black labor unions. In fact, it went further, accepting the idea that piecemeal reform was not sufficient to tackle the apartheid problem, and that a new political system had to be devised. It thus established contacts with the ANC ahead of the government's acceptance of negotiations.

After February 1990, however, the business community no longer appeared to be ahead of the government in thinking about reform. De Klerk had taken the initiative concerning political change, and business was reluctant to entertain the possibility that economic reform, too, must become part of the process of dismantling apartheid. Not surprisingly, businessmen reacted with horror and indignation every time the African National Congress mentioned the word "nationalization." Like the government, they argued that the economic future of South Africa depended not on new forms of economic intervention but on a new commitment to private entrepreneurship in a free market. This commitment to the free market nevertheless did not prevent farmers from complaining about insufficient subsidies or industrialists from asking the government to increase tariffs against foreign competition.

Beyond the rhetoric, representatives of major corporations knew that a postapartheid government facing serious problems—high unemployment, widespread poverty, a very skewed distribution of assets, and an economy controlled by large parastatals and a few conglomerates—was unlikely to simply sit back and wait for a supposedly free market to operate its magic. But they made few attempts to offer counterproposals to the ANC's dreaded policy of nationalizing major economic assets, or to demonstrate in other ways that corporations were willing and able to help solve the country's socioeconomic problems, rendering radical intervention unnecessary. "There is a case for straight welfare," admitted an Anglo-American Corporation official when discussing the problems facing the majority of the black population, "but that is not the business of business."[38]

One of the few initiatives taken by business organizations was the attempt by Nedcor/Old Mutual, a savings and banking corporation, to devise a scenario which would facilitate a transition to democracy in South Africa.[39] Starting from the assumption that a democratic outcome was more likely in a healthy economy, as the experience of other countries indicated, the study offered a plan for stimulating economic growth by tackling directly some of the most pressing social issues, especially housing.[40] The scenario was a business version of the growth-through-redistribution idea supported by the ANC—but with more concern for growth and less for redistribution.

The study argued that the South African economy suffered because of the maldistribution of income and assets created by apartheid and because of fundamental structural weaknesses created by excessive protection, lack of competition, and concentration on the limited domestic market. For growth to resume, both problems had to be tackled simultaneously. Playing down the importance of economic sanctions as the cause of the stagnation of the 1980s, the authors concluded that the real culprit was the low productivity of the economy, grown flabby behind high tariff walls. Increased investment, currency devaluation, and increased expenditure on research and development were among the study's recommendations.

But these reforms alone would not stimulate growth and employment sufficiently in the short run or bring about immediate improvement in the lives of most people. Rather than wait for the benefits of growth to trickle down, government and business should intervene directly. A massive housing program, electrification of the townships and rural areas, investment in education, and the launching of a job corps for the youth would bring immediate benefits and stimulate the economy. The combination of the two measures could lead the country into a period of rapid economic growth, thus facilitating a political transition to democracy.

The idea that South Africa needed both economic growth and an intensification of social programs was hardly new—the government admitted the same. What made the scenario different was the scale of the proposal, and the fact that it entailed considerable costs and a massive mobilization of resources—not simply a piecemeal increase in social expenditure whenever some money could be scraped together for the purpose. The contention that not all economic problems were the result of sanctions was also a departure from the government's position.

The study, unpublished yet widely disseminated through audiovisual presentations, was apparently received with a great deal of interest by the government and the political parties, including the ANC. It was received rather poorly, however, by the business community, which apparently was unwilling to accept the necessity for drastic reform and intervention to stimulate growth.

CONCLUSIONS

Of the three arenas in which the transition process was being played out, the economic one saw the fewest concrete initiatives. Both at the national and local levels, much negotiating was taking place by the end of 1991. The Convention for a Democratic South Africa (CODESA) had met for the first time. In the local arena, a great deal of discussion and experimentation was taking place, and the local authorities of the major metropolitan areas had accepted as inevitable that the cities broken up by apartheid would have to be reunited in one form or another. The negotiations were far from successful, and indeed in June 1992 the initial phase of the process came to an abrupt end when the ANC suspended the talks. The principle that a solution could emerge only from negotiations was nevertheless firmly established.

Not so in the economic arena. There, the idea that negotiations were inevitable had encountered much resistance. COSATU's proposal for an economic forum bringing together government, business, labor, and political parties met a lukewarm, slow response. Some discussions about the possibility of a forum finally took place in May 1992, but the breakdown of CODESA put the future of this and other initiatives on hold.[41] As a result, in the first phase of the transition much of the so-called economic debate consisted of posturing and sloganeering on each side.

Negotiations on economic issues have not been a routine part of the transition to independence in most African countries. (The major exceptions were Kenya and Zimbabwe. In both, an agreement was reached whereby the British government made available funds allowing the new government to purchase land from whites and transfer it to black ownership.) But in all these countries the new government then intervened unilaterally in an effort to repossess the country's wealth, establish control, and theoretically promote development, usually with very poor results. In light of this historical pattern, the reluctance of the South African government and business community to seriously entertain the inevitability of economic reform appeared both puzzling and self-defeating.

A possible explanation was the perception that the collapse of the Eastern European regimes made socialist solutions unthinkable, firmly establishing free enterprise as the only sane option for South Africa. This perception, the government acknowledged, was an important factor in its decision to unban the ANC and start negotiations in 1990. Unfortunately, it also apparently led the government to assume that only political issues had to be negotiated. This was a risky approach. The economic grievances of the black population ran deep, and so did the conviction that steps must be taken to bring about a more equitable distribution of income and assets. The difficulty the ANC encountered in moving away from the idea of nationalization was less a sign that the leadership was wedded to outmoded positions, as the government claimed, than a recognition that economic conflicts must be addressed.

The government also found encouragement in the major international agencies' rejection of state intervention as a viable development strategy. If economic development depended on the health of a private sector unhindered by the shackles of government interference, then it made no sense for the government to negotiate on economic issues with political parties. Economic issues belonged rightly in the private realm, not the public one. The government's task was not to negotiate but to encourage privatization.

Another factor that made it difficult to open a serious debate about the future of the economy was the National Party's attitude toward its own constituency. De Klerk had chosen to play down as much as possible the importance of the change that was bound to take place, seeking instead to reassure whites that the government would protect their interests and that their lives would continue largely unchanged. Opening an arena of negotiations on economic issues would destroy the illusion that apartheid could be eliminated with only minimal disruption in the lives of whites.

The reluctance of business was more difficult to explain. The extremely skewed distribution of income and assets in the country, coupled with the control that a few conglomerates exercised in the private sector, made business vulnerable to attempts at economic restructuring in the future, particularly if the ANC emerged as the dominant party, as seemed likely. By not confronting the issue while the government was still under the control of the National Party, the business community risked being forced to do so later, when it would have to face a much more powerful ANC.

Not only the government and the business community were loath to put economic issues on the agenda immediately; the ANC was not pushing particularly hard for early economic negotiations either, although it had made it clear that it considered policies leading to a measure of redistribution essential. But the Congress was not in a hurry. As a government-in-waiting, it would have power to shape economic policy later, without injecting a new set of contentious issues in the already difficult negotiating process.

This left COSATU as the only organization with a real interest in discussing economic issues immediately, both in order to further what it perceived to be the economic interests of its constituency and to assert its autonomy and importance vis-à-vis its ally, the ANC. The labor unions had become highly politicized during the 1980s and were unlikely to retreat to a purely workerist position at the height of the transition process, when major decisions concerning the future of the country were being made. But COSATU supported the call for a constituent assembly, thus forgoing direct participation in the constitutional process, so it needed to open up an economic arena to have a say in the future of South Africa.

Sooner or later, economic issues were bound to be put on the agenda; the only question was whether this would happen before or after a political settlement was reached. The hope that in the post-socialist era the transition from apartheid could be merely political, leaving the economy untouched, appeared to be based on an inflated assessment of the importance of world trends over the South African reality.

PART 3
The Transition

Negotiating, Nelson Mandela explained in a televised interview shortly after his release, meant being ready to compromise, and to compromise not only on small issues but on major ones as well. Two years later, formal negotiations started at the Convention for a Democratic South Africa (CODESA), yet they did not lead to a compromise; instead, within six months the process had broken down. Neither side was ready to admit that it could not obtain at the negotiating table what it had been unable to get by other means. The African National Congress (ANC) told its supporters that the talks were just one pillar of the liberation struggle and that the goals remained the same. De Klerk continued to assure white voters that the government would not allow them to be dominated by blacks, hence that it would not accept majority rule. These statements, it turned out, represented fixed positions rather than opening moves. Indeed, the main accomplishment of the CODESA process was not to narrow the gap between the two sides but to remove the confusion about the National Party's (NP's) position—the ANC's was always clear—and thus to reveal how wide the gap was.

CODESA failed because it started discussing details before the willingness to compromise existed. The two major adversaries were busy strengthening their positions, not dismantling the barricades. The tortuous process that could have compelled the contending forces to accept the fact they could not negotiate into existence the South Africa they really wanted, but would have to settle for the one they could obtain under the circumstances, never really began.

For several months, nevertheless, the talks at CODESA seemed to be progressing. The government in particular tried to convey the impression that it was flexible by accepting some of the ANC's demands. It had agreed to the idea of an elected constituent assembly set forth by the ANC and supported even by the radical groups that remained outside the process. It had accepted the need for an interim government, so that the National Party would not remain in sole control while elections were organized. Yet no agreement had been reached. The government had simply appropriated the terminology used by the

ANC and applied it to the completely different process it favored. When the confusion was finally dispelled on the eve of CODESA II, it became clear there had been no progress. The talks collapsed.

Although unsuccessful, the first phase of the transition did accomplish something: it had been a learning process for both major organizations, which had started out with unrealistic assumptions about themselves and each other. Both had misjudged the willingness of their followers to be led without asking questions. Mandela and the National Executive Committee had been rebuked by their party on more than one occasion for acting unilaterally, and after the failure of CODESA they had to deal with an increasingly angry and mobilized constituency. De Klerk, whose party had no tradition of challenging the leadership—in the past, dissidents had simply walked out to form new organizations—was able to avoid a revolt of the white electorate only through the referendum to determine whether he should continue negotiations. Having accepted the need for negotiations, however, whites still opposed change that directly affected their lives. It was symbolic of the problem that the residents of a new suburb north of Johannesburg voted yes overwhelmingly in the referendum, yet refused to allow a squatter settlement that had sprung up in their midst either to remain where it was or to relocate elsewhere in the vicinity. De Klerk had a mandate for negotiations, but not necessarily for change.

Also, de Klerk and Mandela had each come to the conclusion that his initial perception of the other had been wrong. The president had seen Mandela's willingness to talk as moderation. The ANC leader in turn had trusted de Klerk as a man of integrity. Both had been forced to revise their views.

Having learned more about themselves and each other, the government and the ANC were no closer to reaching agreement, of course. Indeed, the loss of illusions revealed how complex the situation was and how difficult it would be to find a solution. Realism would nevertheless provide a sounder basis for negotiating once the process resumed.

Devising a new constitution and structuring formal institutions were just the first steps toward conflict resolution in South Africa, however. An even greater difficulty lay in ensuring that the political organizations would accept in practice the constraints imposed by those institutions. For some groups, such acceptance would amount to sliding into political insignificance. Right-wing white organizations fell in this category, for example, and so did some black organizations—radical groups, homeland parties, governments of so-called independent homelands, and possibly even Inkatha, whose capacity to attract votes might well prove limited.

The high level of political mobilization could also make a settlement more difficult. The society had made itself ungovernable in opposition to the white regime, and it risked remaining ungovernable under a black government. The *dream of an active, organized, vibrant civil society protecting its interests against the threat of government domination could lead to chaos rather than participatory democracy.*

Finally, the negotiations would probably not cover all the burning issues the country faced. Economic problems, which the government and the business community insisted on treating as private ones, might never be discussed in the negotiations. The abstract principles of justice and equity for all, which were sure to be incorporated in the South African Bill of Rights, would not settle any issues; they would simply add a new legal dimension to a sphere of conflict that would remain active long after new political institutions had been created.

The process of conflict resolution the country was embarking on thus went beyond the immediate negotiations on which attention was focused. Rather, it had two distinct dimensions: negotiations on constitutional issues, and fitting the country's political, economic, and social conflict into the new institutions. Conflict could not thereby be solved—that was impossible—but it could be transformed from acute and disruptive to chronic and filtered through formal institutional channels.

Chapter 8

The Failure of CODESA

The Convention for a Democratic South Africa (CODESA) opened in December 1991 on a note of hope and optimism. The preliminaries were over, and the serious discussions were about to begin. The government and the African National Congress (ANC) remained the chief players, but many other organizations had been drawn into the process; when an agreement was reached, it would have broad support, it seemed. Not all was perfect, of course. Mandela's bitter outburst against de Klerk, Buthelezi's refusal to attend because the Zulu king was not invited, and the reluctance of some homelands to accept the principle of reincorporation marred the first CODESA meeting. Many organizations on the Right and the Left remained outside the process. And, above all, the ANC and the government brought to the negotiating table antithetical visions of the new South Africa. But then the purpose of negotiations was precisely to overcome differences and reconcile conflicting points of view—problems were to be expected. The mood was buoyant.

Within six months, however, the process had broken down. CODESA was suspended, and it was doubtful whether it would ever convene again, at least in its original form. The political climate in the country had changed drastically. The mood of June 1992 was one of deep anger among blacks and incredulity and confusion among whites. It was as if the opening of February 1990 had never happened. The ANC and the Congress of South African Trade Unions (COSATU) threatened to take their cause to the streets through a concerted program of mass action. The township youth, sidelined as a political force while the ANC leaders talked to the government, were again manning the barricades, both figuratively and literally. The government accused the ANC leadership of having fallen under the domination of the South African Communist Party (SACP), conjuring anew a specter it had pronounced dead two years earlier.

The breakdown was quite sudden. On the eve of CODESA II, on May 14, 1992, it still seemed possible to reach an agreement, and working groups met late into the night. Indeed, when the two sides acknowledged failure the next day, the point of disagreement appeared paltry, a mere difference of a few percentage points in the majority that would eventually be required to amend the transitional constitution. But that was just the tip of a vast submerged iceberg. The talks had broken down not because the negotiators lacked the statesmanship to reach a minor compromise on the size of the required majority but because CODESA was built on the shaky foundations of conflicting goals, misunderstandings, and lack of good faith.

The ANC had entered the process in February 1990 on the assumption that negotiations were a means to achieve the goal that had eluded it for years, namely, that of translating the considerable popular support it enjoyed into control over the governing institutions. It had given up the dream of a revolutionary upheaval sweeping it into power, but not the goal of coming to power. Negotiations, the Congress told its supporters, were simply another pillar of the liberation struggle, another weapon to be used together with the armed struggle, mounting international pressure, and mass action to destroy apartheid. Power would emerge from the ballot box rather than from the barrel of a gun, but the end result would be the same—*Amandla Awhetu* (power to us), as the ANC slogan proclaimed.

For the government, the negotiations were a daring attempt to avoid a transfer of power to the ANC. De Klerk gambled that by taking the initiative he would succeed in negotiating a new power-sharing constitution that would extend political rights to the African population yet would also provide ironclad guarantees against whites having to accept the authority of other ethnic groups or losing control over that sphere of life defined as "own affairs." This, at least, was the promise made by the National Party during the 1989 election campaign.

The ANC finally discovered that the National Party's definition of democracy did not include majority rule. Power-sharing looked dangerously like another constitutional trick, another attempt to save as much white power as possible out of the failure of the apartheid system. This was the root of the crisis: from the ANC's point of view, the solution proposed by the government did not spell the end of apartheid; from the National Party's point of view, the solution proposed by the ANC spelled the end for whites in South Africa.

In the pursuit of their antithetical goals, the two organizations mustered assets, sought alliances, and tried to inject some issues into the negotiating process while removing others. They upheld different ideas of what negotiating meant and how long it should take. They tried to influence what happened at CODESA by taking steps outside it. In the end, it was the way all these elements combined into opposing strategies, rather than the details of a specific agreement, that caused the process to fail and led the country to a dangerous impasse.

THE ASSETS

A serious and essentially unavoidable problem underlying CODESA as well as any other attempt to formulate a new political system was the nature of the assets controlled by the major players. The National Party's strength was institutional control, the ANC's popular support, and Inkatha's ethnic nationalism. Inevitably, each sought a system that would maximize its respective strength.

De Klerk's decision to unban the ANC, release Mandela, and negotiate was an extraordinarily risky move. In retrospect, it is not surprising that P. W. Botha had hesitated and, in the end, refused to take the plunge. The National Party's biggest asset was its complete control over the government and the security forces, and this was exactly what it would have to negotiate away. Stripped of its governmental role, the National Party had limited assets, and they were shrinking. But control over the government and the maintaining of apartheid no longer guaranteed white security and prosperity. The 1980s had brought violence in the townships, war with South Africa's neighbors, costly economic sanctions, and life in a perpetual state of siege. The decision to negotiate was based on a gamble that the failing formal apartheid system could be bargained away as part of a deal that gave protection to, and safeguarded the interests of, the white minority.

Without control over the institutions, the National Party had very little to work with. Its popular support was extremely small to begin with, and for a time it appeared to be decreasing. In the 1989 election it had won only 48 percent of the white vote, and under a system of universal franchise this would probably amount to less than 10 percent of the total vote.[1] To remain an important player in the new South Africa, the National Party needed to get black votes, or to enter into an alliance with black organizations. As the party that had given apartheid to South Africa, however, it was unlikely to see a sudden groundswell of enthusiasm among the people it had previously victimized.

The change in policy also caused white support to decrease even further. All by-elections held after 1990 saw the NP lose votes to the Conservative Party.[2] Some loss was inevitable, but it was probably made worse by de Klerk's leadership style. By entering negotiations, the National Party was reversing the policy it had followed for forty years, a change that was bound to cause dismay among some of its supporters. The party was also a victim of its own propaganda. Having tried to convince white South Africans for years that it had the situation well in hand, it found it difficult to explain why it had decided to negotiate with the ANC and was preparing to give up complete control over the government.

But de Klerk's own style made the situation worse, contributing to a growing conviction among whites that they were being betrayed. Paternalistically, the president sought to reassure the white minority that the government would protect its interests, safeguard its civil service jobs, and prevent black domination, but he never explained what the government was doing or why. Nor did he project a positive vision of the future. The promises sounded increasingly hollow, because the government had already reneged on many. For example, the National Party had sworn during the 1989 election campaign that group rights would be recognized and "own affairs" protected from the encroachment of other groups. It had also promised that group areas would be maintained. But the National Party's constitutional proposals did not provide for group representation, and the Group Areas Act had been repealed. It was obvious the government had started going back on its promises even before the actual negotiations began, as it unilaterally repealed legislation and introduced reforms. At issue was not whether the reforms were good or bad, or whether they protected the long-term interests of whites, but how they had been introduced; many white South Africans were convinced that they had been introduced without a mandate, by stealth, and unjustifiably.

After the ANC was unbanned, political analysts worried for a time about its weakness, wondering whether it would be able to deliver a constituency when an agreement was reached.[3] By late 1991 the situation had been reversed. It was the ANC's turn to worry about the National Party's lack of support and to wonder whether it could deliver a significant white constituency. De Klerk was in a weak position, Mandela told a press conference, but there was nobody else with whom the ANC could negotiate.[4]

In early 1992 dwindling white support led the National Party to emphasize that the new constitution would have to be submitted to a referendum in which whites' votes would be counted separately from those of other population groups. If whites rejected the new charter, the government would go back to the drawing board, even if an overwhelming majority of the total population accepted it. The idea of a white referendum had been broached before, but it was only after the first CODESA meeting that the NP decided to make it a major issue, stressing that in the 1989 election campaign it had made a solemn promise to the white electorate that it was honor-bound to keep.[5] As the ANC quickly pointed out, accepting the government position amounted to giving whites veto power over the entire process. The ANC was in a quandary. If it rejected a white referendum, it could further weaken de Klerk's position, driving more whites into the arms of the Conservative Party; if it accepted such a referendum, it would not only violate all its principles but it would leave itself open to virtual blackmail—the National Party could extract concessions during the negotiations by threatening the possibility of a white veto.

The problem was solved unexpectedly by de Klerk's sudden decision to call for a referendum in March 1992. With negotiations just beginning, whites were not asked to approve a constitution, but simply to give the president an unequivocal mandate to negotiate. The move appeared to solve a problem for both the government and the ANC. It would be easier for the government to receive the approval of the white electorate on the basis of broad and vague principles than on the basis of a concrete constitution embodying inevitable compromises. And as long as the referendum asked whites to decide only whether de Klerk should negotiate on their behalf—not to approve a constitution that would affect the entire population—the ANC could accept the exclusion of other groups more easily; indeed, its objections to the referendum were largely perfunctory.

The 68.6 percent yes vote in the referendum was a great success for de Klerk and the National Party, and even caused the ANC to heave a sigh of relief. De Klerk had an unequivocal mandate, negotiations could continue, and the final agreement would not have to be subjected to a white-only referendum.

But there was a downside to this outcome. The government became overconfident of its ability to manipulate the negotiating process so as to impose its own solution. After steering the white electorate in the desired direction, the government appeared convinced it could do the same with the black parties at CODESA. The referendum victory could complicate the negotiations by making the government more intransigent and manipulative, but it did not make it more willing to accept a political system based on the rule of the majority. Sixty-eight percent of the white electorate was still a very small part of the population under universal franchise.

De Klerk had other important assets he could bring to bear on the negotiations. Only the NP could keep the institutions, and above all the security forces, under control during the transition. If the security forces rejected the government's leadership, the possibility of forming an interim government successfully would vanish, and the potential for violence and chaos would escalate rapidly. There was no guarantee that the National Party could deliver the security forces and other institutions, but certainly nobody else could do it.

Finally, the party still had the ability to manipulate the political situation as well as the negotiating process. This was an extremely controversial issue that created a lot of resentment among antiapartheid organizations, since it gave de Klerk a great advantage. In the past, the government had used secret funds and hit squads to pursue its goals. It claimed that such policies had been discontinued, but there were enough doubts about that assertion to cause the Goldstone Commission to start an investigation into the matter in February 1992.[6] The government had provided support for Inkatha, for other black moderate parties, and at least indirectly for all homeland parties. It could continue funding organizations, and it might even try to buy votes by launching new social programs just before an election. In fact, the ANC's demand for an interim government was in part an attempt to limit the National Party's ability to manipulate the situation.

The ANC's assets were very different from the government's, and they were growing. The ANC's membership was expanding, the divisions between exiled leadership and mass democratic movement were becoming less important, and its negotiators were gaining experience. The patriotic front existed only on paper, but the Pan Africanist Congress of Azania (PAC) and the Azanian People's Organization (AZAPO) were apparently incapable of rallying much support for their hard-line position and thus did not constitute an immediate threat. The ultimatum of May 1991 had been partially met by the government over time: most political prisoners had been released, and the United Nations High Commission for Refugees was helping repatriate the exiles; ministers Vlok and Malan had been demoted to lesser positions; and the National Party had apparently accepted the fact that there would have to be an interim government. The list of accomplishments was becoming longer.

Furthermore, the ANC also remained capable of bringing pressure on the government through mass action. A two-day general strike on November 4 and 5, 1991, called by the ANC, SACP, and COSATU to protest the imposition of a value-added tax on all goods and services, was a resounding success from the point of view of the organizers.[7] It was unclear how often the ANC could call for similar steps before fatigue set in, but in the meantime the mass democratic movement could make normal life impossible. The ANC had numbers on its side.

But the ANC still desperately needed the National Party and de Klerk. On its own, it could not gain the acquiescence of whites, the obedience of the security forces, or the compliance of the civil service. Without the cooperation of the National Party, the transition to a postapartheid South Africa would certainly be violent and chaotic. The ANC could make the country ungovernable, but only the National Party could make it governable for the time being.

THE STRATEGY

For both the government and the ANC, but above all for the former, CODESA was only one part of the strategy to achieve the desired goal. The broader process involved attempts to forge alliances, to determine which issues were up for negotiating and which were not, to create facts on the ground independent of the formal process, and to control the speed of the transition. All this affected the work of CODESA and the political climate surrounding the negotiations.

In this broader process, the government enjoyed many advantages by virtue of its control over formal institutions. Indeed, one of the ANC's problems was that its principal asset, superior popular support, would not become a decisive factor until elections were held. Much of the government's strategy centered on delaying that moment as long as possible and on making sure that a political system curbing the power of the majority had been agreed upon by the time elections took place.

The Alliances

The alliances remained fluid in the period between the first and second CODESA sessions, because neither side succeeded in carrying out its original plan. The failure to forge solid bonds to other organizations was probably a more serious problem for the government, whose support was limited, than for the ANC, which could count on a much larger number of votes in an election. Many of the smaller CODESA parties remained uncommitted, afraid of compromising their future by turning to the losing side. And other parties, Inkatha first of all, tried to play an independent hand. Irreconcilably hostile to the ANC, Inkatha was not the government's faithful ally either.

The National Party failed to forge a stable anti-ANC coalition. At least some of the homeland leaders were not willing to allow the government to negotiate for them a place in the future constitutional dispensation; they wanted to be heard directly and to remain players in their own right. The hope of creating a split between radicals and moderates in the ANC had proved vain—in fact, the very assumptions on which that strategy was based were unwarranted. Mandela, though eager to reach an agreement, was not a moderate. The communists were just as anxious as the so-called moderates to get involved in the negotiations. Furthermore, the government had underestimated the deep emotional bonds that linked the older-generation ANC and SACP leaders, comrades in arms during thirty years of imprisonment and exile. Some of the government's potential allies, particularly Inkatha, had become embarrassments rather than assets. Not only had Inkathagate raised serious doubts about de Klerk's integrity, but Buthelezi had created new problems for the government by demanding that the king represent the Zulus at CODESA.

The ANC's policy had also failed. There could be only two sides to the negotiations, Thabo Mbeki had argued at the time of the Groote Schuur meeting, "on one side [people] who are saying a united democratic and non-racial South Africa and on the other people who are saying a perpetuation of apartheid." But, he added, the ANC expected to have also on its side "people who today are serving within government-created institutions, the *bantustans* [homelands] and so on, but . . . who would want . . . to sit there not as representatives of groups, but as part of that broad formation that makes up that democratic movement."[8] But the patriotic front had started disintegrating even before it was formed, and most homeland leaders were keeping their distance from both sides.

Creating a common front with the PAC and AZAPO was probably an impossible task. Both organizations were divided within, and their members could not agree on any position. But the ANC's own attitude did not facilitate the formation of alliances. The Congress had the arrogance of the dominant movement, and other organizations feared it. Mandela personally tried to maintain good relations with homeland leaders, traditional authorities, and moderate groups, but this policy did not meet the approval of the rank and file. As a result, the ANC had no real allies among other political parties—the SACP was so closely intertwined with the ANC that it could not be defined simply as an ally.

Consequently, no stable blocs had emerged by the time the first CODESA convened, and none did so in the following months. This hindered rather than facilitated the negotiations. In theory, the existence of two cohesive blocs could create an atmosphere of confrontation, encouraging both sides to intransigence, while independent organizations could facilitate an agreement by acting as mediators. In practice, the many small parties, which had little support but nevertheless had to be listened to under the rules of CODESA, only slowed down the process; they make it difficult for the working groups to reach any agreement, while failing to provide a bridge or to suggest compromises.

Most important, some of the homeland organizations introduced delicate issues the principal parties could not raise without forcing a crisis. The most consequential was that of ethnic representation or group rights, which the government could not bring up without being accused of reverting to apartheid, but which some homeland leaders felt free to address in the name of historical identity and self-determination. In this context, the issue of the Zulu king's attendance at CODESA was not trivial, although he was personally only a minor figure manipulated by Buthelezi. Recognizing his right to be at CODESA as the representative of the Zulus meant putting on the agenda the issue of ethnicity as a determinant of political organization.

Buthelezi was not the only homeland leader to have strong reservations about the nature of representation at CODESA and about the convention's goal. President Lucas Mangope of Bophuthatswana attended the first meeting, but only to present an impassioned plea for the recognition of the Batswana nation. He refused to sign the declaration of intent because it called for a "united, democratic, non-racial and non-sexist state in which sovereign authority is exercised over the whole of its territory," thus for the reintegration of the homelands into South Africa.[9] The Ciskei delegation also abstained from signing, and even the Transkei hesitated, withdrawing its objections to the declaration of intent only at the last minute, to avoid being identified with Bophuthatswana and the Ciskei. Together, the representatives of these homelands injected a new issue into the process.

The Meaning of Negotiations

The agreement to negotiate the end of apartheid reached by the government and the ANC was a breakthrough for South Africa, and an enormous change in the two adversaries' positions. But they attached very different meanings to the term *negotiations*. To be sure, the word conveyed to all the idea of a dialogue through which differences would be settled rather than a process in which one side would impose its solution with force. But there the similarity ended. The strategies they were pursuing under the guise of negotiating were quite different. Neither recognized the legitimacy of the other's approach.

For the antiapartheid organizations, the concept of negotiations was broad, comprising the entire process of setting in place a new system of government peacefully. When the ANC talked about negotiations, it referred to the preliminary talks and the convening of CODESA, but also to the election of a constituent assembly and the bargaining there over the new charter. This is what negotiating the end of apartheid entailed for the ANC. The preliminary talks and CODESA were just the beginning of the process, an unavoidable first step to be carried out as quickly as possible so elections could be held and the constituent assembly could complete the peaceful negotiated transition.

But the National Party attached a much narrower meaning to negotiations, referring simply to the process of bargaining among non-elected representatives of various parties and organizations that had to take place before an election could even be considered. The National Party assumed that an election would put an end to all negotiating, and that it was therefore crucial for the parties to agree on all important issues beforehand, lest the majority party be able to impose its views unilaterally afterward. The National Party thus held a pessimistic view of the democratic process, assuming that one party would win an overwhelming majority, control both the Parliament and the executive, and never be forced to compromise to maintain support. Indeed, that had been the situation in South Africa for forty years.

These different definitions of negotiations were not simply a semantic issue. They were based on the government's realization that its bargaining power would be greater before an election than after, and on the ANC's opposite assumption concerning its own situation. The government thus wanted to postpone the reckoning in front of the voters as long as possible, the ANC to hasten it.

Another point on which the views of the two organizations differed concerned the legal framework of the negotiations. The National Party insisted that South Africa had a legitimate government, that there was no vacuum of power, and therefore that any change would have to be introduced according to due process of law under the existing institutions. No matter what CODESA decided, the existing tricameral Parliament would have the final word. The stress on due process under existing institutions gave a particular slant to the government's concept of negotiations. Rather than being a process of bargaining and joint decisionmaking between partners of equal status, although not necessarily of equal power, negotiations became a simple process of consultation of extraparliamentary organizations by the country's legitimate authorities. The government would strive to devise a political system acceptable to all major organizations, but in the final analysis only existing institutions could implement reforms.

This was not the view of the antiapartheid organizations. They simply did not acknowledge the legitimacy of the existing system, and thus did not accept the idea that the illegitimate institutions created by the apartheid regime should have the ultimate responsibility for approving the future political system. Only an elected constituent assembly could do that, and elections for a constituent assembly must be part of the negotiating process.

Issues to Be Negotiated

In theory, what was to be negotiated was simple: a constitutional dispensation for the new South Africa, extending political rights to the entire population and embracing all three tiers of government. But the existing South African constitution complicated the matter. It did not just regulate the exercise of political power; it had a pervasive impact on all spheres of life. The 1983 document established the principles that underpinned much of the day-to-day lives of all South Africans—schooling, medical care, access to housing, loans to agriculture, old-age pensions, and so on. Abrogating the old constitution meant invalidating the existing system in all areas and creating a need for new structures. For example, setting up a new system of education was not a constitutional issue in the narrow sense; nevertheless, writing a new constitution would immediately require the restructuring of education. There was a large gray area, not a clear line, between constitutional negotiations and the formulation of other reforms.

Concerning the narrow constitutional issues, the ANC favored restricting CODESA's role to the discussion of the broad principles on which the constitution should be based, the formation of a short-lived interim government, and the modalities of the elections for a constituent assembly, leaving that body to write the new charter. But the government wanted CODESA to negotiate a constitution based on its power-sharing model, which would have involved tackling the reintegration of the homelands and the setting up of the regions. Although theoretically only transitional, the constitution negotiated at CODESA would be very difficult to amend—the government was holding out for a 75 percent majority, and indeed it was on this issue that negotiations finally broke down.

Neither the ANC nor the National Party wanted broader issues to be discussed at CODESA. It was only special interest groups that tried, unsuccessfully, to argue that CODESA should address problems such as education or metropolitan government. For the ANC, broader issues should wait until a new government was in place. The de Klerk government, however, knew that abrogation of the constitution would create a vacuum in many areas, and it did not intend to leave it to the next cabinet—possibly controlled by the ANC—to settle the issue. Therefore, instead of acting as a caretaker, transitional government, the NP was trying to carry out reforms in many areas so it could create facts on the ground that could survive the change of constitution. This tactic angered the ANC and other parties, increasing the urgency of their demand for an interim government.

During 1990 and 1991, in particular, the government had taken several steps to institute policies that could survive the abrogation of the constitution. These measures would have little impact if a new political system was put in place swiftly, but they could have a far-reaching effect if the transition stretched on for years, as the government hoped.

Three examples will illustrate the government's approach. One, already mentioned, was the passage of the Interim Measures for Local Government Act. It made it possible for the provincial administrators to give legal recognition to new local government structures negotiated among existing councils. Because these new structures would not be strictly a creation of the apartheid government, they stood a better chance of surviving the abrogation of the constitution. However, the government, through the provincial administrators, would also maintain ultimate control over what was acceptable. The formation of the supposedly nonracial Kimberley Council, in which whites maintained disproportionate power, was an example of the kind of fait accompli the government hoped to create.

In the field of education, the government was attempting to transfer control over white schools to parents, yet, again, maintain ultimate say over what was acceptable. Initially, it had given white parents a choice of three models. The one selected by most parents was the so-called B-model, which gave them the right to decide each school's admission policy. However, the government carefully limited the admission of black children, not only by stipulating that at least 50 percent of pupils should be white but, most important, by maintaining funding at a level based on the projections for white enrollment.[10] Furthermore, it was closing down scores of white schools with a high number of vacancies and packing to capacity the remaining ones. This ensured that only a few black students would be admitted to each white school. The policy thus did very little for school integration.

But even this change was not deemed sufficient to protect white schools. In late 1991 the government decided to go one step further, de facto privatizing all white schools by transferring ownership of buildings as well as control over policy to a separate board for each school. The government would pay only teachers' salaries, and each school would have to charge tuition to finance other expenditures. To create a single, integrated school system, a future government would be forced to take back these "private" white schools, undoubtedly opening itself to the accusation that it was nationalizing education.

Another example of how the government tried to create new, difficult-to-change situations before a new political system was in place concerned the allocation of land. The enactment of a new constitution in itself was unlikely to affect either the freehold rights of whites or the communal rights of the homeland populations, since none of the constitutional proposals contained clauses affecting land rights. A new constitution, however, would force the elimination of land institutions tied to the apartheid system, and in particular of the South African Development Trust, which still administered about 1 million hectares (2.5 million acres) of land acquired under the 1936 land act and scheduled for incorporation into the homelands.[11] Some of this land had been under the control of the Development Trust for years.

In November 1991 the government suddenly announced that it was transferring land to Bophuthatswana—a surprising move, considering that the land acts had already been abrogated and thus land should no longer have been earmarked for blacks or whites.[12] This, it turned out, was the beginning of a plan to transfer to the homelands all the land held in trust.[13] The reason, a government spokesman explained, was the need to complete one chapter before beginning a new one. But the chapter had been opened in 1936, and the government had not seen fit to close it for more than half a century. Now, however, it appeared intent on removing from the control of the next administration farms that could be used to foster a land reform program, placing them instead under the control of the homeland authorities, who would thus acquire a new source of patronage. Yet again, the government wanted to create new conditions favorable to its goals.

The ANC was not in a position to follow the government's example in quietly implementing reforms before the transition of power could take place. The only way it could create de facto situations that negotiators could not ignore or reverse was to mobilize its supporters for mass action, that is, the stay-aways, boycotts, and demonstrations which had been the hallmark of the United Democratic Front in the 1980s. Vehemently criticized by the government as an undemocratic attempt to impose the ANC's policies on the country, mass action was simply the more visible, and at times more violent, form of creating facts on the ground open to an opposition movement. It undoubtedly was undemocratic, but so was the considerable amount of maneuvering done by the National Party.

Transitional Institutions and Time Frame

Closely linked to the question of what should be negotiated was that of the duration of the transition process. A quick process leading up to a new constitution, whether through CODESA or an elected constituent assembly, would inevitably restrict the scope of the discussion to immediate constitutional issues and greatly reduce the government's ability to introduce reforms unilaterally. But a protracted transition period, lasting for years, would make it necessary to broaden the discussions, and also it would enhance the National Party's ability to impose new policies while its power remained great.

The ANC, like other antiapartheid organizations, favored a very quick transition. It demanded that the decisions of CODESA be given legal force, superseding the power of the Parliament once and for all, and that the Parliament itself be disbanded within a short time and replaced by an elected constituent assembly. Obviously, the Congress was anxious to move the process out of the existing institutions as quickly as possible, since they represented a playing field where the government had all the advantages.

In early 1992, the ANC drew up a timetable providing for the installation by CODESA of an interim government of national reconciliation in mid–1992, with a constituent assembly being elected by the end of the year.[14] It would probably take at least another year before the assembly finished its deliberations and a government was elected under the new charter. Nevertheless, this would be a swift transition, eliminating the necessity for, and limiting the possibility of, introducing policy reforms until a permanent government was formed.

But the National Party favored a much lengthier process. The first signs of this intention arose immediately after the unbanning of the ANC, with an idea floated by Willem de Klerk, the president's brother, suggesting the necessity for a ten-year transition. The idea received little attention. The common assumption at this time was that a new political system had to be in place by early 1995 at the latest, since the constitution required the Parliament to be disbanded every five years, with a few more months allowed for elections to be organized, and the voters had last gone to the polling stations in September 1989.

At CODESA it became clear that the National Party was indeed looking for a way to prolong the transition. The NP had appeared to accept the idea of an interim government at the opening of CO-DESA—although it preferred the term *transitional government*—but it wanted its formation to be preceded by a referendum of all population groups and by an amendment of the existing constitution giving that interim government legal underpinnings.[15] It was highly unlikely that the government would embark on such a complex and probably lengthy process to create a transitional government lasting only a few months. Rumors that the government was thinking of a ten-year transition acquired new credibility.[16]

The rumors were confirmed when the Parliament opened in early 1992. Both NP General Secretary Stoffel van der Merwe and Minister for Constitutional Development Gerrit Viljoen clarified the government's complex plan. CODESA would negotiate a transitional constitution, similar to the one suggested earlier by the National Party. This constitution would be submitted to a referendum where whites would have veto power—the need for this step was probably removed by the March referendum—and then adopted by the existing Parliament. A new transitional Parliament would then be elected and a transitional government formed according to the rules of the transitional constitution. The permanent constitution would eventually be enacted by the transitional Parliament following the procedures in the transitional charter for constitutional amendment. It would thus take a long time before even the transitional government was formed, and in the meantime the National Party would continue to run the country.[17] As to a permanent constitution and government, the National Party refused to commit itself to any deadline. Viljoen indicated that the transitional government should serve an entire term of office, or even two; if the transitional institutions worked satisfactorily, they could stay in place indefinitely. There was indeed very little resemblance between the ANC's interim government and the NP's transitional one.

The length of the transition period was also a crucial issue. The slow change to an elected and long-lasting transitional government would prolong the influence of the National Party. It would allow the NP to govern the country alone for several more years, introducing more reforms and creating facts on the ground before elections were held. Under the power-sharing transitional government, which would last for an indeterminate number of years, the NP would continue to maintain an influence disproportionate to the number of votes it received. This disproportionate power would probably be perpetuated because it would be difficult to amend the transitional constitution.

The swift transition favored by the ANC would have forced the National Party to share power with others within a few months, thus limiting its ability to enact new policies. The ANC's interim government would do little more than administer the country while elections were held, leaving the responsibility for policy reform in the hands of the future elected government. In the long run, the process would thus be formally more democratic, but in the interim period a constitutional vacuum would be created, with power left in the hands of a nonelected interim government of national reconciliation and of CODESA, also a nonelected body. The danger in such a situation was that if the constituent assembly did not reach an agreement quickly, the country would remain indefinitely under the control of a nonelected body that, the NP pointed out, could rule only by decree.

THE CLIMATE SURROUNDING NEGOTIATIONS

The problems CODESA had to address were undoubtedly complex and contentious. They could perhaps have been resolved by parties convinced of each other's good faith, willing to compromise, and open about their goals. But this was not the case. By the time CODESA convened, the goodwill that permeated initial discussions had dissipated and been replaced by acrimony and suspicion.

The initial public contacts between the ANC and the government took place in an atmosphere of almost unreal cordiality. For a few months, South Africans were treated to surprise after surprise as each side discovered, as a participant in the Groote Schuur meeting put it, that "there was nobody in the room who had horns. . . . We had people sitting in that room who are perfectly reasonable and who are committed to finding a solution."[18] On the front page of newspapers, former prisoners and their jailers, cabinet ministers and newly returned exiles, communists and members of the Broederbond shook hands and smiled broadly at each other. Neither side had let down its defenses, to be sure. The security police still kept a close eye on the ANC and the Communist Party, and they in turn maintained their armed wing and their weapon caches. But there was some trust between the leaders. De Klerk, Mandela declared repeatedly, was a man of integrity. De Klerk appeared to reciprocate the feeling.

The goodwill did not last long. It reached its highest point at Groote Schuur, but it declined sharply thereafter, never to be restored. First came the government's discovery that the idea of separating radicals and moderates in the ANC was not working. The ANC had no intention of allowing itself to be split. The main pressure on the leadership, furthermore, did not come from moderate supporters anxious for a quick settlement but from angry younger members, suspicious that the ANC would sell out and reluctant to abandon the dream of the armed struggle. The point that the communists were an integral part of the ANC and thus of the process was made emphatically when the ANC leadership insisted on keeping Joe Slovo on the Groote Schuur delegation despite strong objections from the government.

The change in the atmosphere surrounding the negotiations, however, was not caused principally by the discovery on both sides that the bargaining would be hard, but by the ANC's growing suspicion that the government was not negotiating in good faith. The turning point came with the signing of the Pretoria Minute on August 6, 1990. A working group had been set up earlier to discuss the problem of the release of political prisoners and the granting of indemnity to exiles, and the Pretoria meeting was convened to ratify the work of the group. The result was an agreement that the ANC would suspend the armed struggle and the government would release political prisoners and allow the return of exiles by the end of the year.[19]

The decision to suspend the armed struggle did not go down well with the ANC's rank and file. The grumbling increased when it became clear that the government had no intention of meeting the dead-line and, in fact, argued that it was not a deadline at all but a target date. Not only had the process become bogged down in red tape, but the government defined political prisoners differently from the ANC. The feeling spread that the ANC had walked into a trap.

At the heart of the crisis was the question whether negotiating meant an open process of bargaining among groups that fully understood the implications of what was being discussed or an attempt by one side to convince the other to sign on the dotted line without reading the fine print. Whether the government had deliberately taken advantage of careless ANC negotiators, cheating them into signing, or whether there was simply a misunderstanding, only persons privy to the government discussions know. But there is no doubt that the ANC interpreted the episode as treachery. Added to the growing suspicion that the government was backing Inkatha and fomenting violence in the townships, the disagreement over exiles and political prisoners led to the ANC's April 1991 ultimatum.

Assisted by the Inkathagate scandal, which forced the government to take some of the steps the ANC had demanded, the impasse was eventually overcome. By the end of the year, the negotiating process was seemingly in full swing again, first with the peace talks and finally with CODESA. But the trust was gone, and the ANC's anger—as Mandela's outburst against de Klerk at the opening of CODESA showed—was very close to the surface, finally erupting after the second meeting.

CONCLUSIONS

The failure of CODESA was not an accident brought about by poor negotiating skills of the major parties or a miscalculation about how far one could push the other side. Such an interpretation, fairly prevalent in South Africa right after the collapse of the process, overlooked the fundamental problems undermining the chances of success. The process failed because the two main contenders were convinced they could win. The initial positions each set forth were not opening gambits but demands on which they would not compromise. The assets they controlled pushed them to seek antithetical solutions: the ANC needed a system that recognized the importance of popular support;

the National Party wanted one based on the manipulation of formal institutions. Fundamental disagreement remained on the meaning of negotiations and its legal framework, on what had to be negotiated, and on the transitional institutions and the timetable of the process. The climate surrounding the negotiations was poor, with suspicion and anger growing within the ANC.

The precise unfolding of the events that precipitated the crisis was in the end less important than underlying conditions in explaining the breakdown. The five working groups met dutifully for months, parties presented their submissions, and periodically a working group would announce that a compromise had been reached, only to be forced to retract the statement when the proposed compromise was rejected by the full parties.

The main goal for the period between the first and second plenary CODESA meetings was to reach agreement on the process that would lead to a new political system. Progress was periodically reported. The government had accepted the need for an interim government and an elected constituent assembly, it seemed. The ANC had agreed that an interim government could not rule by decree, but that it should function under rules established by a transitional constitution. As it turned out, very little had changed. The ANC still insisted that the National Party give up power quickly to an interim government and that a constitution be enacted later by an elected constituent assembly. The government remained adamant that no transfer of power should take place until a full-fledged, although supposedly transitional, constitution had been negotiated among the CODESA participants and enacted by the existing Parliament.

The illusion of progress was fostered largely by semantic confusion. For a long time, very few really understood that the ANC's interim government and the National Party's transitional government were totally different entities, or that the government's elected constituent assembly would come into existence only after a constitution had been adopted and thus that this constituent assembly was not the one sought by the ANC. Certainly, the public did not understand the difference, and the press was often confused. But even ANC negotiators sometimes appeared unsure of what the government was proposing and what had been agreed upon.

Beyond all the confusion, the cause of the breakdown was simple enough, as Ken Owen, the editor of the *Sunday Times*, explained succinctly:

> What happened at CODESA II, if one strips away the propaganda, is that the National Party tried to draw the ANC into an interim government which would have ruled, perhaps indefinitely and under an uncertain constitution, while the parties continued to haggle endlessly over the possession of power.
>
> The ANC, foreseeing the danger that "interim" rule might become more or less permanent, tried to introduce a deadlock-breaking mechanism—a two-thirds majority in a referendum, which would have enabled it to override any combination of the National Party, its satrapies and hirelings, and on this point the Nationalists baulked. Deadlock ensued.[20]

The sudden breakdown of the process after an agreement had been reported to be imminent gave rise to speculation that the government had deliberately misled the ANC, which had discovered only at the last moment that it was walking into a trap. What is certain is that ANC negotiators emerged from CODESA II angry and embittered. Although de Klerk and Mandela attempted to convey the impression that the process had suffered only a temporary setback, it soon became clear that the damage was extensive. While the CODESA management committee struggled to find a way to relaunch the talks, the ANC threatened mass action.

The final break was triggered by a violent incident not directly related to CODESA. During the night of June 17, 1992, inmates of the KwaMadala hostel, an Inkatha stronghold in the Vaal triangle, swept through the nearby township of Boipatong, considered ANC territory, leaving thirty-nine people dead, with more dying of their injuries in the following days. Accusing the police of complicity in the massacre, either by directly transporting the hostel inmates or by failing to respond to warnings of an imminent attack, the ANC held the government responsible. On June 23, it announced that it was withdrawing from CODESA and that it would not consider returning unless the government met fourteen conditions, which included not only steps to stop the violence but also the establishment of an interim government and an elected constituent assembly.[21]

The ANC had accused the government of fostering violence before, but this time the situation was different. The accusations were not simply the posturing of politicians. They were backed up by tremendous anger in the townships, directed at the government and the police, but also at whites in general and even at the ANC leadership for negotiating. In a rare display of solidarity, the PAC and AZAPO sided with the ANC. COSATU called for an intensification of mass action. The struggle against apartheid had moved from the negotiating table back to the streets. No longer united at the center of the political spectrum by fear of the radicals on the Right and the Left, the ANC and the government were again looking at each other as the main enemy.

Chapter 9

Beyond Constitutional Negotiations

In late 1992 agreement on a new constitution appeared quite distant, since the Convention for a Democratic South Africa (CODESA) process had ground to a halt, and bilateral talks between the government and the ANC were just resuming. Whether negotiating the new, permanent constitution of South Africa took two years or ten, however, the transition from apartheid would not be over when the new charter was adopted and a government put in place according to its rules. A long interim period might allow more issues to be tackled before the new system was enacted, but it could not settle the ultimate problem, that of making the new institutions viable. The transition could be considered complete only when it was reasonably certain that most political organizations were willing to work within the limits established by the new institutional setup. For this reason, even a very long interim period would not ensure a successful transition. The new institutions would in the end still have to prove their viability.

There was no guarantee that this second aspect of the transition, the change that went beyond constitutional negotiations, would succeed. The second phase was in fact the most uncertain one. A new constitution would sooner or later be enacted. But it might never harness political activity unless groups that remained outside the constitution-making process were pulled back into it, the major political movements became democratic political parties, and urgent socioeconomic grievances received enough attention to convince the population that the new South Africa had something to offer to everyone, not just to the politicians sitting in the Parliament or in the cabinet.

INTEGRATING GROUPS EXCLUDED
FROM NEGOTIATIONS

No matter how the constitution was eventually negotiated, many groups were bound either to be excluded or to exclude themselves from the process. CODESA gave representation only to political parties, not to other political groupings, although many were important components of both the government and the liberation establishment. Furthermore, many small political parties had not been invited to the opening meeting, and while a substantial number had applied later, most applications were likely to be dismissed on the ground that the applicants could not prove sufficient support. Before the crisis, there was a possibility that CODESA might be broadened to include traditional leaders, in an attempt to pacify Buthelezi and the Zulu king without accepting their contention that the Zulus had a unique place in South Africa or angering other kings and paramount chiefs. But after June 1992, CODESA might never meet again.

Although it was unlikely that negotiations would ever be strictly bilateral, involving only the government and the African National Congress (ANC), or even trilateral, bringing in Inkatha as well, participation would probably be restricted. Even an elected constituent assembly would be fairly exclusive. No matter how many parties qualified to compete in the elections, only a small number was likely to obtain enough seats to influence the proceedings. Finally, some political parties recognized as having "proven support," namely, the Conservative Party (CP), the Pan Africanist Congress of Azania (PAC), and the Azanian People's Organization (AZAPO), had not participated in CODESA and might not join whatever new process was eventually devised.

The organizations that had remained outside CODESA and would probably be excluded from the next phase of national level negotiations fell into several categories. On the Right were the small right-wing extremist groups, dangerous as potentially terrorist organizations, and, more important, the organizations that had opted to play the card of ethnic nationalism, including the Conservative Party, Inkatha, and some homeland governments. On the Left were the PAC and AZAPO, and also the organizations of the mass democratic movement, which were indirectly represented by the ANC, but might come to feel that the decisions taken by the political parties did not reflect their demands. However, the main threat to any settlement negotiated by the ANC and the government probably came from the nationalist organizations, which would also be the most difficult to bring into the process.

The organizations left out of the constitution-making process were unlikely to respect the new system in the future, since they would have no stake in it. Furthermore, many of these groups did not appear to have much support, particularly nationwide, and would have little to gain by participating in an election. They could make themselves heard more easily by direct action than by legal means.

Right-Wing Groups

The right-wing extremist organizations were probably quite small in terms of their numerical support, but could become significant as disruptive forces both during and after the constitutional negotiations. Except for the Afrikaner Weerstandsbeweging (AWB), a well-known organization with a high degree of visibility and substantial support, the right wing was a web of small groups with changing boundaries and somewhat overlapping memberships, endlessly splintering and coming together in new formations.[1] New groups were constantly making an appearance never to be seen again, most probably having turned into another organization.

Strong on khaki uniforms, rhetoric about the *volk*, and nostalgia about the Boer commandos that gave the British so much trouble during the Anglo-Boer war, these groups touched an emotional chord in a large number of Afrikaners. Whether they could also convince many to take an active stand against the political change inexorably becoming a reality was an open question. There was a real dissonance between the imagery and rhetoric of the white extremists and the life experience of their potential supporters. Forty years of National Party (NP) rule had made the Afrikaners into a nation not of self-reliant and rugged farmers but predominantly of government employees. The livelihood of most depended on government jobs, subsidized housing schemes, and pensions. Even the farmers were heavily dependent on government price support programs and low interest rates on farm loans.

Nevertheless, these groups did occasionally go into action, usually by planting bombs against soft targets at night, when they would

cause no casualties. The use of commercial explosives was the hallmark of the white right wing, suggesting that the organizations recruited heavily among miners.

The first wave of sabotage by these groups took place in 1990. The
government easily tracked down the perpetrators, and after a series
of arrests the violence died down. But it resumed in late 1991 amid
predictions that this time the government would find it more difficult
to stop it, because the right wingers were more disillusioned about
de Klerk's policies, more determined, and better organized in small
cells that would prove difficult to dismantle. Whether or not these
groups had changed their organizational structure, their tactics appeared unchanged. The acts of sabotage were still largely a sign of
protest rather than a means to an end. Favorite targets in late 1991
were post offices and private or public white schools that had opened
their doors to black students.

The March 1992 referendum was a defeat for the radical right wing
as well as for the Conservative Party. The AWB in particular had
openly campaigned against the continuation of negotiations, participating widely in rallies and meetings alongside the CP. Yet it was
impossible to reach the conclusion that the right wing was a completely spent force, because it still probably had the capacity to cause
disruption.

The absence of clear goals made the white extremists more dangerous in the short and medium run than in the long term. They
could not forge a movement strong enough to prevent the demise of
white rule, but a small number of determined individuals could cause
considerable damage through acts of terrorism while trying to do so.
If the bombs that exploded at night had been timed to go off during
working hours, the attacks would have acquired a very different importance.

The major question about these groups was whether they had substantial active support within the police and defense forces. There
was no indication at the time of this writing that this was the case.
De Klerk had been able to slowly remove the securocrats of P. W.
Botha from the centers of power, and to replace them with men
whose careers were steeped in politics rather than in the security apparatus. Even the removal of Defence Minister Magnus Malan and
Minister of Law and Order Adriaan Vlok under pressure from the
ANC, thus under conditions that in the rhetoric of the right wing

could be defined as surrender, had not led to a visible reaction on the part of the security forces. Whatever the personal inclinations of individual members, professionalism and discipline still appeared to prevail over political sympathies, and as long as that was true the right wing would remain a potentially destructive force, but not one to stop the transition from apartheid.

Much more threatening to the implementation of an agreement reached between the ANC and the National Party was the spread of ethnic nationalism among all population groups, a phenomenon that was growing rapidly and could no longer be ignored. Support for apartheid was a lost cause, but ethnic nationalism was on the rise. If the white right wing succeeded in becoming part of this wave, it might yet have a future.

Raising the issue of ethnicity in the South African context was a particularly delicate problem. Since the apartheid regime imposed race and ethnicity as the organizing principles for the entire society, the antiapartheid camp reacted by refusing to acknowledge that ethnicity might be a reality affecting social organization and political process in all countries, even in the absence of a government plot. The ANC stood for a nonracial society, and there, as far as it was concerned, the case rested. By late 1991 it had become obvious that the situation was not so simple. While the National Party, realizing that it could never reach an agreement with the ANC otherwise, had dropped its demand that ethnic groups be given an officially recognized role in the new constitution, the demand was being picked up increasingly in other quarters, including some very unexpected ones.

There was no reliable information about the strength of ethnic identification in the daily life of ordinary South African citizens. Survey data were scant and, in the opinion of this writer, highly questionable.[2] Ethnic identity plays a role in all societies, and there is no reason to believe that South Africans were a complete exception. On the other hand, the revolt against apartheid had given rise to a streak of militant "a-ethnicity" on the part of many young South Africans, intermarriage was frequent, and the language of education in many townships depended more on what the local schools offered than on the determination of parents to get their children taught in a specific language. Furthermore, the creation of the homelands probably had a deterrent effect on the development of strong ethnic feelings. It was the government that tried to tag people with a specific ethnic label, "repatriating" them to the appropriate homeland or incorporating their land into it. People were not given a choice, and consequently they resisted.

On the other side of the coin, there were many people whose careers and livelihood depended on the homeland policy, thus on ethnic identification, and many political organizations that existed only because of it. Homeland leaders owed their political careers to the policy. They enjoyed good salaries and all the perquisites of power. Homeland civil servants at all levels drew salaries and pensions, and they worried about being made redundant in the new South Africa, particularly since alternative employment opportunities were virtually nonexistent. For all these people, the change to a united South Africa was threatening. A unitary state was the most menacing scenario, but even a federation would not allay all fears, because the major parties agreed the homelands would become part of broader regions rather than maintain their identity.

The question was whether those who would lose the most from the elimination of the homelands would find a responsive chord when they tried to stir up nationalist feelings. Such a development could not be ruled out. It is true that the National Party had tried for forty years to stimulate ethnic nationalism and that it had failed. But what it had offered under that guise was a blatantly second-class deal. Apartheid had given ethnicity a bad name, but its resurgence in different circumstances remained a possibility.

The organization that pushed ethnic nationalism most unabashedly in the early part of the transition period was the Conservative Party. It had refused to participate in CODESA, at least until the other parties recognized the right of the Afrikaners to self-determination. Unlike apartheid—an ideology discredited abroad and appealing only to whites inside the country—self-determination was a respectable ideal, which enjoyed a renewed popularity because of events in Eastern Europe.

What self-determination meant for the Afrikaners was rather obscure. A *volkstaat*, an Afrikaner homeland, was a dream that might never come true, because the *volk* had no territorial base. There was no way to remove all other occupants from the old Boer republics, and the Afrikaners were not rushing to resettle in Orania or any other remote area to develop their state there. Under the circumstances, the logic of self-determination risked leading to something looking suspiciously like the old apartheid, an attempt to keep apart by political fiat peoples that history had condemned to share the same space. Still, self-determination sounded a lot better than apartheid, and it appealed to other groups.

It also offered the Conservative Party a possible means to establish itself as an important actor in the transition. As a rejectionist party, it had no effect—negotiations were simply going ahead without it. If it joined the process, it faced the same problem as the National Party: its support would be negligible as a percentage of the total vote. But if it formed an alliance with black organizations with a vested interest in self-determination, its prospects might be better. And on the issue of self-determination, the CP was willing to cooperate across the color line, since it meant helping blacks go their own separate way—the party's goal.

Potential allies were multiplying. By the end of 1991 three other groups were also playing the self-determination card: Inkatha, the leadership of Bophuthatswana, and the leadership of the Ciskei. The last one could probably be dismissed as a meaningful ally, because the homeland was very small and Brigadier Oupa Gqozo's hold on power was tenuous. But Inkatha and the Bophuthatswana government had to be taken more seriously. The Conservative Party held talks with all of them.

After Inkathagate, Buthelezi had renounced the attempt to make Inkatha a nationwide movement, falling back instead on Zulu nationalism. The new emphasis had culminated in the decision to ask for separate representation for the king and the KwaZulu government at CODESA, so that the Zulus could participate as a group. Buthelezi had lost the first battle, but he had not given up. In the weeks following the first conference he continued his efforts to win a place for the king, even receiving an endorsement for his position from de Klerk. The Zulus, declared the state president, occupied a special place in South African history and should be represented.[3] It was a dangerous statement. Afrikaners also claimed to occupy a special place in South African history, and any group could elect to do the same. Indeed, if Zulus were represented, all other groups would have to be given the same right. But Buthelezi also met with Conservative Party leaders, who were only too happy to find a black organization sharing their contention that different ethnic groups had the right to special recognition and a special place in the country.

The president of Bophuthatswana, Lucas Mangope, was moving

in the same direction. He had also decided to resist reincorporation unless he could obtain special status for his homeland in the new South Africa. "The history of the Batswana nation," he told the CO-DESA delegates on December 20, "goes back to the eleventh century when we inhabited the greatest portion of the country north of the Orange River and southwest of the Zambesi. . . . It is thus not fair or prudent in terms of our history, our tested principles and values, and our economic performances [sic], to be regarded as just another so-called self governing territory, TBVC [Transkei, Bophuthatswana, Venda, Ciskei] state or product of apartheid. . . . This nation refuses to be ignored or belittled in any way whatsoever."[4] Accordingly, Mangope did not sign the CODESA declaration of intent, because it called for the reincorporation of the homelands.

Mangope did not represent the Batswana nation, nor did Buthelezi represent all Zulus or Treurnicht the white tribe of Africa. But until elections were held, the question of popular support for their positions was less important than their resolve to put on the agenda the issue of self-determination for specific ethnic groups. While the NP during 1990 and 1991 had ostensibly given up the idea that ethnic groups should be represented in the new political system, the demand was being reintroduced by the Conservative Party, Inkatha, and the Bophuthatswana government.

There were signs that the trend was spreading in some unexpected directions. The Transkei leader, Major General Bantu Holomisa, appeared ready to jump on the bandwagon—yet he was considered an ANC supporter, particularly close to Chris Hani and Umkhonto we Sizwe, and he was on record as favoring reintegration of the homelands. Addressing a delegation from CODESA on January 16, 1992, he argued that the Transkei should never be divided among different regions in the future South Africa, and he even set forth a vision of a greater Transkei, extending from "the Umzinkulu River in the east to the Great Fish River in the west." This meant incorporating the Ciskei, a substantial amount of land that was part of white South Africa, and a few fragments of KwaZulu. "Our common historical, cultural and linguistic experience militates against the dismemberment of Transkei as we know it," he argued.[5]

Holomisa's speech illustrated not only the spread of ethnic nationalism but also the expansionism, and thus the conflicts, that would inevitably accompany a nationalist groundswell in the fragmented homelands. Leaders making a strong appeal for the right of their nations to self-determination would certainly not settle for the meager and fragmented pieces of land the apartheid regime had seen fit to give them in the past. They would not recognize the 87 percent of the land occupied by whites as a white homeland. The logic of ethnic nationalism in South Africa led to a scramble for the white land, and for one another's territory, by the homelands.

Left-Wing Organizations

The organizations to the left of the ANC were probably a much more limited threat to the implementation of an agreement. In the short run, at least, they appeared to have lost their way and to have become completely ineffectual. But they were convinced their time was yet to come.

Radical sentiments existed even within the ANC, and particularly among its younger followers. Chris Hani was immensely popular and could rouse a crowd to frenzied *toyi-toying*[6] with the rhetoric of the armed struggle in a way his more sedate colleagues in the National Executive Committee could not. But in the end, the members also accepted negotiations. Chris Hani and Thabo Mbeki, the prototypes of the radical and the moderate in the ANC, tied for first place as vote getters at the ANC national conference in 1991. The number of votes they received, furthermore, showed that most delegates must have cast their ballots for both.

The rhetoric of the ANC Youth League was at times closer to that of the PAC and AZAPO than to the language of the parent organization, suggesting that the youth were open to more radical ideas. However, the Africanist organizations seemed unable to exploit the potential support, while the fringe Trotskyite groups such as the Workers Organization for Socialist Action and the New Unity Movement were practically small clubs of intellectuals. They issued carefully worded and tightly reasoned explanations for why they would not join any forum, but they had no discernible impact on events whether they joined or remained outside.[7]

The weakness of the Africanist organizations was particularly striking, given the crucial importance of the black consciousness movement during the 1970s. A large problem seemed to be the lack of organizational and financial resources to capture the potential supporters. The battle between black consciousness and charterist groups for influence in the black community had been settled since the early 1980s in favor of the charterists. The unwillingness of the Africanists to agree formally to suspend the armed struggle—which was non-existent, anyway—made them ineligible for financial aid from many foreign sources. The PAC's slogan, "one settler, one bullet," with its connotation of race war the leaders never successfully explained away, did not help obtain foreign support, either.

Like all political organizations without much hope of success, the leftist groups tended to choose ideological purity over pragmatism. They were also prone to internal fragmentation and divisions. The PAC in particular could never reach a decision and abide by it, because some group within the organization would denounce it as soon as it had been reached.

Ineffectual in the early part of the transition period, the radical black organizations hoped to become more important in the future. The failure of CODESA gave them a new opportunity, since it vindicated their contention that the negotiating process had been deeply flawed. Even if negotiations eventually succeeded, the ANC could lose its ascendancy at a later stage. It would certainly be part of the next government, and that government was bound to fail to meet expectations when it tried to tackle the country's problems. If it shared power with the NP, it could be criticized for allowing itself to be co-opted; if it formed the cabinet alone, it would be blamed for not doing enough. Such discontent could benefit more radical organizations, but it was far from certain that the Africanists would ever sort out their organizational problems sufficiently to take advantage of future opportunities.

Among the organizations that hoped to benefit from the ANC's future blunders was the South African Communist Party (SACP). Indeed, it was the assumption that the ANC would fail that gave the SACP its raison d'être as a separate organization. In the short run, argued the party, the ANC as a nationalist movement was at the forefront of the struggle and therefore it should be helped. But once in power, as a nationalist organization the ANC would not have a program clear enough, or a working-class base strong enough, to succeed. It was likely to enter into deals with "monopoly capital," and it would not defend the workers' cause as vigorously as it should. The day of the Communist Party would then come.

The Mass Democratic Movement

Trade unions and civic associations posed a different kind of challenge. The issue was not whether they would participate in the constitution-making process—directly or indirectly, they were bound to be part of it because of their close links to the ANC. Rather, the question was whether in the long run they would limit their aspirations to what was admissible under the new charter. The right to form unions and to strike would certainly be recognized in the new system, but it was much less likely that the unions would have an official role in the formulation of economic policy. The ANC itself had emphatically rejected corporatist solutions in its constitutional proposal. If the workerist trend prevailed in the unions, this would pose no problem. Populist aspirations, however, might lead the labor unions to continue a policy of mass action even under a new government. In 1992 the goals of the Congress of South African Trade Unions (COSATU) remained quite far reaching, as shown by its demand for an economic forum in which unions would be involved with government and business in the formulation of economic policy.[8]

Similarly, the new constitution would certainly make it possible for the civic associations to act as lobbies vis-à-vis elected local governments or even the national one, since all parties recognized freedom of association and speech. But at least some elements saw the organizations of civil society as much more than lobbies trying to sway local government actions.

How such aspirations could be accommodated under a new system remained an open, important question. Unions and civics had the ability to disrupt the normal process of government. They had used it successfully against the apartheid regime and could try to use it against the next government, if dissatisfied with its policies. The breakdown of CODESA, furthermore, appeared to be increasing the importance of COSATU and the civics in the transition period. The decision to resort to mass action as a means of putting pressure on the government made the ANC very dependent on the organizations of civil society, which had a much better network at the grass roots. The renewed militancy made it unlikely that these organizations would still be willing to allow the ANC to do all the talking for the liberation establishment once negotiations resumed.

CONVERTING POLITICAL ORGANIZATIONS INTO PARTIES

A complete list of the political organizations operating in South Africa in 1991 would be surprisingly long. Eighteen parties (plus the government delegation) had attended the first meeting of CODESA. Three others had been invited but declined to attend. A few weeks later, the convention's management committee announced it was considering "about twenty" new applications for membership from organizations it declined to name.[9] Admittedly, not all of these were political parties as such—traditional leaders and various interest groups were also seeking membership. Nevertheless, the number of self-described parties remained large, but few of them could be considered such in a democratic political system.

Except for the NP, the parties in the tricameral Parliament probably fit the definition, being independent organizations, not financed by the government, and competing for votes in a relatively open though racially segmented political arena. But the National Party itself did not, because forty years of uninterrupted and virtually unchallenged rule had blurred the distinction between party and state. The NP resembled an African single party more than anything found in a Western democracy. When President de Klerk, opening the Transvaal congress of the National Party in November 1991, assured the audience that the government would never allow the ANC to take over, he provided a perfect example of the extent to which the government and the NP had become one and how oblivious the party was to the undemocratic implications of this identification—imagine an American president reassuring his party's national convention that the government would never allow the rival party to win an election.[10]

The organizations unbanned in 1990 and the homeland movements were also far from meeting the definition of democratic political parties. The latter were emanations of the homeland administrations, invariably led by the chief minister and usually operating as a single party in the respective homeland. The line between party and administration was blurred at best, not because the party controlled the state, as did the National Party, but because the state—or the homeland administration—had simply set up the party. But except for Inkatha, these organizations were not important, and their undemocratic character was unlikely to affect the future political system significantly. The character of Inkatha and the unbanned parties, the ANC in particular, was a different matter.

The ANC was a liberation movement in the midst of a very imperfect transition to a political party. As a liberation movement, it saw itself as the representative of all South Africans, a coalition of people embracing different ideologies and goals but united by the common struggle against apartheid. Since apartheid was evil, the ANC as a liberation movement had to win. Defeat was not conceivable: a political party in a democratic system must be ready to accept defeat and try again, but a liberation movement must never surrender. Operating in a political milieu that deprived the majority of the citizens of political rights, the ANC also considered it not only legitimate but imperative to turn to extralegal means to bring about change, and above all to resort to armed struggle and mass action. In August 1990 the Congress had agreed to suspend the armed struggle, but it continued to emphasize mass action.

None of this was surprising. The ANC could not have been a political party, since it was not allowed to act as one—even after the unbanning, an overwhelming majority of its potential constituents were not enfranchised. The threat to democracy, however, remained. The nature of liberation movements makes a transition to single-party systems easier than the acceptance of democratic competition, as the experiences of other African countries suggest. The change the ANC would have to undergo to become a political party was substantial.

The transformation was also risky. Becoming a political party, as the government argued, meant abandoning the armed struggle once and for all and disbanding Umkhonto we Sizwe, surrendering any arms cache it might still have in the country, breaking up the defense squads that had been set up in violence-ridden townships, giving up all mass action, and probably no longer receiving foreign financing. From the ANC's point of view, taking such steps before political rights were extended to the entire population meant giving up all the means at its disposal to put pressure on the National Party. But the government thought otherwise. There was no longer any need for the ANC to persist in its liberation movement tactics, including trying to set up a patriotic front, argued Minister for Constitutional Development Gerrit Viljoen, because "the apartheid system has been rejected by the government of the day and has already been scrapped entirely in terms of its legislation by the current government, except for the constitution which still has to be replaced."[11]

The ANC's unwillingness to comply with the government's demand that it become a political party rather than a liberation movement was understandable. So was the NP's reluctance to make a clean break between party and government—no organization gives up power voluntarily. The real problem was not the present but the future. The ANC and the NP would confront each other as nondemocratic organizations until election day, when they would have to change suddenly their nature and approach. That would be the most dangerous time.

The transformation of Inkatha from the single party of KwaZulu into a democratic nationwide party presented a different and even greater problem, because it appeared increasingly likely that the IFP would fare poorly in an election. The ANC had a broad, nationwide constituency, although it was worried about its failure to attract substantial numbers of whites, Coloureds, and Indians. Even the NP had made some progress in capturing support among Coloureds—the Indian community kept such a low profile that it was impossible to judge what was happening there—and it was striving to appeal to more conservative Africans as well. But the Inkatha Freedom Party had not succeeded in widening its base of support, as even some of its top officials conceded.[12] By late 1991, badly affected by the revelations that it had received funds from the government and having failed to establish itself as a multiethnic organization, Inkatha had little incentive to turn into a democratic political party. Zulu nationalism was a better card.

TACKLING NONINSTITUTIONAL ISSUES

The transition in South Africa was taking place when issues of justice and equity were receiving very low priority around the world. The name of the game in the decolonization decade of the 1960s had been control of the political kingdom, theoretically making it possible to redress past inequities and promote socioeconomic development. In the 1990s there was a growing consensus that it was the economic kingdom that counted most, not as something to be conquered by politicians but as something to be left to follow its own rules and logic, free of political interference. Politicians should concentrate on democracy and a minimalist, efficient government; the free market would do the rest.

Whatever the merits of such an approach in theory, it was unrealistic to think that the new South Africa could avoid directly tackling some of the most urgent socioeconomic issues. The government could invoke the authority of the World Bank and the International Monetary Fund, recall the lessons from Eastern Europe, and point to the catastrophic conditions of most African economies. The hard reality was that the transition from apartheid represented a period of heightened expectations; that most blacks saw their economic plight to be the direct result of government policy; that the contrast between the standard of living of whites and that of blacks was enormous; and that urban unemployment rates were probably about 40 percent. But it was not these conditions alone that suggested a future government would be forced to address socioeconomic grievances directly. More important, the population was highly politicized and mobilized, and it had learned to use economic weapons in the political struggle. Under these conditions, a purely political transition that ignored economic and social issues was extremely unlikely.

Socioeconomic issues were not a major factor in the constitutional negotiations. They were, however, all too likely to affect the implementation of any political accord and make the prospects for democracy dim no matter what was decided on paper. Unfortunately, neither side's initial position offered much reason for optimism. The attempt by the government and the business community to defend the status quo was unrealistic and shortsighted. The ANC's resort to the magic formula of nationalization appeared equally meaningless. Both were recipes for disaster.

The realities that had to be faced in the transition process were complex and contradictory. Blacks' resentment of white wealth and their own poverty was real, but so were the facts that there were simply not enough black managers and technicians to run the South African economy—apartheid had seen to that—and that many whites, particularly the trained professionals the country needed, would leave if their life-style was threatened. The need to create employment and also to make land available so blacks would not all flock to the cities was indisputable. It was equally indisputable that foreign capital would not be attracted to a country providing no security and profits, and that domestic capital would find its way abroad, no matter what the law said.

Other issues over which conflict was inevitable and threatening to the transition process were the symbolic ones, which touched directly on everyone's sense of identity. In no country has a marked political shift not been accompanied by a change of flags, a new national anthem, the rewriting of history textbooks, the celebration of new national holidays, or the renaming of towns and streets—in other words, by the replacement of the old myths and symbols by new ones. In South Africa, conflict over these issues could be particularly acute because Afrikaner nationalism made such heavy use of symbols and myths.

A foretaste of conflicts to come was offered in November 1991 when a cricket team was invited to play in India, marking South Africa's return to international cricket after a hiatus of more than twenty years. Days later, it was announced that South Africa would also be allowed to participate in the Olympic Games in Barcelona in 1992. The jubilation of whites was quickly replaced by outrage when they discovered that the National Olympic Committee of South Africa (NOCSA) had decided that in Barcelona the members of the national team would not compete under South Africa's flag and national anthem, nor wear the colors and springbok emblem of their predecessors' uniforms. Instead, they would wear colors carefully chosen to eliminate the symbols of any political organization, and the country's anthem and flag would be replaced with those of the Olympic games.

From President F. W. de Klerk to cabinet ministers, white callers on radio talk shows, and newspaper editorial writers, whites were unanimous in their condemnation of the decision, even though it was utterly predictable as well as unavoidable.[13] NOCSA chairman Sam Ramsamy instantly became the object of a hatred whites once reserved for the SACP general secretary, Joe Slovo, or Umkhonto we Sizwe's chief of staff, Chris Hani. The challenge to the old symbols of the national sports teams apparently brought home more clearly than the unbanning of the ANC and the abrogation of the apartheid laws that much was destined to change in the new South Africa.

The years following the formal transition of power to a new government were likely to be very difficult ones for the country. They would undoubtedly be marked by constant discoveries on the part of whites of yet other aspects of life where things could not remain the same, and on the part of blacks of yet other areas where the end of apartheid made little difference. Against the background of an extremely politicized, organized, and violent society, these issues would remain dangerous for many years to come, holding out the possibility of violence, economic disaster, white flight, and long-term instability.

CONCLUSIONS

Constitutional negotiations were just one aspect of the transition process, yet they dominated the political agenda. This focus on formal institutions was to some extent inevitable. Apartheid permeated all governmental institutions, and thus could not be eliminated by the repeal of some laws and the enactment of others but only by the restructuring of the entire system of government. South Africa was not the United States, where the constitution could work equally well whether formal race discrimination was accepted or outlawed. The tricameral constitution could never remain in the new South Africa any more than the web of local councils, management committees, Regional Services Councils, and provincial authorities that characterized the third tier of government.

But the focus on institutional issues went beyond this simple reality. It also reflected the National Party's long-standing faith in constitutional and social engineering. No matter what the demographic realities of the country, institutions could be devised to protect whites. Forty years of constitutional engineering under apartheid had failed to bring about the desired results, but they had not destroyed the conviction shared by the National Party and many white intellectuals that a formula could be found to put an end to black opposition without leading to black power.

While the National Party had not lost faith in the possibility of constitutional engineering, as its convoluted proposal showed, it had come to the conclusion that formal group representation could no longer remain the principle on which the country's political institutions were based. Paradoxically, just as the National Party dropped the demand for group representation, other organizations picked it up. Among them were the Conservative Party and a growing number of homeland officials. Only a short while earlier, the outburst of ethnic nationalism would have played into the hands of the National Party, strengthening its contention that groups had to be recognized in the South African political system. By late 1991, however, the National Party had possibly already moved too far down the road of reform to take advantage of the new mood in the country. The ethnic nationalism the National Party had deliberately tried to foster was finally coming into its own, but it could well lead to an alliance against the National Party.

Ranging from ethnic nationalism to the populism of the labor movement and the militancy of the civics, political mobilization in the society was too high for a new charter to be hammered out by a commission free to pick and choose among models existing elsewhere or to propose new ones. The fifteen-hundred-page report on constitutions published by the South African Law Commission in October 1991 would have less impact on the future of South Africa than the balance of power among the numerous political organizations, both inside and outside the negotiating process. Indeed, too much clever manipulation in the writing of the constitution could well amount to a Pyrrhic victory if the main political organizations did not believe their interests were protected under the new charter. But it was not a foregone conclusion that any agreement reached would be able to satisfy the disparate mobilized constituencies that had joined the negotiations as well as those remaining outside.

No constitutional model in itself would lead to a successful transition to democracy in South Africa. The model proposed by the ANC was good in theory, but it might turn out to be much less so in practice. Majority rule, the government's rhetoric notwithstanding, is a key component of a democratic system. Nevertheless, the exclusion of the National Party from a future government would be a hollow victory, no matter how constitutional it might be. The ANC would not be able to run the country against the establishment that had consolidated its power over the course of the National Party's rule. The security forces and the bureaucracy, in particular, had the ability to disrupt any effort at reform by the ANC, if they so decided.

But power-sharing was no solution either. In the long run, power-sharing is always undemocratic, making it impossible to vote a government out of power and to bring in a new one—the basic requirement for accountable government. But the power-sharing proposed by the National Party was a problem even in the short run, probably making it impossible to carry out any of the reforms the country needed. Neither of the two major models under discussion offered much promise that the political system emerging from a settlement would be successful.

Chapter 10

Liberation and Reformism

"CODESA," declared Frederik van Zyl Slabbert, former head of the Progressive Federal Party and one of the country's foremost liberal pundits, "could be the start of a beginning."[1] The failure of the second Convention for a Democratic South Africa confirmed how uncertain the start was and how far the end. The elimination of apartheid would not be swift or painless. It would be long and contentious, probably accompanied by increasing violence, hatred, and economic decline. And at the end of the day, there might not be the democratic, nonracial South Africa foreseen by the CODESA declaration of intent. The chances that the end of apartheid would mean a transition to democracy appeared more remote in late 1992 than they had been in February 1990. In the climate of suspicion and violence that had developed, neither the government's power-sharing formula nor the African National Congress's (ANC's) demand for majority rule was likely to lead to democracy.

If the government had its way, there would not be a clear break between the old regime and the new. The National Party (NP) aimed at remaining part of the ruling establishment and at blocking reforms threatening to whites' economic standing and way of life. The only steps it had taken to eliminate apartheid were those dictated by other countries, and particularly by the United States through the Comprehensive Anti-Apartheid Act. Once the conditions established by that act had been met and sanctions mostly lifted, the government had focused its attention not on dismantling other aspects of apartheid but on consolidating the position of whites before a new government came into existence. From the de facto privatization of white schools to the formation of the white-dominated, "nonracial" Kimberley Council, the National Party was pushing forward a vision of a postapartheid

South Africa where whites would retain their special and privileged world apart from the rest of the society. It was not a democratic vision.

If the ANC triumphed, there would be change, but probably there would be no democracy either, particularly if the Congress won a large enough majority to form the government alone. The constitutional model advocated by the Congress was not flawed in itself, but it would be implemented under unfavorable circumstances. Problems within the organization and, most important, ·the probable reaction of other groups limited the likelihood of a democratic transition. Despite the statements of its leaders, the ANC in the townships was not a democratic organization. It tried to control entire settlements, and it repressed supporters of Inkatha and often of the Africanist organizations. Certainly, the ANC was not the only organization to blame for this state of affairs. It could hardly be expected to be democratically tolerant of an Inkatha intent on taking over hostels and, increasingly, township areas adjacent to them. But no matter how the fault was apportioned, the situation strengthened the nondemocratic side of the ANC.

The most important obstacle to a democratic outcome under majority rule, however, was not the character of the organization itself but the goals of its enemies. Inkatha had made it abundantly clear it would not accept a political system that did not recognize KwaZulu as a special entity. Buthelezi predicted violence if such a system came into existence, and his prediction had to be taken seriously. Violence would result not from a spontaneous uprising of seven million Zulus defending their national honor, as Buthelezi implied, but from a decision made by a political organization fighting for survival. The record of Inkatha suggested that the threat was not an empty one. Nor was Inkatha the only organization that might reject the verdict of the ballot box. The question of how security forces and white extremists would react remained open.

The chances for a democratic outcome were further dimmed by the fact that the new South Africa was beginning to show some of the most unpleasant characteristics of the old. The state of emergency had long been lifted, but the "hippos," the bulky, yellow-painted armored personnel carriers used by the police in unrest areas, continued to roam the embattled townships. Charred bodies of "necklace" victims were being discovered with increasing frequency. The Boipatong massacre was unique because of its scale, but the fighting

between hostel inmates and township residents was a chronic problem throughout the Witwatersrand. Passengers on commuter trains
to Johannesburg climbed aboard every morning and evening without
knowing whether they would be the next victims of the gruesome
and seemingly pointless attacks that the police declared themselves
unable to stop. Violence in Natal continued unabated.

The beginning of the transition had unleashed a series of secondary
conflicts in the country, as organizations struggled to assert their
positions in the new South Africa. Black-on-black violence stemmed
from these conflicts. The stalling of the negotiating process reopened
the black-on-white conflict in all its bitterness, but without putting
an end to the black-on-black fighting. Violence was unlikely to abate
in the absence of a political solution, but the possibility of such a
solution was made more remote by the violence. South Africa was
caught in a vicious circle.

Relaunching the negotiations was thus the most important step,
not only to reach an eventual political settlement but also to curb the
violence in the short run. Resuming negotiations, however, was not
simply a question of going back to CODESA as if nothing had happened, as the government implied. There was too much anger in the
townships for the ANC leadership to risk such a move, even if it had
been inclined to do so. Nor was it simply a question of the government
meeting the conditions the ANC had set forth on June 23, which
included the establishment of an interim government and a democratically elected constituent assembly. Had the government given in
to those demands, there would no longer be a need for CODESA.
The major parties needed to talk to one another more than ever, but
the modalities of the talks as well as their purpose needed to be
redefined.

Mandela and de Klerk, and other representatives of their organizations, started meeting again in late 1992. But they were doing so
tentatively, outside a formal negotiating framework accepted by all
major parties. The process remained extremely uncertain.

THE SECOND PHASE

In the first phase of the transition, the conflict had revealed itself in
all its complexity, and so had the conflict resolution process. Nego-

tiators had been faced with a series of dilemmas, but rather than solving them they had remained attached to their initial positions. Unless these dilemmas were faced in the second phase, negotiations would fail again.

From a secret dialogue between government officials and the imprisoned Mandela, negotiations in the first phase had broadened to include all political organizations. Even those that had chosen to remain on the sidelines had some influence, since they could threaten the implementation of an agreement. The cumbersome CODESA process was an acknowledgment that the transition could not simply be negotiated among a small number of people. The idea of a quick deal among ANC and National Party leaders—rumored to have been considered initially by both sides—was not realistic, given the level of political mobilization in the country. Mandela discovered very soon that he was not a free agent but part of an organization that would not even allow him to meet with Buthelezi, let alone conclude a power-sharing deal with the National Party.

A pact between ANC and NP leaders alone could not provide a solution, but neither was it realistic to expect that an agreement could emerge from a body as inclusive as CODESA on the basis of consensus among all political groups. Within weeks of its launching, the convention had already shown it could easily become trapped in a bureaucratic swamp. Faced with thorny problems—for example, Buthelezi's demand that the Zulu king participate—the working committees generated subcommittees, enlarged their membership, and modified their terms of reference, all in the vain hope that a different process would somehow remove the need to make painful decisions on controversial issues. Such an approach was unlikely to yield results, and certainly not speedy results. Even before the withdrawal of the ANC, the failure of CODESA II had led to a rethinking of the negotiating mechanisms, with the management committee trying to discover a way to strike a more realistic balance between broad consensus and concrete results.

Finding a solution in the end depended on an agreement between the original participants, the National Party and the ANC, yet the very possibility of such an agreement created resentment among other would-be major players—Buthelezi foremost—who accused the two of conniving to impose a solution on everyone else. Nothing would happen until the ANC and the National Party reached a compromise, but their solution would require the concurrence of at least those groups capable of undermining the agreement's implementation.

Whatever form the negotiations would ultimately take, the dilemma remained. A narrow agreement would not be accepted, and broad consensus might never be reached. The inevitable delay suited the National Party, which was in no hurry to share power with others and even less eager to become an opposition party, but did not suit the ANC or any of the other organizations working toward change.

Of course, the crux of the problem was the substance of the agreement, not the form of the negotiating process. But the government seemed convinced that by manipulating and controlling the process it could also determine the outcome. The negotiating process had thus become an end rather than purely a means. As such, it risked becoming very long indeed.

The ANC's idea that preliminary talks should deal only with very broad constitutional principles, while an elected constituent assembly would enact the constitution, in theory offered a way out of the dilemma. An election would reduce the number of participants by eliminating parties with negligible constituencies. It would also facilitate decisions by making it possible for parties to vote on issues rather than attempt to reach the nebulous "sufficient consensus" deemed necessary at CODESA. The requirement for a two-thirds majority would probably be sufficient to prevent any party from imposing its views and thus forcing compromises. As a negotiating forum, an elected constituent assembly would be less unwieldy, establishing a balance between broad participation and the need to reach an agreement in a reasonable time.

In practice, in the violent, emotionally charged atmosphere of mid–1992, a free and fair election would be impossible. A modicum of peace and trust among the major parties had to be reestablished before voters could be consulted in a meaningful way. Even if peace was restored and elections for a constituent assembly became possible, they would open up a new host of problems, the severity of which would not be known until after the votes were counted. An election showing substantial support for several parties would be the best outcome, eliminating fringe groups but still forcing compromise among the organizations that counted. A landslide in favor of the ANC would narrow the process excessively, increasing the possibility that in the end the new constitution would be considered an imposition by other parties and fail to gain respect. Finally, an election could also drive organizations with large ambitions and limited voter support outside the legal process, increasing the danger of violence and active opposition. Buthelezi was unlikely simply to retire from politics, even if elections confirmed the conclusion reached by opinion polls that his support in urban areas was shrinking to negligible proportions. And white right-wing organizations might become more rather than less dangerous if an election showed overwhelming support for the ANC. No mechanism ensured an easy transition.

As many dilemmas existed concerning the substance of the agreement as concerning the forum in which it would be negotiated. Under the conditions of South Africa, no agreement would satisfy all requirements. The power-sharing formula favored by the government could easily provoke a backlash among ANC supporters, because it was engineered to reduce the power of the strongest party. Coupled with the likely slow pace of reform implemented by an all-party cabinet designed to be stalemated, power-sharing could lead to a disastrous loss of confidence in the government's ability to solve any problems and to a further increase in the already high level of violence.

But majority rule entailed considerable risks as well, particularly if the ANC emerged from elections with an overwhelming majority. One was the danger of run-away reform, without regard for what the country could afford on the basis of its gross national product, or without sufficient attention being paid to the trade-offs between economic investment and social expenditure. The ANC's policy papers highlighted the host of burning socioeconomic problems that afflicted South Africa. The question was whether, in the climate of heightened expectations and pressure from the constituents, the party would be able to make the hard choices concerning what could and what could not be tackled in the short run.

Another major danger was that the ANC's goal to establish a nonracial South Africa would lead it to ignore all vested interests centering on the homelands. Though true that the homelands as apartheid creations had no moral legitimacy and no place in a future South Africa, their reintegration would have to be handled carefully, lest it create considerable resentment and even ethnic backlash. The ANC did not appear very sensitive to this issue. Its repeated call for the disbanding of the KwaZulu police, for example, was as unrealistic as the National Party's call for the disbanding of Umkhonto we Sizwe. Both would have to go, but they could not simply be eliminated.

The pace of the transition process also presented dilemmas. The ANC favored a very quick change, with an interim government in power for only a few months, and a constituent assembly completing its task in only a few more. The National Party wanted a slow change, with a transitional government in power for many years and the interim constitution slowly becoming accepted as a permanent one. The ANC's insistence on speed created unease even among many of its supporters, who did not think the organization was ready yet to take on the responsibility of governing the country. Certainly, the Congress had neither the personnel nor the experience to run a large, complex country like South Africa, but prolonging the power of the National Party would not lead to an accumulation of ANC experience. A quick transition could put in power a new cabinet still completely unprepared to govern, guided by an abstract vision of what ought to be rather than of what was possible with available resources. A slow transition would allow the time for all parties to become acquainted with the limits of government resources and power, but it risked prolonging the imprint of the National Party's policies on the use of those resources and leading to a backlash later on. Neither approach would guarantee widespread support for the new government.

On paper, these dilemmas were not impossible to resolve. The speedy formation of an interim all-party government committed to a far-reaching but realistic program of socioeconomic reforms, for example, would answer most of the problems involved in the transition and create a climate in which a more permanent political system could be agreed upon. In practice, the goals of the various parties, and their vested interests, were too divergent for such a harmonious outcome. The solution to these dilemmas would, in the end, come from a struggle among parties with different resources and strategies. The question was how much of the struggle would take place around the negotiating table and how much in the streets, through violence and repression. Eventually, much of the agreement would have to be reached by the ANC and the National Party. In any event, the transition would be an internal process, not one masterminded by other countries or international agencies. The possibility of decisive outside intervention was remote. None of the parties wanted it, and South

Africa's status as an independent country did not give any organization the right to intervene. There would be no Lancaster House conference temporarily putting the country back under colonial tutelage, as in Zimbabwe, nor a transition supervised by the United Nations, as in Namibia.

Nevertheless, the transition in South Africa did not take place in a vacuum, totally insulated from outside influences. Indirectly, and to a much lesser extent directly, the process of change in South Africa was affected by events taking place elsewhere.

THE INTERNATIONAL CONTEXT

The historical context in which South Africa experienced the transition from apartheid was one of tremendous and unexpected change, marked by the sudden collapse of the world order established after World War II. This was important. If the negotiations had started, for example, after the 1976 Soweto uprising, the transition would have been exposed to a totally different set of circumstances, with the Soviet Union deeply involved in southern Africa, the United States concerned about Soviet expansionism, and both the government and the ANC able to turn to outside forces for support.

The rapid change in the international situation was one reason that the decolonization scenario, which still influenced the thinking of the ANC, could never be wholly duplicated in South Africa. The rest of the continent had reached independence in a world characterized by the cold war, widespread acceptance of state intervention as a means of economic development, tolerance for one-party states, and a strong desire for African and third world solidarity. It was admittedly a mixed set of influences, but it was not inconsequential. African governments could find financing in the West for ambitious state-run development schemes, turn to one or the other superpower for help, and look at one another and at several networks of third world organizations for inspiration and reassurance. Finally, they did not come under great pressure to reform their undemocratic governments—the superpowers and the European countries were much more concerned with the foreign alignments of the African countries than with their domestic policies.

This general climate had an impact on South Africa. The National

Party accepted the idea that state intervention was the key to economic growth and redistribution, with the results discussed earlier. Without ever admitting it, the NP also accepted the blurring of the line between party and state that was typical of the African single-party regimes.

But the government also found in the dominant ideas of the time additional arguments for its refusal to move toward majority rule—it would inevitably lead to an undemocratic regime, it would destroy the South African economy with socialist intervention, and it would open the way to Soviet penetration. The rapid decolonization of the continent nevertheless convinced the South African government that it was no longer possible simply to deny political rights to blacks, thus leading to the creation of the homelands. Whether in its acceptance or its rejection, the international context of the 1960s deeply influenced South Africa, with consequences that carried over into the 1990s.

The thinking of the ANC leadership was molded by the same influences. Although the movement was formed in 1912, it was the dominant ideas of the decolonization period that left the most lasting imprint. The economic principles of the Freedom Charter were the dominant ones of the 1960s, and the charter still influenced the ANC's thinking in the early 1990s. The Congress's approach to foreign relations—Mandela's visits to Cuba and Libya, the expression of solidarity with the Palestinians, the automatic condemnation of U.S. policy toward Iraq—was a throwback to the brave new third world of the 1960s and to the solidarity linking the leaders of the liberation struggle across countries and continents.

Whereas the influences of an earlier period were still strong both on the political and economic structures of the country and on the thinking of the ANC, the world in which the transition was taking place was dominated by a very different set of ideas. During the 1980s a radical change had taken place in the outlook of the international community. Several factors led to a reversal in the perception of which policies were appropriate or at least permissible—economic disaster in Africa, conservative governments in the countries of the North, the failure of the African Marxist-Leninist regimes to bring about even a modicum of political stability and economic viability, and increasing opposition to authoritarian regimes by the urban populations of African countries. Free enterprise became more legitimate than state intervention, membership in the International Monetary Fund and World Bank a more desirable goal than close relations with the Soviet Union, and democracy a universal demand resisted only by a shrinking number of incumbent governments. The collapse of the Eastern European communist regimes completed the metamorphosis. Even the most reluctant African leaders were forced to take note of the change. If the 1960s had been dominated by the politics of third world liberation, the 1980s had opened up the age of Western-induced reformism.

The impact of these changes on South Africa was considerable. The government, by its own admission, was encouraged by the new trends to seek an accommodation with the ANC. Under the new circumstances, the end of white rule no longer automatically meant the triumph of socialism, Soviet intervention, or the presence of Cuban troops. Socialism was so discredited, and the regimes embodying it so weakened, that it was unlikely to win out in South Africa. To be sure, the threat of communism was not the only reason the white regime had clung to apartheid. The most important problem—that whites were a minority in a black country and fearful of losing power and privilege—remained. But that problem could be solved through power-sharing, as long as the ANC was not backed by the force of international communism. The change in the international climate thus made it much easier for the government to move toward negotiations.

The National Party was also quick to embrace the new economic orthodoxy. Suddenly, after building up a huge state sector, heavily subsidizing agricultural production, using the civil service and parastatals to provide jobs for whites, and allowing the private sector to be dominated by a few conglomerates, the South African government became a champion of free enterprise. To the ANC, the conversion looked suspiciously like an attempt to reduce the sphere of government control before handing over power. How much progress South Africa was making in transforming its economy, dominated by state intervention and by the control of a few conglomerates, into a free-market system is an issue open to debate. It was certainly less than the government claimed. But in theory, at least, the country had rejoined the international mainstream, an important goal in its attempt to gain international respectability.

The ANC never discussed whether its decision to seek negotiations was also influenced by changes in the international climate. Mandela, who played the key role in the decision, had been isolated by his imprisonment and possibly less affected than the government by external factors—certainly his behavior immediately after his release suggested that his views of the world and of economic development were rooted in ideas prevalent in the 1960s. The National Executive Committee was not isolated, but the South African Communist Party (SACP), which had a major influence in it, resisted for a long time accepting the changes in the socialist world. As late as mid–1989, the SACP held its congress in Cuba, the last unreformed communist country. Eventually, but still haltingly, the SACP took cognizance of the new climate in the world, but this happened after, not before, the ANC had chosen the path of negotiations.

The organization as a whole strongly resisted accepting the new economic orthodoxy. Its development philosophy was that of an earlier period in Africa, with a strong emphasis on the need for state intervention, including the nationalization of major economic assets. In the government's eyes, the ANC remained attached to the outmoded and totally discredited ideas of an earlier time. The Conservative Party went further, finding in that economic philosophy proof that the Congress was a communist organization.

The ANC's attachment to ideas predominant in an earlier period had a Rip Van Winkle element to it—leaders coming back to political life in South Africa after decades of imprisonment on Robben Island or in exile were picking up where they had left off. But those "outmoded and discredited" ideas persisted for another, more problematic reason: the ANC was not changing its outlook because the problem it was facing had not changed either. In the 1990s, as in the 1960s, the problem was that of terminating apartheid and its legacy.

The National Party could well argue that apartheid was already finished, but things looked quite different from the other side. Even a new political dispensation would not eliminate the economic legacy of white control over almost all assets, and this made it difficult for the ANC to abandon the economics of liberation embodied in the policies of the 1960s—in May 1992 the ANC leadership had been forced by the rank and file to retain the word *nationalization* in its economic policy guidelines. There was no reason to believe that those policies would be more successful in South Africa than they had been elsewhere. Nor was there any reason to believe that black South Africans would easily accept that the end of apartheid should not affect control of economic assets. White refusal to recognize the importance of this issue encouraged the ANC to remain committed to the economics of liberation. Times had changed, yet the logic of the internal situation risked driving South Africa toward seeking quick, blanket solutions to the immensely complicated problems of redistribution and growth—the mistake made by other African countries.

An additional element entered the international context during the transition, namely, the explosion of ethnic nationalism in Eastern Europe. The Soviet Union had collapsed, Yugoslavia had disintegrated, and Czechoslovakia had split. Initially greeted by Western countries with enthusiasm as a means to weaken the Soviet Union, the upsurge of nationalism was later accepted by them as inevitable, despite mounting concern about its consequences.

Demands for self-determination were troublesome in that they upset an established and thus predictable order, but they nevertheless had a legitimacy difficult to refute. And if the nationalisms of Eastern Europe had to be recognized as legitimate, those of South Africa gained an element of respectability. The possibilities were not lost on the country's advocates of self-determination. For example, in December 1991 the government of Bophuthatswana announced an official visit by three "high-powered" delegations from the Ukraine, Latvia, and Kazakhstan.[2] There may not have been much substance to the visit, but the symbolism was unmistakable.

The question nevertheless remained whether South Africa was in a different cycle in relation to ethnic nationalism, just as it was in relation to economic problems. At that particular stage of the transition from apartheid, common opposition to white domination was possibly still much stronger than the appeal of ethnic nationalism. But the world context did nothing to encourage the emergence of a peaceful, nonracial society in the long run.

DIRECT FOREIGN INFLUENCES

South Africa was exposed not only to the diffuse influence of the international context but also to the direct attempts made by a number of Western countries to hasten the end of apartheid. During the 1980s in particular, trade and financial sanctions, as well as cultural and sports boycotts, had helped demonstrate to white South Africans their isolation and the fact that they were out of step with the rest of the world. The sanctions had caused considerable resentment among whites, and they had contributed to the country's economic stagnation, undoubtedly hurting blacks as well. To what extent South Africa's economic problems were the result of sanctions, rather than the consequence of policy choices and structural deficiencies, is a matter on which there is no agreement. But by the government's own admission, sanctions did contribute to change.

With the release of Mandela, the international community's willingness to maintain economic pressure on South Africa disintegrated quickly, despite the ANC's insistence that the time had not yet come for Western countries to modify their policies. The U.S. Comprehensive Anti-Apartheid Act was repealed, the European Community lifted its restrictions, the United Nations put an end to the cultural boycott, and South African sports teams made their reentry into the international arena. South Africa was busy establishing relations with African and Eastern European countries, opening new embassies and trade missions. South African planes could fly over Africa again, and air links severed in the past were reestablished. The Southern Africa Development and Cooperation Council (now the Southern Africa Development Community), originally formed to free its members from dependency on the apartheid regime in Pretoria, was beginning to discuss a future in which South Africa would be part of the organization.

The days of enforced isolation were over, although it remained to be seen how the country would fare in competing in new foreign markets, and, most important, in attracting foreign capital. Political instability had replaced formal sanctions as the major obstacle to foreign investment in South Africa, particularly after the Boipatong massacre.

Despite the ANC's assertions to the contrary, the usefulness of sanctions in encouraging the transition in South Africa had come to an end—some even argued the measures had never served a useful purpose. Sanctions had been an extremely blunt instrument in the first place. As their critics pointed out, they hurt everyone indiscriminately—the government and the white community they were intended to pressure, but also the black population they were supposed to help. To the extent that they worsened the economic crisis, sanctions would not facilitate the transition, since they made whites more desperate to keep what they had and blacks less likely to believe their problems would be solved by growth rather than redistribution. Also, sanctions put pressure on only one side, the government. But the essence of a negotiated solution is that all parties must compromise on their demands. If outside pressure was to help, it had to be applied to all sides, not just to one.

With the end of sanctions, the probability of a direct attempt by other countries to influence the transition in South Africa appeared limited. First, neither the government nor the ANC, nor indeed any of the other parties, wanted outside intervention in the negotiations. Second, the more the conflict revealed all its complexities and ramifications, the less obvious the solutions became. It was one thing to put pressure on the South African government to abrogate the apartheid legislation, but a very different one to make suggestions about a political system that could tackle the maximum number of problems while causing a minimum of disruption and open opposition.

If there was one point on which all political organizations in South Africa agreed, it was that the role of the international community in the transition process was limited. South Africa was a sovereign, independent country with a legitimate government, not a colony, the National Party insisted. The parties to the conflict were all internal to South Africa, and foreign powers had no reason to get involved. The government had problems even accepting the assistance of the United Nations High Commission for Refugees (UNHCR) in organizing the return of the exiles, giving in only when the long delays in the operation created much friction with the ANC. But originally the government saw only one role for the foreign community, that of providing observers when elections were held, so that the fairness of the poll could not be questioned.

The ANC's position was similar, not because it deemed the government legitimate but because it considered itself capable of handling the negotiations alone. It welcomed the assistance of UNHCR with the exiles, and, suspicious of the government, it also favored the presence of foreign observers at the elections. What the ANC really wanted from the international community, however, was the continuation of sanctions to maintain pressure on the National Party. This it failed to get.

The breakdown of CODESA and the outcry over the Boipatong massacre prompted the government and the ANC to rethink their positions concerning foreign intervention in the process. Both asked for a meeting of the United Nations Security Council to discuss the escalating violence in South Africa. Both were interested in the presence of observers from the United Nations, the European Community, the Commonwealth, or the Organization of African Unity. Foreign experts were invited to assist the Goldstone Commission with its investigations and to advise on how best to maintain peace during mass action. Nevertheless, none of the initiatives discussed in the aftermath of Boipatong included the possibility of foreign mediation in the negotiations. The role of outsiders was to be limited to studying the problem of violence.

The foreign community thus remained unlikely to directly influence the initial phase of the transition, as South Africans tried to choose their political institutions. It could be expected, however, that later, when the new government tackled policy reform, international agencies would have a considerable impact. Already, IMF and World Bank missions were visiting South Africa and carrying out studies in preparation for future intervention. The full weight of the international community would be brought to bear on the country when it started applying for development assistance and loans. This worried the ANC, which correctly perceived that international agencies were more likely to support the policies of minimal reform backed by the National Party than its own plans for economic liberation. Direct international pressure had helped the ANC pursue its goal of political liberation during the 1980s, but was likely to thwart its policies of economic liberation in the 1990s.

A DIFFERENT TRANSITION

White control in South Africa lasted much longer and was much more thorough than in any other part of the continent. The presence of a large white population, over half of which considered itself indigenous, maintained the pattern of domination established in Africa during the colonial period long after it had disappeared elsewhere. Indeed, for more than thirty years South Africa stood against the current, unchanged on a continent in turmoil.

White domination affected the entire society. No corner of the country remained untouched. What white South Africans liked to define as the third world in their midst was not a traditional peasantry but a new, semiurban lumpenproletariat surviving on the margins of an industrialized country. The traditional society existed only in the pages of the glossy brochures published by homeland governments and travel agencies in the hope of attracting tourists in search of the exotic.

This deeply unbalanced society was reaching the end of white rule in a world that had advocated the end of apartheid, but was in reality extremely hostile to black demands for transformation. Earlier, the West had been tolerant of African demands for redistribution through state intervention, while the socialist countries were definitely supportive. But in the early 1990s the West spoke only the language of structural adjustment. The former socialist countries were busy establishing ties to Pretoria; receptive to the white regime, they looked with deep suspicion at the ANC, because it had received support from the now-defunct communist parties. African countries theoretically remained on the side of the liberation movement against the white government; in practice, they were trying to undo the damage inflicted in the past by their own politics and economics of liberation. They were experimenting with democracy with varying degrees of enthusiasm, and, in need of foreign assistance, they were submitting to the demands of the international agencies and painfully trying to wean their economies from state intervention and subsidies to the logic of the market place.

The ANC, still struggling for political and economic liberation, was definitely out of step with the times. But the times were definitely out of step with the reality of South Africa. Blacks had been dispossessed politically and economically, not by the forces of the market and the logic of election results but by superior power. The argument that only economic market forces, rather than government-enforced policies of redistribution, should allocate resources in the future was deeply ironic under the circumstances. The National Party's contention that the political market forces of elections could not be allowed to allocate power unhindered, but that political control needed to be redistributed more equitably between majority and minority, made the irony very bitter indeed. The continued appeal of liberation politics and economics was not surprising in the South African context. No matter how late the transition came, liberation still had a logic. It was a dangerous logic, as experience elsewhere showed, but it addressed the felt needs of most black South Africans better than the logic of cautious reform and structural adjustment. The country was buffeted between two sets of demands, neither of which appeared likely to address its problems satisfactorily.

South Africa in transition from apartheid stood at the confluence of a number of internal and external currents working at cross-purposes. The simple black-on-white conflict that had made the country a pariah state in the past had dissolved into a much more complex set of crisscrossing cleavages fought out and negotiated in different arenas. These conflicts did not lend themselves to simple solutions, and even less to clear-cut moral judgments. The combination of internal conflicts and external influences created a unique configuration. Under the circumstances, it was pointless to look for parallels with models of transition found in other countries and at other times. Only one thing was predictable in South Africa: the country would undergo a different and difficult transition.

Notes

CHAPTER 1

1. For a recent discussion of the concept, see Jeremy Cronin, "Inside Which Circle?" *Transformation*, vol. 10 (1989), pp. 70–78.

2. Peter L. Berger and Bobby Godsell, "South Africa in Comparative Context," in Peter L. Berger and Bobby Godsell, eds., *A Future South Africa: Visions, Strategies and Realities* (Boulder, Colo.: Westview Press, 1988), pp. 267–98.

3. One five-volume study, in particular, acquired enormous popularity among liberal intellectuals in this period; see Guillermo O'Donnell, Philippe C. Schmitter, and Laurence Whitehead, eds., *Transitions from Authoritarian Rule* (Washington: Woodrow Wilson International Center for Scholars, 1986).

CHAPTER 2

1. South African Institute of Race Relations, *Race Relations Survey, 1989–90* (Johannesburg, 1990), p. 550.

2. Ibid. The Conservative Party won thirty-nine seats, and the Democratic Party thirty-three.

3. According to the 1983 constitution, new elections had to be called within five years of the previous election, with an additional six months allowed for organizing them.

4. The terms *verligte* and *verkrampte*, which were made part of the South African political lexicon in 1966 by Willem de Klerk, F. W. de Klerk's brother, can be translated literally as "enlightened" and "narrow-minded." That translation is extremely misleading, however. *Verligte* NP leaders were not liberals; they were simply more flexible supporters of the policies of the National Party and more realistic about what could be achieved. The *verligte* concept of race relations, explained Willem de Klerk in 1972, was "equality in diversity," while integration was emphatically rejected. The *verligte* position has evolved

since then, but *pragmatic* still appears a better translation of the term. See Willem de Klerk, "The Concepts 'Verkramp' and 'Verlig,' " in Nic Rhoodie, ed., *South African Dialogue* (Philadelphia: Westminster Press, 1972), pp. 519–31.

5. Willem de Klerk, *F. W. de Klerk: The Man in His Time* (Johannesburg: Jonathan Ball Publishers, 1991), p. 17.

6. Hermann Giliomee, *The Parting of the Ways: South African Politics, 1976–82* (Cape Town: David Philip, 1982), p. 160.

7. De Klerk, *F. W. de Klerk*, p. 100.

8. Ibid., p. 28.

9. "De Klerk Will Not Apologise for Apartheid," *Natal Witness*, May 2, 1991.

10. On removals, see Laurine Platzky and Cherryl Walker, *The Surplus People: Forced Removals in South Africa* (Johannesburg: Ravan Press, 1985).

11. Heribert Adam, *Modernizing Racial Domination* (University of California Press, 1971). Adam defined apartheid as "a pragmatic race oligarchy."

12. Interview with the *Rand Daily Mail*, August 1, 1978, reprinted in J. H. P. Serfontein, *Brotherhood of Power: An Exposé of the Afrikaner Broederbond* (Indiana University Press, 1978), pp. 254–56.

13. In November 1991 a major dispute erupted between President F. W. de Klerk and former president P. W. Botha over the tape recording of Botha's first meeting in July 1989 with the imprisoned Nelson Mandela. The former president reportedly wanted the tapes in order to disprove claims that he had set the course of reform followed by de Klerk. The National Intelligence Service claimed the tapes had been destroyed as useless. De Wet Potgeiter and Mike Robertson, "De Klerk in Row with PW," *Sunday Times*, November 17, 1991, p. 1.

14. Interview with *Rand Daily Mail*, in Serfontein, *Brotherhood of Power*, p. 254.

15. Quoted in de Klerk, *F. W. de Klerk*, p. 25.

16. The expression "narrow and slippery ledge" is taken from Viljoen's interview with *Rand Daily Mail*, in Serfontein, *Brotherhood of Power*, p. 254.

17. See South African Institute of Race Relations, *Race Relations Survey, 1986*, part 1 (Johannesburg, 1986), p. 161.

18. See "Abolition of Racially Based Land Measures Act," chapter 7, "Norms and Standards in Residential Environments," *Government Gazette*, vol. 312, no. 13341 (June 28, 1991), p. 46.

19. De Klerk, *F. W. de Klerk*, p. 28.

20. The bulletin, dated June 21, 1990, was leaked to the press several weeks later. See Edyth Bulbring, "No Govt Mandate to Unban the ANC, Says NP Document," *Business Day*, August 16, 1990.

21. The first nonwhite member, an Indian, reportedly joined in November

1991, and the first NP meeting in a black township, organized by the Indian member, was held in January 1991. Boeti Eshak, "More Firsts for Mixed-Race NP," *Sunday Times*, January 27, 1991, p. 13.

22. Peter Fabricius, "Time for Leaving Big Decisions to Leaders," *Star*, September 4, 1990, p. 1.

23. The proposal is discussed in chapter 5.

24. Gerald Reilly, "Public Servants Fear for Job Security," *Business Day*, October 21, 1991, p. 4. In 1989, among the top 857 civil service employees, 2 were black, 6 were Indian, and 6 were Coloured. Of the top 100,000 positions, 80.5 percent were occupied by whites. See Pierre Hugo and Louise Stack, "Whites in the South African Public Service: Angst and the Future," in Pierre Hugo, ed., *Redistribution and Affirmative Action: Working on the South African Political Economy* (Halfway House, South Africa: Southern Book Publishers, 1992), pp. 56–57.

25. The problem was thoroughly documented in Carnegie Commission Report, *The Poor White Problem in South Africa* (Stellenbosch, 1932).

26. Hermann Giliomee and Lawrence Schlemmer, *From Apartheid to Nationbuilding* (Cape Town: Oxford University Press, 1989), p. 120.

27. Ibid., p. 104.

28. Calculated from figures in South African Institute of Race Relations, *Race Relations Survey, 1988–89* (Johannesburg, 1989), pp. 395–96.

29. Craig Charney, "The National Party, 1982–85," in Wilmot G. James, ed., *The State of Apartheid* (Boulder, Colo.: Lynne Rienner, 1987), p. 16.

30. "Hospitals Open to All, but Manpower, Finance in Way," *Star*, May 17, 1990, p. 1; and Brian Stuart, "44 White Hospitals Open to All Races," *Citizen*, May 18, 1990, p. 7. The fourteen departments of health are divided as follows: one for each of the four independent and six self-governing homelands, one "own affairs" department for each of the population groups represented in the tricameral Parliament, and one ministry, the one that announced desegregation, to take care of those health issues considered to be "general affairs."

31. See, for example, Esmaré van der Merwe, "Racism Rife at OFS Hospitals," *Star*, March 12, 1991; "Hospital Apartheid Still Alive," *Business Day*, March 14, 1991, p. 1; Esmaré van der Merwe, "Apartheid Alive at Hospitals," *Star*, March 14, 1991; and "Government Silent as Race Row Rages in Free State Hospital," *Star*, March 14, 1991.

32. Esmaré van der Merwe, "Blacks Prefer Segregated Wards—Hospital MEC," *Star*, March 6, 1991; and "Why Blacks Not Ready for 'White Side,' " *Sowetan*, March 5, 1991, p. 5.

33. Annette Seegers, "Apartheid's Military: Its Origins and Development," in James, ed., *State of Apartheid*, p. 144.

34. Ibid., p. 165.

35. P. W. Botha became prime minister in September 1978 and state president in September 1984, after the new constitution abolished the former position. The entire period from 1978 to 1984 is termed here the Botha presidency.

36. For an overall account of the death squad saga, see Patrick Laurence, *Death Squads: Apartheid's Secret Weapons* (Johannesburg: Penguin Books, 1990).

37. The Harms Commission report was released on November 13, 1990. Lengthy summaries of the report were published in the following days by all major newspapers. See especially Fred de Longe, "Harms: Review of Covert OPS-FW," *Citizen*, November 14, 1990, p. 1; and Norman Chandler, "Prosecutor and Executioner," *Star*, November 14, 1990, pp. 14–15.

38. The conclusion that police death squads did exist came to light in a court judgment against police lieutenant general Lothar Neethling, who had brought a defamation case against two South African weeklies that had linked his name to reports about death squad activities. The judgment raised questions about the credibility of the Harms Commission report. See Brendan Templeton and Cathy Stagg, " 'Coetzee's Death Squads Are Fact,' " *Saturday Star*, January 19, 1991, p. 1.

39. Laurence, *Death Squads*, p. 27.

40. Billy Paddock, "CCB Report Reveals Ire within NP over Malan," *Business Day*, March 18, 1991.

41. Eddie Koch and Anton Herber, "Police and Inkatha to Block ANC," *Weekly Mail*, July 19–25, 1991, p. 1.

42. "Press Statement by the State President, Mr. F. W. de Klerk, Pretoria, July 30, 1991," p. 4. The cabinet reshuffle was announced on July 29, 1991.

43. Serfontein, *Brotherhood of Power*, p. 29.

44. Ibid., p. 14.

45. Ibid., p. 101.

46. Among cabinet ministers who were supposedly members of the Broederbond were Gerrit Viljoen, Stoffel van der Merwe, Hermanus Kriel, Barend du Plessis, Dawie de Villiers, Kobie Coetsee, and Pik Botha. See David Breir, "ANC May Govern but Broeders Plan to Rule," *Sunday Star*, February 25, 1990.

47. *Church and Society: A Testimony Approved by the Synod of the Dutch Reformed Church* (Bloemfontein: Pro Christo Publishers and General Synodical Commission, 1987), pp. 20–21.

48. A splinter group formed the Afrikaanse Protestantse Kerk in 1987. See South African Institute of Race Relations, *Race Relations Survey, 1987–88* (Johannesburg, 1988), pp. 226–27.

49. This position, known as the Vereiniging Testimony, was taken by the black NGK churches in March 1989. The moderator of the white NGK ap-

peared to accept it, but the church rejected it de facto by restating the position taken in 1986.

50. Dries van Heerden, "The End of the NGK," *Sunday Times*, June 21, 1990.

51. Statement by W. D. Jonkers, from the documents of the National Conference of Churches in South Africa, November 5–9, 1990.

52. Cathy Thompson, "Geref Kerk Attacks Rustenburg Summit," *Citizen*, January 18, 1991.

CHAPTER 3

1. African National Congress, *Joining the ANC: An Introductory Handbook to the African National Congress* (Johannesburg, May 1990), p. 5.

2. On the ANC as liberation movement, see Marina Ottaway, "Liberation Movements and Transition to Democracy: The Case of the ANC," *Journal of Modern African Studies*, vol. 29 (March 1991), pp. 61–82.

3. Some of these points are raised in Charles Simkins, *The Prisoners of Tradition and the Politics of Nation Building* (Johannesburg: South African Institute of Race Relations, 1988), pp. 30–31.

4. Chris Hani, Umkhonto we Sizwe chief of staff, admitted in an interview that "our people inside the country, in fighting . . . to mobilize thousands into active struggle, neglected a basic area of struggle under conditions of fascist or police state: the need to have underground structures which are unknown to the enemy." *New Nation*, February 9–15, 1990, pp. 6–7.

5. Stephen M. Davis, *Apartheid's Rebels: Inside South Africa's Hidden War* (Yale University Press, 1987), p. 57.

6. Ibid., p. 58.

7. Howard Barrell, *MK: The ANC's Armed Struggle* (Penguin Books, 1990), p. 64.

8. A list of NEC members distributed at the 1991 ANC national conference in Durban listed thirty-seven names (thirty from the Kabwe conference and seven co-opted in 1988), but indicated five as deceased. The list omitted, however, the names of the three co-opted in February 1990, namely Nelson Mandela, Walter Sisulu, and Govan Mbeki.

9. See *Star* and *Business Day* reports on the conference, December 17 and 18, 1990: Shaun Johnson and Patrick Lawrence, "Mandela Gets Tough on Internal Strife within the ANC," *Star*, December 17, 1990; Mike Robertson, Tim Cohen, and Alan Fine, "April 30 Is Our Talks Deadline, Says the ANC," *Business Day*, December 17, 1990, p. 1; and Alan Fine and Mike Robertson, "ANC Conference Brings Home a Lesson in Leadership," *Business Day*, De-

cember 18, 1990. The discussion is also based on typescript resolutions that were distributed at the conference.

10. Tom Lodge, "State of Exile: The African National Congress of South Africa, 1976–86," in Philip Frankel, Noam Pines, and Mark Swilling, eds., *State, Resistance and Change in South Africa* (Johannesburg: Southern Book Publishers, 1988), pp. 247–48.

11. In an interview with the *Washington Post* on June 26, 1990, only parts of which were published, he declared that "the ANC is a coalition . . . of people of various political affiliations. Some will support free enterprise, others socialism. Some are conservatives, others are liberals. We are determined solely by our determination to oppose racial oppression." (Unpublished.)

12. Lodge, "State of Exiles," p. 236; and Davis, *Apartheid Rebels*, p. 204. A discussion of Marxist and Africanist tendencies in the ANC appeared in an interview with Pallo Jordan, ANC's director of information; Patrick Lawrence, "A Long, Stormy Marriage, but Divorce Unlikely," *Star*, September 11, 1990. For ANC's view of Africanism and black consciousness, see Francis Meli, *South Africa Belongs to Us: A History of the ANC* (Harare: Zimbabwe Publishing House, 1988). For a more detached view, see Gail Gerhart, *Black Power in South Africa* (University of California Press, 1979).

13. Mike Robertson, "Mandela Defends Private Meetings," *Business Day*, December 17, 1990.

14. Barrell, *MK*, p. 32.

15. Ibid., p. 42.

16. The various phases of this relationship are outlined in Barrell, *MK*, chaps. 3, 4.

17. "ANC Admits It Cannot Intensify Armed Struggle," *Star*, January 19, 1990.

18. The paper, dated January 1990, has been circulated in typescript form. Further indications of Slovo's thinking can be obtained from his interviews with South African newspapers, including Dries van Heerden, "Comrade Slovo: The Man without a Guilty Conscience," *Sunday Times*, February 18, 1990, p. 5; Gaye Davis, "Face to Face with Joe Slovo," *Weekly Mail*, February 16–22, 1990; Patti Waldmeir, "Control—Not Ownership—Is Aim of ANC Economic Policy," *Star*, March 2, 1990, p. 8; "Restoring Socialism," *New Nation*, March 16–22, 1990, p. 10; and David Greybe, "Slovo Says SACP Supports a Mixed Economy in SA," *Daily Mail*, June 29, 1990.

19. See Stephen Ellis and Tsepo Sechaba, *Comrades against Apartheid: The ANC and the South African Communist Party in Exile* (London: James Currey, 1992), pp. 195–97. See also "South Africa: The Party Faithful," *Africa Confidential*, January 12, 1990, p. 1. Much of the content of the article is corroborated by other sources.

20. South African Institute of Race Relations, *Race Relations Survey, 1991–92* (Johannesburg, 1991–92), p. 15.

21. "ANC Says It Now Has 500,000 Members," *Citizen*, June 17, 1991. The figures were provided officially by the ANC.

22. Mark Swilling, "The United Democratic Front and Township Revolt," in William Cobbett and Robin Cohen, eds., *Popular Struggles in South Africa* (London: Review of African Political Economy, 1988), p. 93.

23. See Rob Lambert and Eddie Webster, "The Re-emergence of Political Unionism in Contemporary South Africa?" in Cobbett and Cohen, eds., *Popular Struggles*, pp. 20–41. See also Steven Friedman, *Building Tomorrow Today: African Workers in Trade Unions, 1970–1984* (Johannesburg: Ravan Press, 1987); and Johann Maree, ed., *The Independent Trade Unions, 1974–84: Ten Years of the South Africa Labour Bulletin* (Johannesburg: Ravan Press, 1987).

24. Cited in South African Institute of Race Relations, *Race Relations Survey, 1987–88* (Johannesburg, 1988), p. 232. The statement was issued at a conference organized in Lusaka, Zambia, by the World Council of Churches.

25. Use of the term *black-on-black violence* to denote the fighting in the townships has been condemned by liberals and radicals alike as blind acceptance of government propaganda, but the term is justified. There is no doubt that the fighting pitted black factions against each other. Furthermore, the violence was often perceived as black-on-black by local inhabitants. Anyone who sought an explanation of the violence from local residents has heard about ethnic strife and rivalry among black political organizations. Whatever the government's responsibility for the fighting, black-on-black violence was a fact.

26. Address to the congregation in St. George's Cathedral, Cape Town, March 27, 1991, as transmitted on the South African Press Association (SAPA) PR Wire Service, March 28, 1991.

27. The South African Institute of Race Relations estimated that the membership of the independent African churches associated with two so-called moderate groups, the Reformed Independent Churches' Association and the Zion Churches in South Africa, totaled about seven million. See South African Institute of Race Relations, *Race Relations Survey, 1989–90* (Johannesburg, 1990), p. 291. These figures are rough estimates at best.

28. The report was not released. The quotation was provided by Director of Information Pallo Jordan at a press conference held during the congress. See also "The ANC Blamed for Violence, Nzo Warns," *Citizen*, July 4, 1991, p. 1; Esmaré van der Merwe, "ANC in Disarray, Says Report," *Saturday Star*, July 6, 1991, p. 1; and David Breier, "ANC Shambles Outlined by Departing Nzo," *Sunday Star*, July 7, 1991, p. 7.

29. "Movement Can't Ignore Ethnicity, Warns Mandela," *Sunday Star*, September 29, 1991.

CHAPTER 4

1. Tony Sterling, "Strike the Zulu and Face His Wrath—Buthelezi," *Citizen*, September 14, 1990, p. 8. Appeals to Zulu nationalism were a standard part of his speeches; examples are innumerable. For particularly strong appeals, see also his address at the unveiling of the tombstones of Inkosi Bekayiphi Sibiya and of Inkosi Mtshekula Sibiya, Kwakhiphunyawo ("Buthelezi Pleads for Zulu Unity in Democratic SA," *Citizen*, July 23, 1990); and his speech at the King Shaka Day celebrations in Stanger ("You Can't Annihilate the Zulus: Buthelezi," *Citizen*, September 25, 1990).

2. The *inkatha* was a traditional ceremonial object, a bundle of grasses and snake skins representing "the good spirit of the tribe, binding all together in one, and attracting back any deserters." L. H. Samuelson, quoted in Gerhard Maré and Georgina Hamilton, *An Appetite for Power: Buthelezi's Inkatha and the Politics of "Loyal Resistance"* (Johannesburg: Ravan Press, 1987), p. 227.

3. Cited in ibid., p. 57.

4. "Secretary-General's Department Report," in Inkatha YeNkululeko YeSizwe, Annual General Conference, Ulundi, July 13–15, 1990, p. 2.

5. The borders between KwaZulu and Natal were gerrymandered so that the townships of the cities and towns of Natal would be located in the homeland. This was true in other parts of the country as well.

6. After the breaking of the Inkathagate scandal, the government admitted having provided funds for UWUSA since its launching. See Phillip van Niekerk, "The Money That Vanished," and Drew Forrest, "UWUSA Is an SAP/Inkatha Project," *Weekly Mail*, July 26–August 1, 1991, p. 1. The last official payment to the organization was made on July 31, 1991. "UWUSA Given Last Official Police Payment Yesterday," *Business Day*, August 1, 1991.

7. John Aitchison, "The Pietermaritzburg Conflict: Experience and Analysis," University of Natal, Centre for Adult Education, Pietermaritzburg, n.d., p. 11.

8. Ibid., p. 12.

9. Inkatha, through its Inkatha Institute, favored the socioeconomic interpretation of the violence. See Gavin Wood, "Black Violence: A Comprehensive Analysis," Inkatha Institute, November 1989.

10. Zulus and Xhosas, closely related ethnic groups speaking mutually intelligible Nguni dialects, were the two largest ethnic groups in the country, numbering, respectively, 5.3 million and 5.6 million, according to the 1985 census. However, 3.5 million Xhosas were considered to be citizens of the independent homelands of Transkei and Ciskei, and thus excluded from official South African statistics, which led to the impression that Zulus were by far the largest group in the country. Department of Foreign Affairs, *South*

Africa, 1989–90: Official Yearbook of the Republic of South Africa (Pretoria: Government Printers, 1990), p. 80. Buthelezi was often referred to as the leader of seven million Zulus, a figure based on estimates of population growth since 1985 and probably somewhat inflated.

11. In late September, for example, the morgues in the Johannesburg areas held 478 bodies of violence victims, still unidentified and unclaimed after several weeks. Linda Burns, "Morgues Held 478 Unclaimed Bodies," *Business Day*, September 21, 1990.

12. "6 Councillors Killed, 404 Have Quit," *Star*, March 2, 1991; and Phillip van Niekerk, "All Transvaal Councillors Now Members of Inkatha," *Weekly Mail*, March 28–April 4, 1991.

13. Michele Vermaak, "Sisulu: Forces Killing Blacks at Random," *Citizen*, September 8, 1990.

14. David Breier, "Gov't, ANC in 'Third Force' Allegations," *Sunday Star*, September 23, 1990, reporting comments by MK head Joe Modise.

15. Ibid.; and Erik Larsen, "Third Force May Be ANC Dissidents, Say Police," *Citizen*, September 24, 1990, p. 4.

16. "Press Release by the Honourable Mr. Justice R. J. Goldstone, Chairman of the Commission of Inquiry, regarding the Prevention of Public Violence and Intimidation," May 27, 1992, p. 1.

17. Human Rights Commission Press Statement on Goldstone Commission Report, May 28, 1992.

18. Brian Stuart, "Goldstone Censures Govt for Handling of His Report," *Citizen*, June 2, 1992, p. 4.

19. See Drew Forrest, "Secrets of Hit Squad Camp Revealed," *Weekly Mail*, December 13–18, 1991, p. 2. The allegations confirming the training were not denied by either Inkatha or the security forces, although Inkatha claimed that personnel were simply being trained for VIP protection as a result of the threat posed by the ANC.

20. A good summary of all these points is found in Buthelezi's address to an Inkatha Freedom Party mass rally, Jabulani Amphitheatre, Soweto, February 23, 1991.

21. Eddie Koch and Anton Harbor, "Police Paid Inkatha to Block ANC," *Weekly Mail*, July 19–25, 1991, p. 1.

22. The accuracy of black opinion polls in South Africa is totally unknown, and it will remain so until elections are held. Furthermore, some polls are also held for political purposes and are thus highly suspect. Nevertheless, all surveys of urban blacks, no matter the organization carrying them out, concur in the conclusion that support for the Inkatha Freedom Party is very low. See summary of studies in Gavin Evans, "Who'd Win If SA Voted Today?" *Weekly Mail*, March 22–27, 1991; "ANC Would Win One-Man, One-Vote Election, Says Poll," *Star*, July 2, 1991, and July 23, 1991, p. 17; and

John Aitchison, "The Opinion Polls: How Do the Parties Fare?" University of Natal, Centre for Adult Education, Pietermaritzburg, October 1991.

23. On the origins of the PAC, see Gail M. Gerhart, *Black Power in South Africa: The Evolution of an Ideology* (University of California Press, 1978).

24. Ibid., p. 231.

25. Ibid., p. 227.

26. "Appeasement Never Wins: PAC," *Citizen*, February 19, 1990.

27. Speech by Barney Desai, president of the Pan Africanist Movement, at a special congress held in Bloemfontein, March 10, 1990. The Pan Africanist Movement was formed in December 1989 as an internal wing of the banned PAC, and merged back into it a few months later at the Bloemfontein congress.

28. SAPA Wire Service, March 5, 1990.

29. "An Official in Britain," *New Nation*, July 13–19, 1990, p. 7.

30. Gavin Evans, "PAC Rides High—but Its Bluff May Be Called," *Weekly Mail*, May 11–17, 1990, p. 13.

31. Tshokolo wa Molakeng, "PAC's Stand on Talks Dries Up Its Meagre Funds," *Weekly Mail*, December 14–19, 1990.

32. Gary van Staden, quoted in "The Outbidding Position," *New Nation*, July 13–19, 1990, p. 7.

33. The adoption of the name Convention for a Democratic South Africa broke a stalemate and much confusion on what the conference should be called. The government referred to a multiparty conference. The ANC insisted on an all-party conference. The PAC would not go beyond preconstituent assembly talks in order to underline how narrow the topic to be discussed was.

34. Mandela's press conference of December 1, 1991, from author's transcript of tape.

35. The best known of these were the Workers' Organization for Socialist Action and the New Unity Movement, radical, Trotskyite-oriented groups with a tiny and rather intellectual membership.

36. The Black Consciousness Movement of Azania, based in Harare, represented the ideology outside South Africa.

37. SAPA, March 4, 1991.

38. See Cassandra Moodley, "Mandela and Azapo Discuss Solidarity," *Weekly Mail*, February 23–March 1, 1990; Moodley, "We Should Talk to Each Other First—Azapo," *Weekly Mail*, March 9–15, 1990, p. 10; Moodley, "Mandela Meets Azapo for Talks and a Common Front," *Weekly Mail*, March 30–April 4, 1990; and Kaizer Nyatsumba, "Bold Azapo Bid to End Township Strife," *Star*, June 8, 1991.

39. The Coloured parties represented in Parliament were the Labour Party, which controlled a large majority of seats in the House of Representatives,

and the Democratic Reform Party, the small official opposition. In May and June 1991, the National Party won over a number of Labour MPs, and in February 1992 it became the majority party in the House of Representatives. Eight Indian parties won seats in the House of Delegates. Solidarity eventually formed the administration with the support of smaller organizations, and the National People's Party became the official opposition. Only the majority party and the official opposition in the House of Representatives and the House of Delegates were invited to participate in CODESA.

40. The self-governing homelands and their parties were KwaZulu (Inkatha Freedom Party), KwaNdebele (Intando YeSizwe Party), KaNgwane (Inyandza National Movement), Lebowa (United People's Front), Gazankulu (Ximoko Progressive Party), and Qwaqwa (Dinkwankwetla Party).

41. See South African Institute of Race Relations, *Race Relations Survey, 1989–90* (Johannesburg, 1990), pp. 550–52.

42. The independent homelands were Transkei, Bophuthatswana, Venda, and Ciskei, also called the TBVC states, after their initials.

43. In 1989–90 Bophuthatswana revenue was broken down as follows: R 1.55 billion from own revenue, R 0.53 billion from the central government, and R 0.19 billion from loans. South African Institute, *Race Relations Survey, 1989–90*, p. 450.

CHAPTER 5

1. See Arend Lijphart, *Power-Sharing in South Africa* (Berkeley: University of California, Institute of International Studies, 1985), pp. 52–66.

2. The writing of Arend Lijphart was particularly influential in South Africa. See his *Power-Sharing in South Africa*, particularly the section on "Optimal Constitutional Guidelines for South Africa," p. 80.

3. See F. van Zyl Slabbert and David Welsh, *South Africa's Options: Strategies for Sharing Power* (St. Martin's Press, 1979). At the time of the book's publication, Slabbert was the head of the Progressive Federal Party, and the book reflects the ideas that shaped the party's constitutional guidelines. See also the section on "Progressive Federal Party Proposals," in Lijphart, *Power-Sharing*, p. 66.

4. Lijphart, *Power-Sharing*, pp. 54–55.

5. Although it was illegal not to register, only 60 percent of Coloureds and 80 percent of Asians did so, according to official figures. Independent studies concluded the percentages were even smaller; South African Institute of Race Relations, *Race Relations Survey, 1984* (Johannesburg, 1985), pp. 123–24. Only 30.9 percent of registered Coloured voters (18 percent of potential voters) and

20 percent of Asian voters (16 percent of potential voters) actually participated in the election; ibid., pp. 127–28.

6. "National Party Position Paper Number 1: Power Sharing (and Related Concepts)," compiled by Dr. Stoffel van der Merwe, MP, July 1986, p. 2.

7. Ibid., pp. 2–4.

8. "Group Security: Proposer's Speech by the Minister of National Education, Mr. F. W. De Klerk, M.P.D.M.S.," in National Party, Federal Congress for Freedom and Stability, *Speeches by the Proposers and Seconders of Motions, 13th August, 1986* (Durban, August 12–13, 1986), pp. 27–31.

9. See Gerhard Maré and Georgina Hamilton, *An Appetite for Power: Buthelezi's Inkatha and the Politics of "Loyal Resistance"* (Johannesburg: Ravan Press, 1987), p. 43.

10. On the involvement of Natal businessmen, see ibid., p. 164; and Graham Linscott and Arthur Kônigkrâmer, "Genesis," *Indaba* (Cape Town: A Leadership Publication, 1987), pp. 21–26.

11. Lijphart, *Power-Sharing*, pp. 76–77; and Maré and Hamilton, *Appetite for Power*, p. 164.

12. Linscott and Kônigkrâmer, "Genesis," pp. 24–26; and Lijphart, *Power-Sharing*, p. 9. Lijphart, a strong advocate of consociationalism, gives high marks to the Buthelezi Commission proposal.

13. Maré and Hamilton, *Appetite for Power*, p. 166.

14. Ibid.

15. The government, in fact, even tried to block the Buthelezi Commission, claiming that KwaZulu had no right to discuss the affairs of white Natal. See Linscott and Kônigkrâmer, "Genesis," p. 24.

16. See KwaZulu-Natal Indaba, *Constitutional Proposals* (Durban, 1986).

17. Ibid.

18. National Party, "Proposed Plan of Action of the National Party—Election, 6 September 1989," (n.p., n.d.), pp. 6–7.

19. Ibid., p. 6.

20. See National Party, "Constitutional Rule in a Participatory Democracy: The National Party's Framework for a New Democratic South Africa," Pretoria, September 4, 1991.

21. Ibid., p. 9.

22. Ibid., p. 16.

23. Brian Stuart, "Minority Rights, Not Special Privileges, Says Viljoen," *Citizen*, May 12, 1990, p. 8.

24. "Constitutional Rule in a Participatory Democracy," p. 9.

25. See African National Congress Constitutional Committee, "A Discussion Document on Structures and Principles of a Constitution for a Democratic South Africa," Belville, Centre for Development Studies, April 1991.

26. African National Congress Constitutional Committee, "A Bill of Rights for a New South Africa," Belville, Centre for Development Studies, 1990.

27. See Albie Sachs, *Protecting Human Rights in a New South Africa* (Cape Town: Oxford University Press, 1990).

28. From President de Klerk's speech during the budget vote debate, issued by the South Africa Communication Service and carried on SAPA Wire Service, May 2, 1991.

29. Democratic Party, National Congress, "Discussion Document on Constitutional Proposals," Capetown, November 15–16, 1991. See also the discussion of the paper in Ben MacLennan and Martin Challenor, "DP in Crucial Shift on Constitution," *Saturday Star*, November 16, 1991.

30. See Edyth Bulbring, "Revealed: Inkatha's Plan for New Constitution," *Sunday Times*, December 1, 1991; and "IFP Releases Flexible Draft Constitution," *Star*, December 16, 1991.

31. "Address by Mangosuthu Buthelezi, Chief Minister of KwaZulu and President, Inkatha Freedom Party to the Amakhosi of KwaZulu," issued by the Chief Minister's Office, Ulundi, on SAPA PR Wire Service, September 13, 1990.

32. Statement issued on March 24, 1990, by the Chief Minister's Office, Ulundi, on SAPA Wire Service.

33. Buthelezi's address in Umlazi, December 15, 1991, was carried on SAPA Wire Service.

34. Examples are innumerable. In addition to the National Party's own long history of constitutional and political engineering, both opposition white parties and social scientists were imbued in a similar tradition. For example, see Lijphart, *Power-Sharing*; Slabbert and Welsh, *South Africa's Options*; Hermann Giliomee and Lawrence Schlemmer, *From Apartheid to Nation-building* (Cape Town: Oxford University Press, 1989); and, more recently, Fanie Cloete, Lawrence Schlemmer, and Daan van Vuuren, eds., *Policy Options for a New South Africa* (Pretoria: Human Sciences Research Council, 1991). Among non–South African writers, see Donald Horowitz, *A Democratic South Africa? Constitutional Engineering in a Divided Society* (University of California Press, 1991); and Samuel Huntington, "The Secret of Success Is Secrecy," *Sunday Times*, February 17, 1991.

35. See Gavin Woods, "Toward a New Constitution for South Africa: Why the IFP Rejects a Constituent Assembly," *Clarion Call*, vol. 1 (1991), pp. 12–15.

36. The government started indicating its acceptance of some form of interim arrangement in mid–1991. See, for example, de Klerk's speech to Parliament during the budget vote debate, May 2, 1991, cited in note 28.

37. Convention for a Democratic South Africa, "Terms of Reference for Working Groups for Codesa," December 20–21, 1991.

38. The conference was attended by five parliamentary parties (NP, DP, Labour Party, Solidarity Party, and National People's Party); three anti-apartheid organizations (ANC, SACP, and Natal Indian Congress); six parties from the self-governing homelands, including Inkatha; and four delegations representing the governments of the independent homelands. And the government had its own delegation, separate from the National Party's.

39. "Speech by the State President, Mr. F. W. de Klerk, at the First Session of CODESA, World Trade Center, Kempton Park, 20 December 1991," p. 2.

40. Ibid., p. 4.

41. Shaun Johnson, "Fiery First Round As Leaders Clash over MK," Saturday Star, December 21, 1991, p. 1.

42. See "Press Statement by the State President, Mr. F. W. de Klerk," Pretoria, July 30, 1991, annex A.

43. See Brian Stuart, "FW Meets 23 Who May Be NP's First Coloured MPs," Citizen, May 23, 1991; Peter Fabricius, "21 Coloured MPs Walk over to NP," Star, May 24, 1991; Patrick Laurence, "The Browning of FW's Nats," Star, May 31, 1991; Michael Acott, "FW's Land Reforms Give His NP the Keys to Two Houses," Star, May 27, 1991; and Michael Morris and Shaun Johnson, "Sensation as 'House of Hendrickse' Is Toppled," Star, February 1, 1992.

44. In his closing speech, Mandela admitted that in some areas the ANC had "entered discussions with homeland leaders without proper consultation with our grassroots members in that particular area. We must assure you that this mistake will be attended to." Closing speech to the ANC National Conference, Durban, July 7, 1991, p. 5.

45. The National Party initially resisted the inclusion of SACP members in the delegation at Groote Schoor. It finally had to accept the presence of Joe Slovo, but it continued to argue, unsuccessfully, that the communists be dropped from the negotiating team. The government had fewer problems accepting the presence of a separate SACP delegation at CODESA.

46. Soon after his release from jail, Mandela talked most homeland leaders into boycotting a meeting called by de Klerk, but a few months later it became clear that the government had turned the tables on the Congress and that it had opened a dialogue with the homeland leaders. See Helen Grange, "Homeland Leaders Deny ANC Pressure," Star, April 6, 1990; Patrick Laurence, "On the Road to Black Unity: De Klerk Loses Out as Local and Homeland Leaders Look to the ANC," Saturday Star, April 14, 1990, p. 11; "3 Homelands behind ANC, Says Mandela," Star, November 12, 1990; and Shaun Johnson, "Counting One's Allies Too Soon," Star, November 15, 1990. But the dialogue between the ANC and the homeland authorities resumed later.

47. David Breier and John MacLennan, "How Dingane and Pik Broke the Ice," Sunday Star, May 6, 1990, p. 2.

CHAPTER 6

1. Department of Foreign Affairs, *South Africa, 1989–90: Official Yearbook of the Republic of South Africa* (Pretoria: Government Printers, 1990), p. 127.

2. South African Institute of Race Relations, *Race Relations Survey, 1988–89* (Johannesburg, 1989), p. 513.

3. In South Africa, municipalities buy electricity in bulk from Eskom, the producer, and resell it to households at a profit. White councils often also resell to black councils at a profit, and these in turn resell to the black households. Electricity tariffs are thus higher in the townships. For example, the Johannesburg Council in 1988 bought electricity from Eskom at 7 cents per unit, but Soweto paid 9.7 cents per unit. See Mark Swilling and Khehla Shubane, "Negotiating Urban Transition: The Soweto Experience," in Robin Lee and Lawrence Schlemmer, eds., *Transition to Democracy: Policy Perspectives, 1991* (Cape Town: Oxford University Press, 1991), p. 230.

4. Urban Foundation, "Policies for a New Urban Future: Informal Housing," part 1, "The Current Situation," Johannesburg, August 1991, pp. 6, 7.

5. Tania Levy, "Transvaal Townships Owe R 1bn," *Business Day*, April 4, 1991; "R 410-m to Go to Non-Viable Black Councils," *Star*, March 27, 1991; and "Unpaid Rents Bill Now R 1,5-bn," *Citizen*, June 4, 1992.

6. Esmaré van der Merwe, "More Councils Collapse," *Star*, April 8, 1991, p. 1; and "New Campaign against Black Councillors," *Citizen*, December 10, 1990, p. 1.

7. Robert Cameron, "The Institutional Parameters of Local Government Restructuring in South Africa," in Chris Heymans and Gerhard Tötemeyer, eds., *Government by the People* (Cape Town: Juta and Co., 1988), p. 49.

8. A chronology of desegregation is found in Urban Foundation, "Policies for a New Future: Tackling Group Areas Policy," March 1990.

9. Peter Fabricius, "Govt May Outlaw Segregated Facilities," *Star*, March 19, 1991.

10. White schools were given the option to open their doors to members of other race groups if a large majority of parents voted to do so. These open schools, known as Model B schools, did not receive additional funding from the government, and thus took very few black children.

11. This was typical of the National Party's policy in this period. All moves toward decentralization were accompanied by an attempt to limit the choices open to local actors. For example, during 1990 the government decided to give white parents a voice in deciding whether "their" school should be desegregated, but offered them a limited choice among three prescribed models and left the final decision to the minister of education. On the National

Party's philosophy of local government, see also de Klerk's comments in Brian Stuart, "Local Power Sharing—FW," *Citizen*, May 8, 1990, p. 1.

12. Council for the Coordination of Local Government Affairs, Chairman Dr. C. Thornhill, "Report and Recommendations of the Investigating Committee into a System of Local Government for South Africa," Johannesburg, October 25, 1990. (Hereafter the Thornhill Report.) On the report, see also Bureau for Information, "Manifesto on Local Government," SAPA PR Wire Service, October 25, 1990; and Edyth Bulbring, "Principles for Local Govt Set Out," *Star*, October 26, 1990.

13. "Abolition of Racially Based Land Measures Act, 1991," *Government Gazette*, vol. 312, no. 13341 (June 28, 1991), chap. 7, p. 98. See also Ismail Lagardien, "Law to Scrap Group Areas Sparks Protest," *Sowetan*, May 28, 1991; Jo-Anne Collinge, "Local Government at Crossroads," *Star*, June 13, 1991; and Brian Stuart, "World Watches FW Sign Away Apartheid," *Citizen*, June 28, 1991.

14. National Party, "Constitutional Rule in a Participatory Democracy: The National Party's Framework for a New Democratic South Africa" (Arcadia, P.O. Box 56503, September 1991), pp. 2–3.

15. Ibid., p. 16.

16. Ibid.

17. Ibid., p. 17.

18. Ibid.

19. Urban Foundation, "Policies for a New Urban Future," pp. 6, 7. The number of Africans living in informal housing was greater than the total white, Asian, and Coloured population of the metropolitan areas. The voting devices suggested by the National Party would thus have a major impact on the composition of the local councils.

20. Rehana Rossouw, "Civics Start Learning to Govern," *South*, August 15–21, 1991.

21. See John MacLennan and Abbey Makow, "New Group Is a Threat to ANC," *Star*, May 2, 1991; and "UDF Denies Formation of Civic Body Is Result of Rift," *Star*, May 18, 1991. See also SAPA PR Wire Service report on "Civics," May 12, 1991; and ANC Youth League, "Press Release re: National Civic Movement," SAPA PR Wire Service, May 14, 1991.

22. "Press Statement by the Administrator of the Transvaal, Mr. Danie Hough," SAPA PR Wire Service, December 13, 1990. The statement included the text of the agreement signed by ANC representatives on behalf of a number of civics.

23. "Struggle at the Local Level," *Mayibuye: Journal of the African National Congress*, vol. 1 (December 1990), p. 29.

24. See ANC Press Statement, "ANC Delegation Meets Government on Local Government Matters," SAPA PR Wire Service, January 9, 1992.

25. Technically, the Soweto Civic Association was represented by the Soweto People's Delegation, a structure that the civic association, restricted by the emergency regulations of the time, had set up in December 1988 to negotiate the end of the rent boycott. For simplicity's sake, only the term Soweto Civic Association is used here. See also Swilling and Shubane, "Negotiating Urban Transition," pp. 223–58.

26. "The Greater Soweto Accord Explained," *Sowetan*, October 5, 1990, p. 11.

27. Jo-Anne Collinge, "Soweto Sliding into Dark," *Star*, August 16, 1991, p. 13.

28. Ibid.

29. Reported on SAPA PR Wire Service, October 1, 1991. See also "Inkatha Left Out of Cast Talks," *Citizen*, October 28, 1991.

30. Jo-Anne Collinge, "Cast Rejects Plans for 'Racial' Chamber," *Saturday Star*, April 13, 1991; and Collinge, "Soul-Searching for Strategy to Define 'New' Local Government," *Star*, April 15, 1991.

31. Tania Levy, "Support Is Growing for Local Assembly," *Business Day*, August 19, 1991.

32. This discussion is based on the debates during the meetings of the chamber on October 9, November 13, and December 4, 1991, and on the documents provided there.

33. "Interim Measures for Local Government Act, 1991," *Government Gazette*, vol. 313, no. 13373 (July 12, 1991).

34. African National Congress, "Press Statement on the Interim Measures for Local Government Bill," SAPA PR Wire Service, June 10, 1991. On the bill, see "Local Govt Bill to Thwart 'Frustration,' " *Star*, June 13, 1991.

35. Peter Wellman, "Kimberley Breaks New Ground," *Star*, February 10, 1992, p. 13; and Patrick Bulger, "ANC Warning over 'Twinned' Councils," *Business Day*, June 8, 1992.

CHAPTER 7

1. Nineteen percent of the estimated value of fixed assets was owned by public authorities, 15 percent by public corporations, and 23 percent by general government agencies. See Stephen R. Lewis, Jr., *The Economics of Apartheid* (New York: Council on Foreign Relations Press, 1990), p. 155. In 1983, 80 percent of the value of shares listed on the Johannesburg Stock Exchange (JSE) was controlled by seven companies. See Fuad Cassim, "Growth, Crisis and Change in the South African Economy," in John Suckling and Landeg White, eds., *After Apartheid: Renewal of the South African Economy* (London:

James Currey, 1988), p. 4. By 1989, four companies (Anglo-American, The Rembrandt Group, SA Mutual, and Sanlam) controlled 80.7 percent. See Barry Streek, "Big Four Control 80.7% of Shares of JSE," *Business Day*, April 20, 1990. In 1990 Anglo-American claimed to control "only" 30 percent of the market capitalization of the JSE, not 45 percent, as often claimed. See Andrew Gill, "Anglo Calculates Extent of Its 'Control' of the JSE to Be Only 30%," *Business Day*, July 11, 1990.

2. For a summary of the early debates, see Witney W. Schneidman, "Who's Where in the Debate on 'Nationalization' in South Africa," *CSIS Africa Notes*, no. 114 (July 1, 1990). The same arguments were repeated endlessly.

3. Michael D. McGrath, "Income Redistribution: The Economic Challenge of the 1990s," in Robert Schrire, ed., *Critical Choices for South Africa: An Agenda for the 1990s* (Cape Town: Oxford University Press, 1990), p. 94. The figure is for 1980; the gap may have closed slightly since then.

4. On the issue of dualism in the South African economy, see Lewis, *Economics of Apartheid*, p. 129.

5. Urban Foundation, "Rural Development: Towards a New Framework," Urban Debate 2010, no. 4 (September 1990), p. 19.

6. SACTU eventually turned into an exiled organization, existing in little more than name alongside the ANC. After the unbanning of political organizations, SACTU was officially disbanded, opening the way for the alliance between the ANC and COSATU. For a brief summary of SACTU's history, see Steven Friedman, *Building Tomorrow Today: African Workers in Trade Unions, 1970–84* (Johannesburg: Ravan Press, 1987), pp. 26–36.

7. Ibid., pp. 149–79.

8. Ibid., p. 438.

9. Eddie Webster, "The Rise of Social-Movement Unionism: The Two Faces of the Black Trade Union Movement in South Africa," in Philip Frankel, Noam Pines, and Mark Swilling, eds., *State, Resistance and Change in South Africa* (Johannesburg: Southern Book Publishers, 1988).

10. Vera von Lieres, "NUM Grows Despite Job Cutbacks," *Business Day*, May 8, 1991; and von Lieres, "Numsa More Than Double '87 despite Huge Job Losses," *Business Day*, June 19, 1991.

11. See Devan Pillay, "NACTU's 3rd Congress: What Prospects for Unity?" *South African Labour Bulletin*, vol. 15 (November 1990), pp. 54–61. At the congress, NACTU claimed a membership of 258,000.

12. Wage settlements reached by black unions, according to one study, resulted in an average wage increase of 81.5 percent between 1985 and 1988. See South African Institute of Race Relations, *Race Relations Survey, 1989–90* (Johannesburg, 1990), p. 663. The ratio of African to white wages in mining, which had been 1:19.8 in 1970, was 1:5.7 by 1985; in the same period in

manufacturing the ratio changed from 1:5.8 to 1:3.9. See Lewis, *Economics of Apartheid*, p. 176.

13. Avril Joffe, "COSATU: Economic Policy Conference," *South African Labour Bulletin*, vol. 15 (June 1991), p. 42.

14. Vera von Lieres, "Metal Workers Win Increases of up to 15%," *Business Day*, August 1, 1991, p. 1. This followed the enactment of new legislation that removed training programs from the exclusive control of the government. See Andre Kraak and Karl von Holdt, "The Training Strategies of Business and Government: New Opportunities for Unions?" *South African Labour Bulletin*, vol. 15 (June 1990), pp. 16–22.

15. On the charter, see Devan Pillay, "The Workers' Charter Campaign," *South African Labour Bulletin*, vol. 15 (January 1991), pp. 37–44; Vera von Lieres and Patrick Bulger, "Cosatu Spells Out Demands for New SA," *Business Day*, April 4, 1991, p. 1; and "Cosatu's Plan to Protect Workers," *Citizen*, April 4, 1991, p. 8. For a broader discussion, see Drew Forrest, "Rival Currents at Work in Cosatu," *Weekly Mail*, April 5–11, 1991, p. 17.

16. Eddie Koch, "Unions Want Their Own Seat at the Groote Schuur Table," *Weekly Mail*, May 11–17, 1990. See also Drew Forrest, "Cosatu Demands Talks on Economy," *Weekly Mail*, May 30–June 6, 1991, p. 14; Tyler Parry, "Cosatu to Review Its Role in Tripartite Alliance," *South*, May 29–June 5, 1991, p. 23; and Chiara Carter, "Cosatu Affirms Political Independence," *South*, August 1–7, 1991.

17. The election of unionists to top ANC positions caused a major debate within COSATU concerning whether such dual leadership was permissible. The 1991 congress of COSATU answered the question in the affirmative. See Drew Forrest, "Unity-Conscious Cosatu Comes of Age," *Weekly Mail*, August 2–8, 1991, p. 15.

18. African National Congress (ANC), Department of Economic Policy, "Discussion Document on Economic Policy," paper prepared for the DEP workshop, Harare, September 20–23, 1990; and ANC, Department of Economic Policy, *Draft Resolution on ANC Economic Policy for National Conference* (University of the Western Cape, Centre for Development Studies, 1991).

19. ANC, "Discussion Document on Economic Policy," p. 5.

20. Ibid., pp. 8–9.

21. Ibid., p. 16.

22. Ibid.

23. See African National Congress, "ANC Policy Guidelines for a Democratic South Africa," as adopted at the National Conference, May 28–31, 1992.

24. See ANC Land Commission, *ANC Land Commission Workshop: A Discussion Document* (University of the Western Cape, Centre for Policy Studies, 1990).

25. Privatization was preceded by commercialization, to make the corporation viable without government subsidies. Once that was done, shares were sold to employees and on the stock exchange, completing the privatization process. The first parastatals to be privatized were Iscor, the steel producer, and the South African Transportation Services (SATS). Others, including the telecommunication system, were still in the process of commercialization at the time of this writing. In all cases, commercialization and privatization had led to the retrenchment of thousands of workers. This was particularly true for SATS, which had been used by the government to provide employment for Afrikaners through a system of job reservation.

26. See Independent Development Trust, "The First Year," Cape Town, August 1991.

27. Billy Paddock, "R 1bn Will Create 59000 Jobs—Govt," *Business Day*, August 28, 1991; and Rohan Minogue and others, "CP No, Others Praise R 1-bn Plan to Aid Poor," *Citizen*, August 28, 1991, p. 1.

28. Studies estimating malnutrition on the basis of family income provided the higher figure. The lower figure was reached through anthropometric studies correlating weight, height, and age of children, which the government's Committee for the Development of Food and Nutrition Strategy for Southern Africa described as "sporadic, incomplete and according to incomparable norms."

29. For an overview of these land laws, see Michael Robertson, "Dividing the Land: An Introduction to Apartheid Land Law," in Christina Murray and Catherine O'Regan, eds., *No Place to Rest: Forced Removals and the Law in South Africa* (Cape Town: Oxford University Press, 1990), pp. 122–36; see also Michael de Klerk, ed., *A Harvest of Discontent: The Land Question in South Africa* (Cape Town: Institute for a Democratic Alternative for South Africa, 1991).

30. Republic of South Africa, *White Paper on Land Reform* (Pretoria: Government Printers, 1991), p. 1.

31. Ibid., p. 13.

32. Peter Delmar, "ANC Reacts with 'Outrage and Deep Disappointment,'" *Business Day*, March 13, 1991.

33. A "declaration" protesting the white paper was issued on March 19, 1991, by twenty-four organizations ranging from the moderate to the radical. They included centers for legal studies at three major universities, organizations dealing specifically with the land issue, human rights groups, development NGOs, student groups, and so on.

34. N. T. Christodoulou and N. Vink, "The Potential for Black Small-Holder Farmers Participation in the South African Agriculture Economy," paper presented to a Conference on Land Reform and Agricultural Development, Newick Park Initiative, United Kingdom, October 1990. Note that Christodoulou was the general manager of the Development Bank of Southern Africa, and

that the paper was prepared with the assistance of the bank staff, making it a bank document rather than a study by one individual.

35. Under the land acts repealed in 1991, 13 percent of the land was theoretically reserved for blacks. This included the land set aside under the 1913 act, and that added later under the 1936 act. In reality, the purchase and transfer of additional land under the 1936 act had not been completed. Part of the land acquired under the act was still controlled by the trust, and in some cases even rented out to white farmers. The Development Bank study estimated that two million hectares of the land acquired under the 1936 act had not been distributed. Later, the bank admitted that the amount of undistributed trust land was smaller, only about one million hectares.

36. The total number of communities involved in these efforts is uncertain, because the process was not centrally coordinated. To the author's knowledge, in early 1991 thirteen communities in the Transvaal, Natal, Eastern Cape, and Border Region (East London) were being supported by the Transvaal Rural Action Committee. The Grahamstown Rural Committee dealt with another ten communities in the Border Region. In general, these communities fell into two categories: those who had been pushed out of their land when considered a "black spot" in a white area; and those whose land had been incorporated into a homeland. On the problem of displacement, see Laurine Platzky and Cherryl Walker, *The Surplus People: Forced Removals in South Africa* (Johannesburg: Ravan Press, 1985); and Christina Murray and Catherine O'Regan, *No Place to Rest: Forced Removals and the Law in South Africa* (Cape Town: Oxford University Press, 1990). See also Dawn Barkhuzen, "Give Us Back Our Land—or Else," *Sunday Times*, September 29, 1991, p. 43.

37. For a summary of the dominant viewpoints, see Merle Lipton, *Capitalism and Apartheid: South Africa, 1910–1986* (London: Wildwood House, 1986), chap. 1.

38. Quoted in Di Paice, "The Great Debate," *Leadership*, vol. 9 (April 1990), p. 29.

39. The study was not published, but its results were widely disseminated through a lengthy presentation of the various transition scenarios. The study was first presented to government and major political parties, then to business groups, the press, academics, and so on. This summary is based on notes taken by the author during a presentation to the foreign press on September 17, 1991. Some indications of the main ideas are found in Riaan de Villiers, "Crusader," *Leadership*, vol. 10 (June–July 1991), pp. 52–56.

40. The idea that transition to democracy is facilitated by economic growth was taken from Guillermo O'Donnell and Philippe C. Schmitter, *Transitions from Authoritarian Rule: Tentative Conclusions about Uncertain Democracies* (Johns Hopkins University Press, 1986)—possibly the most quoted, and misquoted, book in South Africa in this period.

41. Linda Ensor, "Keys to Lead Govt in Talks with Labour and Business," *Business Day*, May 18, 1992; and Billy Paddock, "Economic Forum Gets Govt Support," *Business Day*, May 19, 1992.

CHAPTER 8

1. The composition of the electorate was still undetermined and could easily have a significant effect on an election's results. First, population statistics were not accurate, by the government's own admission. Second, the number of black voters would be much smaller if the population of the independent homelands did not participate in an election, or if those votes were counted separately. Third, a large number of blacks, five million by the government's estimate but possibly much more, did not even have an identification card, which made registration more difficult. Adding to these factors the demographic composition of the population, with a much higher percentage of blacks being under eighteen, the white electorate would probably end up as a much larger percentage of the total than its demographic weight suggested.

2. A by-election in Umlazi, Durban, in June 1990 saw a 23 percent swing in favor of the Conservative Party, although the National Party made up some of its losses and narrowly retained the seat by taking votes from the Democratic Party, whose share of the votes went from 27 percent to 8 percent. In November 1991 a by-election in Virginia, Orange Free State, saw the Conservative Party increase its vote from 47 percent to 62 percent and take the seat. The by-election in Potchefstrom, Western Transvaal, in February 1992 registered an 11 percent swing in favor of the CP. See "Umlazi Vote Stuns Nats, Crushes DP," *Star*, June 7, 1990; Cathy Thompson and Tony Sterling, "Smashing CP Win in Virginia," *Citizen*, November 29, 1991, p. 1; and "Potch Sounds Alarm for Nats," *Star*, February 20, 1992, p. 1.

3. See, for example, Hermann Giliomee, "Battle Revolutionaries Can't Win," *Star*, June 10, 1991.

4. Press conference of December 1, 1992, from author's notes.

5. The National Party's 1989 electoral platform stated, "The National Party also undertakes to place before the electorate any new constitutional principles before such principles are finally implemented." National Party, "Proposed Plan of Action of the National Party, Election 6 September 1989," p. 3.

6. Following repeated allegations published by the *Weekly Mail* that the Defence Force had provided covert training for Inkatha operatives, using

educational institutions and consulting groups as fronts, the Commission of Inquiry into the Prevention of Public Violence, headed by Justice Richard Goldstone, announced on February 3, 1992, that it would start an investigation into current government funding of such activities. Minister of Defence Roelf Meyer supported the investigation.

7. Research by the Labour Monitoring Group at the University of the Witwatersrand showed very high levels of support. Regionally, they ranged from a high of 98 percent on both days in Port Elizabeth and Uitenhage to a low of 67 percent in East London. In terms of economic sectors, absenteeism ranged from more than 90 percent on both days in the financial sector to a low of about 45 percent in the personal services sector. See Glen Adler, Judy Maller, and Eddie Webster, "The Labour Movement's Show of Strength," *Business Day*, November 12, 1991.

8. Thabo Mbeki, "Press Lunch Address," April 3, 1990, transcript of taped remarks.

9. Convention for a Democratic South Africa, "Declaration of Intent," December 20, 1991, Isando, South Africa, p. 1. See also Peter Fabricius, "Historic Declaration of Intent Launches Summit," *Saturday Star*, December 21, 1991; and Mike Robertson, Edyth Bulbring, and Charles Leonard, "What's Being Debated and Where the Different Parties' Loyalties Lie," *Sunday Times*, December 22, 1991, p. 2, for the positions of various delegations.

10. David Breier, "Open School Policy: The Catch," *Sunday Star*, September 16, 1990, p. 4.

11. For more detail, see *South Africa, 1990–91: Official Yearbook of South Africa* (Pretoria: Department of Foreign Affairs, 1991), p. 177.

12. The annexation was announced in the *Government Gazette* of November 1, 1991. See "More Land for Bophuthatswana," *Star*, November 1, 1991.

13. "Press Statement by the Minister of Regional and Land Affairs, Mr. I. de Villiers, on the Transfer of Certain Land to Bophuthatswana," SAPA PR Wire Service, November 1, 1991.

14. The idea was contained in a formal statement by the National Executive Committee, released on January 8, 1992, on the occasion of the eightieth anniversary of the founding of the ANC. See Jo-Anne Collinge and Peter Davies, "ANC Wants Poll for Constituent Assembly in 1992," *Star*, January 9, 1992, p. 3. Earlier, Cyril Ramaphosa had indicated that the interim government should not last more than eighteen months. Mike Robertson and Edyth Bulbring, "10-year Joint-Rule—FW," *Sunday Times*, December 22, 1991, p. 1.

15. "Speech by the State President, Mr. F. W. de Klerk, at the First Session of CODESA," World Trade Center, Kempton Park, December 20, 1991.

16. See Robertson and Bulbring, "10-year Joint-Rule."

17. This explanation of the process was set forth by Stoffel van der Merwe at a press briefing held in Cape Town on January 27, 1991, and it was confirmed by Gerrit Viljoen at a press briefing the following day.

18. "Press Lunch Address by Thabo Mbeki," Cape Town, April 3, 1990, pp. 5–6.

19. "Pretoria Minute," *History in the Making: Documents Reflecting a Changing South Africa*, vol. 1 (November 1990), pp. 21–22. In special cases requiring individual consideration, the date was April 30, 1991. One of the misunderstandings concerning the minute was that the government claimed the dates were simply "targets," hence flexible, while the ANC interpreted them as deadlines.

20. Ken Owen, "Codesa Fails Because It Asks the Wrong Question," *Sunday Times*, May 24, 1992.

21. See Esther Waugh and Peter Fabricius, "Meet Our Demands or No Talks, Says ANC," *Star*, June 24, 1992.

CHAPTER 9

1. For an overview, see Helen Zille, "The Right Wing in South African Politics," in Peter L. Berger and Bobby Godsell, eds., *A Future South Africa: Visions, Strategies, and Realities* (Boulder, Colo.: Westview Press, 1988), pp. 55–94. At the time, Zille put the AWB membership at fewer than 10,000, with 150,000 people willing to attend meetings and 500,000 silent sympathizers. All these numbers had probably increased.

2. Some data are presented in Hermann Giliomee and Lawrence Schlemmer, *From Apartheid to Nation-building* (Cape Town: Oxford University Press, 1989), pp. 166–69.

3. "FW Backs Zulu King for Codesa," *Citizen*, January 11, 1992, p. 1.

4. "Address by His Excellency Kgosi Dr. L. M. Mangope, President of the Republic of Bophuthatswana, on the Occasion of the First Meeting of CODESA," December 20–21, 1991.

5. Quoted by SAPA, January 16, 1992.

6. *Toyi-toyi* is a kind of dance step that ranges from a slow shuffle to a rather wild war dance, to express anything from jubilation to defiance.

7. See Mike Robertson, "Who's Who on Far Left of Political Spectrum," *Sunday Times*, December 15, 1991.

8. Mike Siluma, "Cosatu Set to Seek Representation at Negotiations," *Star*, January 21, 1992.

9. Mandy Jean Woods, "Right-Wing Group Barred from Codesa," *Saturday Star*, January 11, 1992.

10. Fred de Lange, "NP Won't Let ANC Take Over: FW," *Citizen*, November 8, 1991, p. 1.

11. Interview with the *Republic of South Africa Policy Review*, January 1992, released on SAPA PR Wire Service, October 24, 1991.

12. Edyth Bulbring, "Inkatha's Biggest Worry—Being Left Out in the Cold," *Sunday Times*, November 3, 1991, p. 17.

13. See, for example, Carol Hills, "Craven Slams Flag, Anthem Move," *Citizen*, November 9, 1991; "Sam and Jay," *Citizen*, November 13, 1991, p. 6; David Beattie, "SA Bound for Olympics," *Star*, November 7, 1991, p. 1; and "FW Slams Dumping of National Symbols," *Star*, November 8, 1991, p. 2.

CHAPTER 10

1. Frederik van Zyl Slabbert, "Codesa Could Be Start of Good Beginning," *Sunday Times*, December 29, 1991.

2. SAPA Wire Service, December 4, 1991.

Index

Abolition of Racially Based Land Measures Act of *1991*, 119
Adam, Heribert, 27
African National Congress (ANC), 1–2; accountability issue, 47; banning of (*1960*), 73; churches and, 60–61; coalition strategy, 110–11, 164–65; CODESA, 112–13, 153, 154, 158–59, 162–63, 164–65, 166–68, 173–78, 201–02; Coloureds and, 60–61; communists in, 53, 54; constituent assembly proposal, 8, 105, 106, 171, 202–03; constitution-making process, 2–9, 13–14, 90, 99–101, 105, 110–11, 171–72, 173, 198–200, 202–03, 204; controversy caused by Mandelas, 49–50; COSATU, alliance with, 58, 137, 138, 139; covert operations against, 33, 36; death squads and, 34, 35; "decolonization" perspective, 15; de facto situations, capacity for creating, 171; democratic shortcomings, 47, 199; divisions within, 3, 6–7, 11; economic restructuring and, 133, 140–43, 146, 151, 208–09; election of leaders, 46; financing for, 44; government in exile, 45–47; history, 42; homelands and, 82; homelands reintegration issue, 203–04; ideological orientation, 48; IFP and, 65–68; interim government issue, 8, 106; international context and, 206,

207–09, 210, 211–12; land reform policy, 141, 142–43; leadership figures, 47; as liberation movement, 43–45; local government restructuring and, 121–25, 127, 129, 130; majority rule proposal, 14, 99–101, 196, 198–200, 203; mass democratic movement, relationship with, 43, 56–58, 61–62; membership of, 46, 55–56; National Executive Committee, 45–48, 54; nationalization policy, 132, 133, 140–41, 142, 208–09; PAC, relationship with, 75–76; Patriotic United Front, 76, 110–11; political party, conversion to, 44–45, 191–92; pressure on government, capacity for, 163; SACP, relationship with, 52–53, 54, 55, 188; on sanctions against South Africa, 210; smaller groups, attitude toward, 11–12; time frame for constitutional change, 171–72, 173; unbanning of, 1, 2; underground operations in South Africa, 45; Youth League, 73, 187. *See also* Black-on-black violence; Umkhonto we Sizwe; United Democratic Front
Afrikaner Broederbond, 24, 36; decline, 37–38; National Party and, 37; purpose, 36–37
Afrikaner Volkswag, 79–80
Afrikaner Weerstandsbeweging (AWB), 79, 181, 182

241